THE PSYCHOLOGY OF CHRONIC ILLNESS

THE
PSYCHOLOGY
OF
CHRONIC ILLNESS

THE HEALING WORK OF PATIENTS, THERAPISTS, AND FAMILIES

ROBERT SHUMAN

BasicBooks
A Division of HarperCollins*Publishers*

Published by BasicBooks,
A Division of HarperCollins Publishers, Inc.

Library of Congress Cataloging-in-Publication Data
Shuman, Robert.
    The psychology of chronic illness : the healing work of
patients, therapists, and families / Robert Shuman. —
1st ed.
        p.   cm.
    Includes bibliographical references and index.
    ISBN 0-465-09534-8
    1. Chronic diseases—Psychological aspects. I. Title.
RC108.S48   1996
616' .001'9—dc20   96-10957
                                                        CIP

96 97 98 99 ❖/HC 9 8 7 6 5 4 3 2 1

For Sheila
Companion, lover, wife, generous bearer of gifts, soulmate

CONTENTS

PREFACE

D URING THE NIGHT, if another world enters the one in which we ordinarily live, we call it a dream. When it enters in daylight, we often call it illness.

The purpose of this book is simple. I want to describe worlds of illness and healing adequately enough to make some helpful difference to those, be they patient or physician, family or friend, nurse or therapist, who cannot evade a confrontation with suffering. I would like readers to get a feel from the inside of the worlds of illness and to better grasp the experience of chronic illness and disability as it is lived by those afflicted. If at times the piling up of detail seems irritating, frustrating, or even repetitive to the reader, it may be that I am accomplishing my purpose. For that is what it feels like to those who are ill, to those who live, love, or care for them and each other, and to the clinicians with whom they work.

My book is drawn from the fruits of personal experience and the testimony of others living with illness, pressed through the sieve of my own reflections. I offer neither theory nor proof. The volume is not a program for research. There are no recipes for treatment or recommendations for cure. I have tried to avoid jargon. This book expresses ideas to which I am committed, worked out in relationships with people—patients, family, friends—with whom I am deeply engaged. I want the book to be of interest and value to the professional yet accessible to the student and a more general readership as well.

Chronic illness is common. It is likely that many of the individuals seen by any physician or therapist in clinical practice, though they may not be seeking treatment or therapy for chronic illness, live in families in which chronic illness is present, nearby, or at some distance. It is important, therefore, for people helping people, be they professionals or not, to have some sense of the illness experience, an awareness of its impact on individuals and families, and a knowledge of therapeutic attitudes and approaches that may help either to ease the suffering or to help those afflicted to pursue the opportunities for good that chronic illness can present.

Many fine therapists and physicians attempt to work collaboratively with each other and with their patients diagnosed with chronic illness. I hope they will find this book a congenial supplement to their efforts. But I also hope this book will be read by the professional, often a general practitioner, whose practice incidentally includes those with chronic illness or for whom collaboration with other providers is difficult to achieve. For it is this clinician who, often without much collegial support and operating outside of university or medical settings, bears much of the weight of giving care, as do the individuals and families he or she meets.

Moreover, there are few caregivers, friends, family members, psychologists, social workers, counselors, or physicians who, whatever their orientation or however their work is structured, cannot help individuals and families living with illness to:

learn behaviors that support recovery and good health practices, facilitate relaxation and relief from pain, and increase the possibility of sensible compliance with medical recommendations;

receive support in managing the multiple impacts of chronic illness on work, relationships, roles, and resources;

speak of the suffering, fears, anxieties, anger, and grief that
accompany chronic illness and disability; and

hold onto or recover hope, meaning, and morale during the
punctuated or continuing presence of illness or disability.

In this book, I offer clinicians and other interested readers a
sense of how people with illness get on. I encourage readers to
examine and reflect upon their own personal and professional
histories, attitudes, and encounters with illness and disability. I
hope my material assists therapists, friends, physicians, and
family to make sense of and translate the protean "stuff" of illness
experiences into clinical imagination and empathic understanding. Some individuals wish to cope with their illness; others
want to make something of it. In either case, psychotherapy can
be of some use.

The Psychology of Chronic Illness is an invitation to think about,
to imagine, to feel, and to encounter the experience of illness differently. There are as many "maps" of the experience of chronic
illness as there are people who are ill. The same is true of all psychologies, theories of human nature, and other umbrella concepts intended to cover the particulars of the lives of all individuals and families.

Chief among our commonalities is our uniqueness. I've tried
to stay close to experience; at ground level, peculiarities and
paradoxes are what we find. As a result, it is likely that within
these pages the reader will find contradictions and ambiguities.
So be it. Chronic illness is not a topic easily pinned down and
neatly peeled open for the examining eye.

I am particularly grateful to several people for the support
they have given me over the years and the encouragement they
have offered on behalf of this book. Among them are Lynne
Smilow and Jonathan Felsman, Patty and David Straus, Mark
Horowitz and Abby Seixas-Horowitz, Jan and Al Schwartz,
Patricia Berry, and, more recently, my editor, Eric Wright.

Also, with love, my parents, Harold and Evelyn Shuman, and
my wife's parents, Emanuel and Zelma Felsman.

Of course, my children, Rebecca and Daniel, loving their dad,
accepting his limitations, following their own ways.

And, unconditionally, Sheila.

CHAPTER 1

A Simple Twist of Fate

Illness is the experience of living through the disease.
Arthur Frank, *At the Will of the Body* (1991)

THIS IS HOW I remember it. On a spring day in 1979, I left my car at a local service station for a minor repair. As I walked three-quarters of a mile home, I noticed that I stumbled as the toe of my left foot seemed to drag behind me and stub itself on the ground. I wondered whether passing drivers or even my neighbors might think me drunk. I let the incident pass and was bothered no more except for an occasional trip on the stairs.

At that time, I was a practicing psychologist at a children's hospital, married for eleven years, and the father of two children. Our family owned and participated in a movie theater and its internationally respected resident stage magic company. One of my roles was to change the metal letters on the theater marquee every weekend night. As the seasons rolled into summer and fall, I experienced more and more difficulty keeping my footing as I hauled the wooden crates full of letters down to the street from the upstairs workshop where they were kept. On Sunday show days, costumed as a toy soldier, I stood on a small platform behind a stand at which I sold souvenir programs. My leg and back would become strained before the curtain was raised and I could get down from my perch. Quickly changing into another costume, I rushed backstage to assist with props and make a brief appearance during one of the magic tricks.

But more and more often an unexpected urge to urinate could not be denied, and I would run to the bathroom. There were even several times when I wet myself, but I managed to conceal the stain. I spoke of these events to no one. I just carried on, assuming that most of my symptoms were psychological. The tightness around my abdomen, difficulty sleeping through the night, my urinary problems, my fatigue, parathesia, irritability—were these not characteristic of anxiety disorders?

On Thanksgiving Day that year, I could no longer carry on as if nothing were wrong. I had been swimming in a warm indoor pool, and when I got out of the water, my strength was sapped. I could barely stand or walk. Only later did I learn that an early test for multiple sclerosis was to place people in warm baths and observe the temperature's effect on their bodies.

A severe back spasm the next day brought me to the hospital, and after reporting on my recent symptoms, I was admitted. I entered the hospital for an evaluation to rule out, as my wife saw annotated on an admitting sheet, a spinal cord tumor. Two days later, following several evaluative procedures of varying levels of discomfort, I was discharged with a diagnosis of viral lesions of the spinal cord. I did not know that this was a label for the cause of the symptoms that were to be diagnosed three years later as multiple sclerosis. My life, it seemed to me, remained unchanged. I accepted with apparent unconcern the incidents that once in a while literally tripped me up. I just chalked them up to the spinal cord lesions and put them out of mind. I had too busy a life to think about what had never occurred to me at all— the possibility that I might, in fact, be ill.

The idea of illness was not remotely in my mind. Physical illness was not a part of my family or personal history. As a child and young adult, I was rarely ill, nor could I recall serious illnesses among my immediate family. Even the death of my grandfather when I was thirteen seemed more a function of his old age (he was seventy-four) than of the cancer from which he had suffered.

Three years later, in 1982, on a blazing hot summer weekend, my wife, my children (then ages eleven and eight), and I climbed down an embankment toward a small lake in the White Mountains of New Hampshire. Shockingly, I could not make my way back up the small slope. I had no strength in my legs, and my wife had to support me on her back and arm and drag me back to our car. Returning to Massachusetts, I entered the hospital for a second time. I left with a diagnosis of multiple sclerosis.

By Labor Day I was unable to ride a bike or walk for more than fifty yards without collapsing of fatigue, and an assortment of other symptoms had appeared. I had frequent episodes of urinary urgency and occasional incontinence. My wife reminded me and pleaded with me to go to the bathroom before leaving wherever we happened to be, but I hated the feeling of powerlessness that accompanied the realization that I needed to do such a thing. Consequently, I often neglected to make sure I didn't have to go, and accidents occurred. In 1982, for example, I attended my brother and sister-in-law's wedding in New Jersey. I was taking medication to increase the holding capacity of my neurogenic bladder. I ate and drank during the festivities without regard to the risk, putting faith in my new prescription.

How relieved I was that the drug worked so effectively that I never had to make my way to the rest room at all. On the way home, however, the dam broke. Through New Jersey, Connecticut, Massachusetts, I peed and peed, helpless to control the flow. My pants, my socks, my seat, all were soaked, making it impossible, from my point of view, to make my way to the men's room at a highway stop. Even if I managed to change my clothes, the upholstery was thoroughly drenched; nor did I know whether my bladder had finally emptied.

I learned a lot that day. I learned about helplessness and pride, about the limits and luxury of embarrassment when more important concerns are present, and about the power of the body to assert its dominance in the presence of rational and therapeutic controls.

During the next three years, my life was filled with changes that at the time I did not connect with my illness diagnosis. After all, I told myself and others, the worst part of my MS was the sadness that unexpectedly caught me on spring days when other people, alone or with partners or family, rode their bikes along the country roads and seaside ways around our town. The sense of freedom and spontaneity that such sights invited reminded me of my losses, and I attempted to keep my grief from spreading beyond the images in which I contained it. My wife freely admitted her own fear and pain, but I insisted that I was really not "in denial," as she suggested.

Yet within three years after diagnosis, I left the magic show and community with which I had been intimately involved since I was twenty-one years old, resigned from the hospital where I had worked for seven years, stopped the practice of psychotherapy, took a position as director of the nonprofit Institute for Human Evolution(!), resigned from that role to start up a magazine for parents, and, when that endeavor was not successful, resumed work as a psychotherapist in collaboration with a neuropsychology practice associated with a neurology group.

On a winter night in 1985, I placed my Apple IIc on the kitchen table, put a filled teapot on the electric stove, and began to write a book to help individuals, couples, and families cope with the effects of multiple sclerosis. When I next looked up from the monitor, the water in the unheard whistling pot had evaporated and the pot was welded to the cooktop. I wrote with passion and ease of the difficulties, dynamics, and strengths of people with chronic illness, drawing upon the lives of the people with whom I worked in therapy. Yet not even when the manuscript was published was I able to imagine or acknowledge that any of the events of the previous few years were linked to my own experience of, and coming to terms with, my chronic illness.

Only gradually, blessed with the love of my wife and the compassion, patience, and honesty of friends, through my work as a psychotherapist and as a patient, from my encounters with clients and students, as a result of following my own heart and mind, and with the aid of unexpected grace, has a broader tapestry unfolded. The colors, textures, and darker shadings of illness have revealed themselves.

Nearly thirty million Americans have been diagnosed with a

chronic medical condition that limits their activities, including 25 percent of people between the ages of forty-five and sixty and over 45 percent of those over sixty-five. If we assume that the average household includes two people, then sixty million are directly affected by chronic illness. Add on the extended family members and intimate friends who share its burdens, and it is easy to imagine that chronic illness touches over one hundred million Americans.

Many of these individuals and families will go to professional health care providers for relief from the physical and psychological distress meted out by chronic illness. Unfortunately, a large number will not receive the solace they seek. For despite its ubiquity in their own lives and in those of their patients, most physicians are not sensitive to what it is like to live and suffer with chronic illness. Nor are most therapists.

The ethical demands of professional caregivers, observes Edmund Pellegrino (Kestenbaum, 1982), "are rooted in the phenomenology of illness" and an understanding of "the assault of illness on the person" (p. 33). Yet few therapists who live with illness have described its effect on their professional work or explored the fact that their affliction may influence how they think about human meaning and behavior. As one reviewer, Charles Brenner, noted, the book *Illness in the Analyst* (Schwartz & Silver, 1990) was the first "to discuss at length the important and often vexing technical problems posed by an analyst's illness." Physician accounts are greater in number but rarely make the connection between the doctor's own experience and the care of his or her patients.

In one early encounter with a neurologist during my journey toward diagnosis, I told him that I thought my symptoms were signs of anxiety. "Is there anything you're anxious about?" he quite pleasantly and sensibly asked.

"No," I replied, which was both true and not true. But before any further questioning on his part or reflection on mine, I was up on his examining table being tapped by his hammer, stroked by a feather, and pricked with a pin. During the next three years, through the entire process of diagnosis, when I was visited by posses of residents, wheeled along corridors by attendants, and seated in laboratories for tests, no physician, nurse, technician, social worker, or psychologist ever offered me that question a second time. And when I was told I had multiple sclerosis—whether with kindness or concern I can't remember— nobody asked again. Of course, self-reliant and resourceful as I was, I did not suggest that, perhaps, now I might actually be anxious.

WHAT IS CHRONIC ILLNESS?

Caveat: Chronic illness is, of course, not the description of it.

A chronic illness is one in which a person's symptoms continue over a long term to impair his or her ability to continue with significant activities and normal routines. Medical treatment is frequently of limited effectiveness and contributes at times to both the physical and psychological distress of individuals and their families. Chronic illness typically impacts a person's sense of his or her body, orientation toward time and space, ability to predict and control life course and events, self-esteem, and feelings of personal motivation and mastery.

Many individuals and families absorb the shocks of illness with resourcefulness and resilience. The ongoing and increasing demands of illness overwhelm others, who undergo ever greater suffering and despair. And there are those who knit together well-made lives out of the threads that fate has spun. For them, the illness experience is a source of significant meaning and spiritual worth.

The diagnosis of a chronic illness is the outcome of a complex web of interactions between, at a minimum, physician and patient. Other individuals—family members and friends of the patient, other health care professionals, insurance company employees, and managed care personnel—are often involved as well. In fact, the patient may not be present for the great majority of the encounters that result in agreement that his or her afflictions or signs are consistent with a particular diagnosis. The process can take years and may not be resolved until death and autopsy. Even then, people placed within one nosological group may be shifted to another as legal battles are fought over the financial consequences of the assignment of disease causes and classifications, as demonstrated by cases of mortality apparently related to tobacco use, drinking, exposure to asbestos, breast implants, and mining.

Two central events that shape the illness experience are the decision to seek care and the receipt of a diagnosis. Whether an individual decides to go to a physician depends on the meanings that pain and distress have for that person and his or her family. Some people, owing to their occupation or personal history, accept physical pain and discomfort as a normal part of life. As long as they can function in the roles they consider important, they dismiss the need for a medical consultation. Others read pain or unusual sensations as signs that something is wrong.

The way in which illness is configured typically begins in one of two ways, or a combination of the two. In the first, an individual complains of some sort of physical distress of uncertain origin. In the other, a medical professional, friend, or family member observes in the individual changes in physical functioning, biological markers, or behavior that fall outside of what was previously seen as typical or normal. It is not that hard to accept the argument that "illnesses" such as hyperactivity, alcoholism, dysthymic disorder, drug addiction, and chronic back pain are social constructions, whether one agrees with the validity or pragmatics of the diagnosis or not. That cancer, lupus, Parkinson's disease, arthritis, or Alzheimer's might be products of a similar process of negotiation is not as easily admitted but should not be surprising. As Charles Rosenberg (1992) reminds us, the social construction of illness, "in an important sense . . . is no more than a tautology, a specialized restatement of the truism that men and women construct themselves culturally. Every aspect of an individual's identity is constructed—and thus also is disease" (p. 306).

Past experience, level of comfort, cost, and the accessibility of care are other important variables that influence the entrance of individuals into medical settings. The ease or difficulty of the process affects the illness itself, adding or removing levels of distress. It is probably impossible to separate those somatic complaints that result from the underlying pathology of tissue and organ, framed as a disease, from those that arise from the emotions, strains, and social and political context in which the illness experience is first embodied and formed.

The realities of sickness and care are jointly constructed by patients, physicians, families, and the culture out of the psychobiological experiences of the ill person. The interested parties, lay and professional, sick and well, patient and healer, negotiate diagnosis, prognosis, treatment methods and goals, fees, degrees of disability, concerns about compliance, and so forth. From these transactions, some individuals emerge with a "chronic" illness, and it is with them and their families that I am concerned.

People build their own world of meanings when they are diagnosed with chronic illness. They struggle to make sense of the accompanying motley of symptoms and signs, prognoses and changes that cloaks their distress. It seems commonplace by now to recognize that people don't suffer from diseases; they live their own idiosyncratic experiences of illness. Yet one must constantly remember that it is not the disease that is to be treated, but the person who is to be offered care. It is not chronic pain, multiple sclerosis, rheumatoid arthritis, Parkinson's disease, or cancer that I suffer from. It is my body that aches, my husband's bladder that leaks, my mother's hands that can't move with their customary ease, my friend's legs shuffling as if weighted by lead, and my child who can't breathe without a machine. So powerful is the naming of disease, however, that it is easy to fall into looking at people with illness from the viewpoint of their designated malady.

Illness is an event that makes a painful difference in the world we take for granted. For some people, their lives are irrevocably damaged. For others, the cracks in their world are patched up. And there are those for whom a former world falls apart and something new replaces the old.

All too often, patients are told what a sickness *should* mean for them—in terms of treatment, disability, changes in lifestyle. Objectively, such an assessment may be accurate. If, however, it does not speak to the felt truth of the patient's experience, it is useless. Worse, such a report may be recalled as an instance of intrusion without respect, of communication without listening.

Despite differing diagnoses, individuals who share similar

physical limitations or personal situations typically have more in common with each other than they do with those suffering from the same disease. Most medical care, self-help associations, professional organizations, and systems of reimbursement, however, are organized around disease entities and diagnostic schema. Yet it is necessary for caregivers and others to follow the lead of those who are ill, as well as for the ill to collaborate with those who have the power to pay and the authority to treat.

A colleague who works with children with juvenile diabetes and their families was asked by a urologist to speak to a group of men recently diagnosed with prostate cancer. When she protested that she knew nothing about the disease, the physician remarked, "So what, you can give them hope." He knew that more important than her knowledge or expertise with a particular medical diagnosis was her ability and experience helping people cope with newly threatened worlds. Healers are people who can make a difference in the world of another to lessen suffering, restore morale, and relieve pain.

WORLDS MADE AND UNMADE

"I feel as if I am looking at the world, at myself, through broken glass," Tom reports. "I've felt that way ever since I was diagnosed with cancer. I'm young, I have a lot to look forward to, a lot I want to do. I have played by the rules just like my parents taught me to, and now my bubble's burst.

"What's my 'bubble,' you ask? I think it's the belief that my life is supposed to go along a straight road if I live a straight life, that I could take for granted, naive as that sounds, a lot of things. That I'd get sick when I got old, not now. That I could keep my body in shape with the right food and exercise. That I could plan on things being a certain way in the future if I did certain things now. But with this damn cancer, that's not the way it is. The bubble has burst. There's glass all over the floor, the furniture, my bed, and I'm getting cut and all of us, my wife, my children, my parents, we're all bleeding."

For many people, as with Tom, chronic illness is the experience of a world that is dramatically changing. Tom experiences his situation as catastrophic although significant people continue to exist in his life as before and much remains unchanged by his illness. His world, however, is altered. The world that might have been, could have been, should have been, can no longer be.

As a consequence of the illness's symptoms and his need for medical treatment, Tom is not able to continue with the same employment as before. His income is likely to decline, and his wife will probably have to work longer hours in a physically demanding job. As a result, despite his new physical limitations, Tom will have to assume a measure of the care that his wife now provides for their children and his ailing mother-in-law. Owing to Tom's concern about his ability to drive safely, physician and physical therapy appointments have to be scheduled to fit his wife's already crowded schedule. The financial budgeting he and his wife have to undertake and the increased fatigue they both experience force them to cut down on the time they spend with friends. The leisure activities the two enjoyed before, both as individuals and as a couple, required time and fitness, and each has less of both. There are fewer opportunities for intimacy between Tom and his wife, and when they do take place, expressions of anxiety and concern about the present and future predominate.

Although nearby relatives and friends offer and provide some degree of both emotional and logistical support, Tom is reluctant to accept their help because he does not know how he could reciprocate their kindness. At the same time, he notices what he thinks is a worsening of symptoms. He's reluctant to share his worries and to cause even more distress to those he loves. Tom often awakes early in the morning—the time he calls "the hour of the wolf"—and wonders what has and will become of his family and himself. He puts off falling back asleep, fearing that he will awake to one more trouble in a world gone wrong.

Distress is the most common human response to the discovery of discrepancies between the present world and the former world that was taken for granted. Colin Parkes (1993) suggests that the life events most inimical to our continued well-being are those that force us to make significant, lasting, and often abrupt changes in what we had assumed to be permanent about our world. This is a description of chronic illness, even when its onset proceeds more slowly. The very chronicity of certain illnesses and disabilities makes it likely that unexpected and physically limiting effects, as well as many other unanticipated changes, will continue to arise over time. It is painful to fully face the implications of having the set realities of one's everyday life suddenly become unstable. The departure of the old certainties, as expressed in the powerful images Tom used, can be as disorienting, painful, and devastating as any material loss might be.

It is important, of course, for clinicians to focus on what remains constant amid the multiple changes, cascading losses, endangered meanings, fears, and anxieties that chronic illness may bring. It is, however, essential to all—patients, families, therapists—to look straight at the "facts on the ground," while still giving comfort and proffering hope. The clinician has a moral imperative to respond to people with illness from the angle of its world-unmaking capacity

> for the assault of illness on humanity is not simply physical, it is ontological, affecting our very image of ourselves—our being—and our circumstance—our world. Illness is a transformation of our being-in-the-world, it is not only that; it is an attack upon it, a deformation of it, because it threatens our integrity. (Kestenbaum, 1982, p. 33)

CHAPTER 2

The World of Everyday Life

We need a dream-world in order to discover the features of the real world we think we inhabit.
　　　　　　　　Paul Feyerabend, *Against Method* (1978)

IN THE ABSENCE of threat or wonder, we take everyday life for granted. Reality becomes transparent. It is as ubiquitous, forceful, and invisible as gravity or air. I see right through it onto my next event, encounter, or aim. In the world of everyday life, I expect and imagine myself to be wide awake and give my attention to the matters before me. I suspend my doubts that the world could be other than it is. I take for granted my body's ability to act and follow through on the projects and aims that mean something to me. I have a sense of self and identity, a "me," an "I," which assumes a fundamental sameness and continuity. My social relations with others are based on the assumption that others can understand my experience because they are similarly, although not identically, situated within the world of everyday life. The time perspective of everyday life is a shared social construct as well, making possible joint projects and common expectations.

Yet, as with Tom, everything I take for granted is in danger of being scuttled by chronic illness. In the aftermath of a storm, it is difficult to survey the loss and identify the resources available to cope with the damage without an appreciation of the lives and terrain that existed prior to the storm's arrival. Life with illness bears some resemblance to what was there before, but so much may have changed. "I don't feel like myself," or, "I feel like my life is coming apart," persons with illness may say. Among other things, they are speaking of the feared replacement of the familiar thoughts, feelings, sensations, projects, memories, and plans of their former everyday world. What was substantial now seems set upon shifting sands.

Illness assaults the world of our everyday life, a world we inhabit without much conscious thought. The largely unexamined presumptions of what our world "is" and how it "works" enable us to get on with our business in that world. Its features, knit together into a routine way of taking action and making meaning, make up much of the fabric of our lives. If we were to look at our everyday world too closely, its smooth operation would probably fall apart. It is through this world that one initially experiences illness, and it is the coherence of this world that illness most directly threatens.

Thus, starting with a firm grip on the features of everyday life will give us a better purchase on the shifting terrain of illness. The world of daily life is largely one of meaning. Meanings help us to connect one thing with another. The "world" is, in fact, "the web of meanings that allow the individual to navigate his way through the ordinary events and encounters in his life with others" (Berger, Berger, & Kellner, 1974, p. 12). We recognize patterns amid clutter.

We are guided through this landscape by an assortment of bodily habits and dispositions, mental images, internal voices, and emotions. Each acts in and upon the others, shaping and reshaping personal and larger social, cultural, and environmental realities. In the world of dreams or delirium, no other person needs to exist, but neither a person nor the world has much meaning apart from the other. There is no question that rocks can exist in a world without people, but their *meaning*, if it could be said to exist at all, would be entirely different.

The concept of life-worlds (Schutz, 1945/1970) provides a useful construct with which professionals, patients, and families can approach the task of rebuilding a world that has been changed by illness. The life-world each person inhabits is unique, defined by his or her biography, body, personal store and stock of knowledge and meanings, and interactions with the worlds of others. Individuals and the world "co-constitute" each other. As I act in and upon the world, the world, in its turn, influences and impresses itself upon me. I initiate a conversation with my wife in the morning, for example, that leads me to feel emotions of anger and affection and to reflect upon some meanings of marriage and masculinity. Later in the day, as I listen to a woman upset about the behavior of her husband, I hear overtones in her expressions of distress that I might have missed or dismissed before. My response to her concerns, in turn, may contribute to some difference in how she approaches her life, and thus to some difference in her world.

The notion of a person without a world is difficult to imagine. The shipwrecked Robinson Crusoe keeps a diary for an imaginary audience of others whom he may never meet. He delights in his solitary commerce with his man Friday. Prospero, the deposed duke of Milan, is ruler of spirits and powers on his enchanted isle, yet he discovers a wish to return to the world and to engage it as he has not done before.

ACTING "AS IF"

Contemporary life particularly demands that individuals be proficient in a "wide-awake" style of consciousness. But it is precisely this quality of consciousness that chronic illness typically undercuts. There is little on-the-job opportunity for dreams, reveries, or reflections. One learns to manage emotions and to separate work and private life. We are often expected to interact with others in such a way as to minimize knowledge of their individuality as persons and avoid the pain that comes with the hierarchies of power and the arrivals and departures from workplace settings. We are encouraged to handle many tasks simultaneously in as rapid and efficient a manner as possible and to take on life's difficulties as problems to be solved rather than as unavoidable trials of God, ill fortune, or fate. But for someone with illness, pain, medications, fatigue, restlessness, and other sensations and symptoms make it particularly difficult to attend to the matters at hand and the things that need to get done.

I have a neurogenic bladder, a not uncommon accompaniment of many illnesses, disabilities, and treatments. This means I sometimes experience urinary urgency. When I have to go, I *have to go*. I find it difficult in some circumstances to focus on what people are saying or to pay attention to whatever else I'm supposed to be doing if I don't know where the toilets are or how accessible they'll be. I have learned that I can't rely on my previous ability to "hold my water." Before getting in my car, or upon arrival at my destination, I sense my body and lightly press on my bladder to check out whether I need to go to the bathroom. I survey the territory and make mental calculations and notes about the "where" and "how" of getting relief. Even when I wear an external catheter and leg bag, I don't have full confidence that they'll work, and I touch and look for signs of wetting.

My anxious sensory and cognitive scanning is common among those with neuromuscular disorders or gastrointestinal distress. People who suffer nausea or chronic pain also engage in a constant process of shuttling their attention between body demands and social and environmental constraints. Are the chairs firm? Can I lie down if I need to? Will there be time or space to move around or stretch? Can I get out? Deciding whether to accept an apparently simple invitation to travel can turn into a fretful dilemma packed with ambivalence and apprehension.

I recall one occasion when my wife and I stepped inside the house of a friend we had not seen for many years. Our flight had been without personal incident, and I was happy to be finally near a toilet for my own use. Instinctively, I touched my pants leg to check on its dryness. It was not wet, but looking down I noticed I was standing in a small puddle leaking from my socks. The cap on the bottom of the leg bag had come undone. Daydreams recur of accidents and embarrassments, past memories of episodes that felt shameful. The characteristic effect of trauma, thoughts simultaneously intrusive and constricting, is at work in individuals with chronic illness as well.

People with chronic illness engage in a difficult struggle to act "as if" they are "all there." Such performances can be quite exhausting. Often told, "But you look so good," by others just learning of their illness, they fight to keep the facts of their life— fatigue, colostomy, pain, for example—from intruding on their many roles. Those with chronic illness become quite skilled at impression management and learn, sometimes cruelly, with whom they can be themselves. Ironically, the coping style that may be most successful in dealing with situations of danger, embarrassment, frustration, or uncertainty—"low monitoring/high blunting" (Miller, 1990)—itself calls for a conscious effort that takes attention away from the wide-awake world.

As Good (1994) points out in describing the effect of chronic pain on a particular individual, "it is only through 'tremendous effort' [as the patient describes his struggle] that he can attend to what is for most of us our paramount world. . . . His attention and preoccupations are absorbed by his pain" (p. 125). That "tremendous effort" often leaves little energy for even the small bits of daily business that constitute the most automatic of routines. "Habit," William James (1890) said, ". . . is the enormous flywheel of society." For those with chronic illness and their families, that wheel turns neither smoothly nor well.

In the world of daily life, we take much for granted. Unless we are traveling in a foreign country, we don't bother to think that most of what we say will be intelligible to others. We rarely question that we will wake the next day, and we therefore leave many tasks, promises, and business still undone at nightfall. We assume that when we do spring out of bed in the morning, not only will there be a floor, but our legs will work to set us upon it and stand. We typically suspend our doubt about the rules of whatever world we inhabit. In the two hours we may spend in the world of the theater, for example, we are able to accept a passage of days, weeks, even years or centuries, taking place onstage. At the same time, we believe that the actors engaged in swordplay or exchanging gunfire will not kill each other or those of us sitting in the audience. We exercise common sense and afterward return to the world in which we lived before.

We do what we can to maintain the "plausibility" (Berger, 1967) of the everyday world in the face of facts to the contrary—the collapse of a bridge or road, the sudden death of a friend, illness—through rationalizations, rituals, the reassurances of significant others. But with illness, doubt is no longer as easily suspended, nor does common sense retain universal appeal. We are unsettled when the plausibility of our world no longer holds.

"Since my diagnosis," Tom reflects in a brief moment of respite, "the way I think about, see, and hear everything seems changed. What I used to believe in, what I used to think was important, doesn't seem as relevant as it once did. Before I got sick, I thought of life as this big film that I automatically assumed was real. When I entered a theater to see a film, I didn't think about what was happening on the screen as a series of rapidly projected separate images. I just got lost in it.

"Now I know that so much of what I took for granted is not guaranteed to be or to happen. It's weird. There are a lot of times when the movies don't seem real in the way they used to. Just about anything can break the illusion for me, and there are fewer and fewer moments when I forget myself and react to the movie as if it's not just something being shown through a projector." The suspension of doubt that previously characterized Tom's experience of the world has been ruined by his illness. He no longer automatically assumes much about anything.

The plausibility of our culture, as with every other, is reinforced by a matrix of social practices. Most people have little cause or incentive to question basic beliefs. The dominant ideologies become embedded within our bodies and minds through the policies of the institutions we create, our styles of child-rearing, our ways of relating to each other, the kinds of entertainment we enjoy, the content of our conversations—indeed, all the features that make up the world of everyday life. Inevitably, as Geertz (1983) remarks, "those roles we think to occupy turn out to become minds we find ourselves to have" (p. 155).

BEING SICK

Illness can both subtly and more drastically limit or even overthrow much of what people assume to be true in their expectations of and relations with others. The sick role in our society makes it acceptable for individuals with illness to be exempt from performing or taking part in customary duties. To maintain this license, as well as the financial and other benefits that may accrue to being sick, a person must be seen as making a good-faith effort to get well, with the help of an authorized, competent health care professional. Those with a chronic illness, however, may be subject to periods of exacerbations and remissions, how well or sick they feel may change on a day-to-day basis, and medical treatment may be of little value to them. The personal and social consequences of entering into the sick role can be quite problematic.

Among the symptoms of Jack's illness, for example, were fatigue, severe headaches, and an overall feeling of malaise. On his well days, he appeared to be in good health, alert and fully functional. On his bad days, however, he felt so wretched that he could barely get out of bed, and he was certainly unable to drive to his office or attend even the briefest of meetings. As a result, his manager at work saw only the "healthy" Jack and found it very difficult to accept the explanations he gave for his absences, particularly since there was no firm diagnosis of his illness at the time.

When he was able, Jack pushed himself to work to make up for lost time and, he admits, to disprove other's doubts about the legitimacy of his illness complaints. Jack was concerned about how he was perceived by his manager. The pace at which he worked contributed, he believes, to more frequent illness episodes, which further undermined his manager's confidence in him. Since the workplace was becoming an area of ever greater discomfort for Jack, he began to question his commitment to his job. He wondered whether he was indeed both exaggerating his symptoms and using them to avoid work. The quite substantial pride and pleasure he had once taken in his work and in those for whom he worked were now menaced by his illness experience, as well as by the reactions of others.

Individuals like Jack recognize that they are seen differently by others, however they are known to themselves. Although words like "cripple" are no longer acceptable, terms such as "handicapped," "disabled," and "physically impaired," though subject to much dispute, are widely used. They carry substantial psychological, social, cultural, political, and financial weight. Many individuals with chronic illness are wary of the consequences of the diagnosis given to them for a variety of reasons, including the biases of others and the limiting of medical coverage and insurance. They may believe, often with justification, that others do not understand their illness and believe them to be hypochondriacs or malingerers.

Chronic illness brings more distressing results. Its impact on dating, marriage, family interactions, and sexuality can be quite dramatic, often in ways that we might not typically think of. "I'm just a twenty-five-year-old woman," offers Charlene, "working my way through business school, hoping to be done with this cancer stuff. For a year before my diagnosis, I thought I had a cold I couldn't get rid of. I had tired myself out from running around with full-time college and a part-time job and keeping up with a social life. Unfortunately, I never had night sweats to speak of and wasn't that concerned about the way I was feeling. It never really occurred to me that I could be that drastically sick at the age of twenty-four. I've always thought of myself as a kid. I never thought kids got cancer. I know better now.

"The problem that really bothers me right now is that I've been engaged for over a year to a man I've been dating for five and a half years. I worry about marrying him because my insurance situation is shaky at best. I think to myself that if I were to get sicker and we were married, he would get billed for my hospitalization debts. If I'm not married, nobody is responsible but me, so if I die, who can they go after about the money? It's morbid, but I worry about the consequences of not considering it. Still, do I allow my illness to take away the chance to be married?"

Individuals with chronic illness and their families spend a great deal of time engaged with the health care system. The domain of medicine has its own attendant beliefs and ways of working, and the interactions between people in the worlds of illness and those in the world of health care can be quite wearing. To cope in the provinces of home, work, friends, and community while taking on and off the role of patient is one more strain on an individual's attempts to maintain a life reasonably similar to the one that existed prior to illness.

Ellen, burdened with severe rheumatoid arthritis, feels that most people in her life think she's a smart, warm, straight-talking woman—except those who treat her illness. At work, she's very competent. She knows her job, and she speaks up when she needs to. With all the vagaries of chronic illness, Ellen feels in greater control when she has more information. She believes that some doctors and even their receptionists think she is checking up on them when she asks about her symptoms, her prognosis, her medications. When Ellen walks into the HMO, she's sure they're thinking, "Oh, no!" She feels as if her questions are treated as complaints. She uses up a great deal of energy imploring professionals to give her the time she needs to ask her questions. By the time she's finished with her appointment, she often feels worse than when she came in.

The normal transactions that take place within families and among friends and coworkers become loaded with new meaning and can carry a moral weight when someone is living with chronic illness. Ellen is especially conscious of her limitations when her friends make plans for activities in which she can't take part. They talk about playing tennis or going for walks. She is aware that she is cut off from much of their lives together. Though she recognizes that her isolation is no one's fault, she nevertheless feels differently now about herself and her friends.

FALSE IDOLS

The ideologies of progress, individuality, and health are among those that strongly affect our attitudes toward illness. Modern society's elimination of a range of social and medical ills lends much credence to the argument for progress. Most modern people assume that human culture, over the long run, is improving, as demonstrated by the feats of technology, science, and the power of rational thought. Those who doubt the value of these apparent goods and point to higher populations, greater poverty, and increased environmental destruction are often dismissed as moral softies, political Neanderthals, or neo-Luddites.

We easily forget that the concept of human progress is recent. Not more than three hundred years ago, and in traditional and fundamentalist cultures today, human history is imagined as a fall from an original state of grace or a descent from a once-upon-a-time golden age. In this view, the evolution of humanity is inconceivable except as a result of divine intervention. Individuals may take steps along a path toward perfection, but any success they experience typically occurs in spite of, rather than because of, the existing social order. So difficult is the real evolution of being and consciousness, according to some traditions, that its attainment is possible only after many lifetimes of effort.

The belief in the ideology of progress continues despite what Danieli (1989) calls a "fourth narcissistic blow" to humanity's self-love (in addition to the three that Freud proposed make it difficult for people to accept psychoanalysis—Copernicus's solarcentric universe; the human membership in the animal world implied by Darwin; and Freud's own suggestion that the individual ego is not even master in its own house): "I believe," Danieli writes, "that Nazi Germany gave humanity the fourth, the *ethical blow*, by shattering our belief that the world we live in is a just place in which human life is of value, to be protected and respected" (p. 456).

The belief that "for every problem, there is a solution," is a cliché with which we are all familiar. It is a message, as many critics have noted, that is reinforced by the facile endings of so many television shows and the barrage of advertising for goods that promise to fulfill so many desires or remedy so many ills. Our unquestioned commitment to the ideologies of progress and health contributes to the drive of many physicians to leave no treatment stone unturned or intervention untried. Patients, too, are often willing to undergo whatever miseries the attempted cure may bring. For a number of people with chronic illness and their families, I believe it is an unexamined and unwarranted attachment to a belief in progress and a problem-solving orientation, as much as a hope for recovery, that keeps them searching for a cure despite disappointments. The grip that these taken-for-granted ideologies have on us also adds to the anger some feel toward their physicians and other care providers when their condition does not improve.

People apply the ideology of progress to their own life courses, devising career plans and strategies with long-term goals to launch and maintain themselves on continuously upward trajectories of economic and personal growth. Not doing better is often taken as a mark of personal inadequacy rather than as ill fortune, an act of God, or the distributive justice of the bell-shaped curve. This ideology is ironically expressed by Garrison Keillor's description of Lake Wobegon as a town where "all the children are above average."

Consistent with the belief in progress and the evidence of our century, our attitude toward ourselves is contradictory. We assume that the person we were yesterday is pretty much the person we are today, and we make promises and commitments in the good-faith belief that some identity exists between our current impulses and what we will want tomorrow. The fact that our body, its workings, and its surroundings appear to be pretty much the same from day to day confirms the soundness of our naive assumption.

In actuality, we often make excuses, tell lies to ourselves and others, and scramble to make good on our word. We imagine that changes in love or fortune can lead to a radically different world, and we claim that the world we once inhabited has changed. The person we take ourselves to be is no longer consistent with the self we imagined we once were. Fortunately or not, however, most of us manage to maintain on a day-to-day basis a relatively coherent account of ourselves. We project into the near future a self with aptitudes, dispositions, and commitments reasonably congruent with those of the person we claim, without reflection or pretext, to be today. Consistent with our everyday sense of self, Erikson's (1959) classic definition of identity is "the accrued confidence that one's ability to maintain inner sameness and continuity is matched by the sameness and continuity of one's meaning for others" (p. 89).

Attempts to maintain a stable identity and live by a secure set of rules are, however, put to the test when confronted by the ideologies of our present moment. We are offered workshops and books that offer us the opportunity to "create" our lives the way we want them to be. We live in a time characterized by rapid social change and a belief in continuous improvement. Not only who or what we are but who we intend to be is a source of great importance as well as anxiety in a culture like ours. Little wonder that authors refer to the "saturated self" (Gergen, 1991), "peculiarly open identities" (Berger, Berger, & Kellner, 1974), and so on. The times seem to require that our identities be fluid, complex, self-aware, singular, and autonomous.

Many people believe that health, like progress, is a good to be pursued at whatever cost. Health care expenditures continue to climb; discomforts are medicalized; variations in bodily chemistry are identified as symptoms; aging, with its accompanying deterioration of bodily function, is seen as a collection of serious diseases; and the diagnosis and treatment of the body through procedures, technologies, and drugs are major targets of investment and sources of profit. Meanwhile, children are hungry.

"At least I've got my health," someone says. Well, that is true. If I want to identify values more important than health, however, I might suggest beauty, friendship, love, wisdom, gratitude, courage, truth, simplicity, and so on. To move from being fixed on a cure for the body to an openness to the healing of the person or the soul can be a profound shift for patients and clinicians alike.

In our society, with its emphasis on differentiation, purposefulness, accomplishment, personal responsibility, and individuality, we tend to experience our selves as separate from others. The self's boundaries are set by the outer skin and run by a central authority called "I." From Ben Franklin to Horatio Alger to the entrepreneurial heroes, celebrity stars, and infomercialists of today, the idea of the self-made man has resonated powerfully within the American psyche. The public's attitude toward each person's responsibility to avoid "lifestyle" diseases does not show much sympathy for those who suffer.

Ideologies of individuality and autonomy have been analyzed and rebutted by progressive political critics, feminist scholars, proponents of communitarian philosophies, and many in the fields of family and community therapy and medicine.

In practice, however, many therapists are ambivalent. They

do not want to "blame the victim," but they are oriented toward "empowering the individual." Therapists often seem more fearful of enmeshment than of moves toward differentiation and are uncomfortable with supporting dependency. Taking personal responsibility for the "sameness and continuity" of the self and its actions can be difficult in a culture that seems to be at odds with itself. It is especially so for people living with the uncertainties and changes of chronic illness.

"When I got ill with emphysema," Frank told me, "I knew that it was probably a result of all the smoking I had done since I was twelve. No one said it directly, but I know that people were blaming me for ruining my health, and some had a hard time feeling badly for a guy who from their point of view had no self-control. No self-control? Listen, I fought in two wars, I worked shifts and sometimes double shifts busting up my back and shoulders in pretty hard factory jobs for almost forty years, I drank some, never hit anybody, raised three kids, two of whom went to college, stayed married for thirty years. After we got divorced, I let my wife have the house, and I helped her out. Now some doctors and nurses are telling me I don't have self-control?

"In the back of my mind, to tell you the truth, I think maybe this is some kind of punishment from God for not doing all the right things in my life. I'm not so old, and I was just beginning to look forward to retirement. Maybe God said, 'Look, the guy did some good things, but he did do some bad things too, so I'll let him be able to see the good (like my grandchildren), and then he'll die before he gets to enjoy too much for himself.' I admit I got a lot of self-control, but I've been a sinner too.

"I tell my grandchildren, who really are feeling terrible about this, that when I was a kid in high school, and then overseas, that everybody smoked, they gave cigarettes away. We didn't know how bad it was. They just can't understand why when I did find out, I just didn't quit, even if it was hard. They said that in school they learned you can do what you want to do, that you're in control of your life. They think most poor people are probably losers. I know they get some of that from their parents, my kids, because I taught them how important hard work is and not to rely on anyone else to do the job for you. So I guess I've kind of hung myself on my own noose."

The word *stigma* has had an interesting career. Its earliest use was to refer to the marks left by burnings and cuttings on, for example, traitors or criminals. One was "branded" for life, both to remind oneself of one's misdeed and to warn others of a crime and a person to be avoided. The "mark of Cain" and the "scarlet letter" are biblical and literary variants, respectively, of this practice. Later the meaning of stigma was reversed: it referred to the wounds Christ experienced at his crucifixion from the nails that pierced his hands and feet and the crown of thorns that tore his brow. Spontaneous bleeding, rashes, or swelling in those body sites were said to have occurred among some saints as well as common folk. The visible symptoms of disease among those who bore their suffering with dignity by God's grace were also characterized as stigma. Now the term has reversed itself again. Many dictionaries make little reference to its Christian meaning and allude only to words like *stain*, *blot*, and *disfigurement*. While certain illnesses—cancer and tuberculosis, for instance—have lost some of their identity as stigmas, individuals with other medical difficulties, such as AIDS or chronic fatigue syndrome, have come under social suspicion.

The people of many traditional cultures, on the other hand, suffer profound shock and disorientation when confronted by modern ideologies of the self and their noncommunal spirit. For some of them, life takes place within an "ensouled" world in which the distinctions between a deceased grandparent and a living grandchild are profoundly different from our own. Reliance on objects and values outside of oneself—a particular piece of land, a ritual, a way of being toward each other—seems to them part of the natural order of things. We often forget that ancient and powerful critiques of beliefs and assumptions of independence and self-sufficiency are found in traditional religions. Indeed, the notion that humanity is essentially dependent on another source of being for its very existence is perhaps the simplest truth of sacred wisdom.

Illness in such a context can be seen as an attempt by the divine to crack the ego's illusion of separateness. Unless one opens up the field of therapeutic exploration to include the question of ultimate dependency and personal and family beliefs about spirituality and the sacred, opportunities may be missed to identify significant and unexpected fears, as well as resources for healing. Making individuals or families responsible for their illness or health can strengthen one kind of self but, paradoxically, may run the risk of weakening their spirit. "The only real difference between people," writes Arthur Frank (1991), "is not health or illness but the way each holds onto a sense of value in life" (p. 134).

CHAPTER 3

My Body Is Always with Me

> ... prayer barely out, heavy numbness seizes
> limbs, soft breasts enclose in bark, hair
> in leaf, arms branch, feet (so swift)
> root; head, a tree-top; but her splendor remains ...
>
> Ovid, *The Metamorphoses*

MY BODY IS ALWAYS with me. Awake or sleeping, well or ill, in infancy or old age, during puberty or pregnancy, the ultimate fact that "I" am embodied never goes away. Because I have a body, I am alive, lusty, and limited. I am dependent on the environment and others and subject to the certainties of aging, loss, and death. Bound as I am within my body, suffering indignities and experiencing joys, I can still enter with empathy into ways and possibilities of being that exist beyond my own. If you are in pain, I try to imagine your suffering. Crippled, I dream of running. Grown old, I picture my youth.

Personally, I am glad that I maintain a body image that is probably incongruent with how others see me. When I greet my patients in my office, they may notice a slight stiffness in my posture or gait. Soon, of course, I sit down and my body displays no appearance of illness. But anyone who is around me when I am at home or who encounters me in the street sees the movements and bearing of an entirely different body and, therefore, another "me." Because of the weakness and spasticity of my legs, I am unable to stand straight, and I tire easily. Exhausted after a small bit of cooking or cleaning up in the kitchen, I lean on the sink. I shuffle or limp through the yard and literally pull myself up the stairs. Yet, despite these conditions, and making no conscious effort to "see" myself differently, I still picture my frame in my mind's eye as I remember it before MS took hold.

When I am around strangers or when I meet people—clients, for example—in unexpected situations, I am thrown into a heightened degree of self-consciousness and can no longer deny the true nature of my carriage. I might make a mildly self-deprecating joke about my condition that is more an expression of my own discomfort than an (unnecessary) attempt to put them at ease.

Such encounters can produce quite a jolt in individuals with illness. The body, its appearance, its posture, its very existence, is experienced as something unfamiliar, unexpected, strange. Getting a glance in a mirror at oneself in a wheelchair evokes unexpected emotions. The shock of finding that our formerly domesticated companion, our body, has become an alien being is described in Franz Kafka's *The Metamorphosis* (1925, 1979). The opening of the story, when Kafka's Gregor Samsa awakes one morning in his bed and discovers that his human body has been transformed into a huge insect, is unforgettable.

For most people in our culture, the body is experienced as background. For those in ill health, however, the body often becomes the dominant figure to which our intentions and projects must yield. The spontaneous action we may have enjoyed before the arrival of illness now requires careful thought. Walking up and down stairs, a simple task once carried out with unconscious ease, may be accomplished only by grasping a handrail and raising oneself step by tiring step. Getting in and out of bed, emptying the bladder, moving and turning so as to minimize pain or nausea, the range of motions involved in sexual activity, all require special concentration and effort.

We exist through our bodies. We set out in them from birth to navigate the world and use them to express and satisfy our preferences and dispositions. Gradually, through the inevitable process of socialization, we learn which bodily actions on the "outside" and states on the "inside" (later characterized as feelings, moods, intuitions) bring pleasure to ourselves and others. Some motions and meanings are not welcome in particular families, physical environments, or social milieus; others are offered no opportunities to emerge. Events and encounters with the natural world, exhilarating, frightening, and commonplace, sculpt and shape our body, its movements, our emotions, and our mind.

Thus, the winnowing out of a repertoire of acceptable postures and gestures, thoughts and words, inevitably leads to a complex and tightly woven fabric of habitual movement and familiar and intimate sensation that we characterize as "me" or "I." Our bodies come to serve, in Merleau-Ponty's phrase, as a "living envelope of our actions" (Moss, 1978, p. 77), incarnating the meanings that guide us through our lives. With our bodies, we make our mark upon others and in turn are formed by their deeds. The body is the medium through which we make and have a world.

We take for granted the ability of the body to perform the routine actions of everyday life. In a fluid suite of actions that require little or no conscious attention, we turn the ignition key, engage the gears, press the accelerator pedal, and drive off. We talk and walk, carrying a cup of hot beverage with no fear of tripping, falling, or spilling. We type, focused on finding the right word without giving our fingers the least thought. We read, engrossed in the plot and rarely concerned about the neurophysiology and biomechanics of vision. We forget the intention, limbs, and practice we once employed to master such everyday skills. These well-practiced ensembles of movement and meaning—"kinetic melodies," in A. R. Luria's phrase (Moss, 1978, p. 81)—are built up over time through ordinary use and intentional practice.

In general, however, except when displaying its strengths, enjoying sensory pleasures, or acquiring new skills, we give the body little notice. We take its existence and service for granted and forget how much its tissues contribute to our sense of self, identity, and personality.

Thus, gradually, through common usage, each person's body "disappears" from consciousness, rendered secondary to our attention to other, more important concerns. The corporeal quality of being recedes. The experience of a place (usually "in my head," in our culture) that is "I" becomes more dominant. The "I" becomes one thing, the body another. The figure of the ego establishes its relationship to the ground of the body, just as a general observes his troops. The body overthrown is the unconscious, a living embodiment of possibilities unexpressed. The body becomes an instrument in service to its master's aims.

With the onset and progression of chronic illness or disability, however, the relationship between the body and the "I" is altered. The absent body becomes present in a way that the self does not intend. Our attention is yanked away from the "I-witness" world of everyday life to the body-focused world of illness and pain.

BODY AS GROUND, BODY AS FIGURE

It is this change in the gestalt of consciousness and being-in-the-world that is central to the experience of illness. After all, the person who has no signs or symptoms of the tumor that grows treacherously and unknown deep inside his brain neither experiences nor construes himself as ill, despite the threat the growth poses to his existence. Van den Berg rightly states, "The transformation of the body from an instrument to a problem is a good indicator of a move from the world of everyday life to that of illness" (Kestenbaum, 1982, p. 23).

The experience of illness arises primarily from the ways I and others use and respond to my body in relation to a range of favored or constrained attitudes and movements that exists within my social world. The gravity of my illness is shaped by what my body means to me and what I use it for as much as by the clinical symptoms it presents. Just as our bodies are affected by how we think and feel about ourselves, our identities are similarly influenced by how we experience our bodies.

Bound by no rules, disrespectful of authority and limits, the illness does what it pleases. One is never quite sure how one's body may present itself from one day to the next. One is possessed by a shape-shifter, a being of indeterminate appearance who makes the familiar strange and the strange familiar.

There are those for whom the passage from a world of good health to one of illness is sudden and frightening, the spasm of pain or the terror of paralysis that grabs hold and may never let go. For others, the malady wears and pulls more slowly, but no less insistently, as the powers and functions of the body fall away, whether as single threads or in clumps. Some people are crippled, disfigured, disabled, or bent. Many appear ambulatory and functional, look well, and don't feel too bad. Few are untouched.

Most people notice when they're not feeling quite right or like themselves. But for the "well-bodied," such notice is usually not a matter of continuously conscious concern or obsession. Individuals or families who focus apprehensively on bodily sensations and processes, in the absence of a medical diagnosis, may well be characterized as "the worried well," hypochondriacs, or "somatizers."

Those living with illness, however, find it hard not to stay tuned in to swings in sensation and waves of unease. The ill body insists that we attend to it. People living with chronic illness need to be alert to variations and fluctuations in physical signs and symptoms. "I would prefer not to monitor my 'in-house' systems," as one engineer with Parkinson's disease put it. "But I can't just turn off the key and walk out the door."

During the first few years following my diagnosis, I learned to recognize and adapt to a baseline level of somatic disturbance. I now distinguish between the ongoing sensory "noise" of MS and the alterations in body feeling or function that indicate an exacerbation. Changes in weather, minor colds or infections, and fatigue are influential variables. Multiple sclerosis draped my body in a stranger's cloak for the first years following the onset of illness. That impression has been replaced with a wary and tenuous familiarity, which will surely disappear in turn with the disturbances of a major exacerbation or clear evidence of deterioration.

IN THE HANDS OF OTHERS

Not only are deeds disrupted or bodies impaired when illness or accident throw up obstacles to the smooth flow of intention, action, and thought; our images of body and self suffer fissures and fractures as well. What illness wreaks upon our bodies influences how we are touched and perceived by others. Medical care is not the only way in which the bodies of those with illness are handled by others. Parents, partners, and friends often participate in the provision of care. They assist with injections, intravenous hookups, tubes, and bags and aid in the washing and cleaning up that may accompany the difficulties of the ill. A helping hand in walking, a literal shoulder to lean on, eyesight for the blind, arms that push wheelchairs, fingers and palms that give massages, hugs, and simply touch, are all extended out of love and kindness from most, as well as guilt and necessity from others. As caring as such ministrations may be, however, many are the kinds of actions that anyone but an infant or toddler usually performs on his or her own.

To be vulnerable to discomfort or harm and in need of the protection and service of others reverses the expected capacity of most adults to take care of themselves. Surges of pride that shove away proffered help or refuse to acknowledge the need for assistance are not to be simply dismissed as failures to cope but rather seen as expressions of a wish for autonomy that ought to be taken seriously, and with great respect. The uncontrollability of the body provokes feelings of helplessness and shame. The help that others furnish stirs up emotions of a similar kind.

Some who ail prefer that their bodies be approached, and their privacy breached, by strangers. They may wish to spare their family or companions from having to do the dirty work of bodily care. Others want to protect their loved ones from struggles with their own feelings of embarrassment or shame. On the other hand, many individuals with illness prefer the touch of familiars over that of those whom they know less well. Many families assume that they will provide the kinds of care to their afflicted loved one that other families believe are best offered by professionals. Whatever the preference may be, once again the simple and sometimes punishing fact is that such concerns are real and ongoing in the life of the one confronted with illness. For the ill, embarrassment is a luxury.

Body images are as much a product of our engagement with our personal, social, and cultural worlds as any other detail of our lives. The image I have of my body does not come from a clear-eyed stance I take outside of myself, as if my body were a subject to be captured by a camera. The idea that the photograph is more objective is a fiction, for photographs themselves must be looked at to be seen and the act of looking is itself an interpretive event. Rhetorical attempts to persuade me that I look different from how I sense myself to be will fail.

To display the unique self that inhabits the body structure we have in common, people employ an extravagant range of practices with religious, cultural, social, familial, or solely personal significance. Much of this activity is motivated by a wish to give notice of our own individuality, as well as to mark the similarities and differences between the groups with which we identify and those of others. In our own culture, our bodies are sculpted by workouts, diets, and plastic surgery and decorated with clothes, jewelry, makeup, and tattoos. We fashion ourselves through exercise, diet, and costume to measure up to or at least approach our ideals of attractiveness and health. What some find beautiful evokes disgust and fear in others.

A Western physician, for example, might perceive a "diseased" body as either a problem to be diagnosed and solved or a beautifully designed machine in need of surgical or chemical repair and cleaning. Dancers think of their bodies as instruments to be mastered for the performance of art. A boxer acknowledges his body as a potential source of great fortune and glory and conditions it to weather the punishment of his sport.

Healthy bodies are described in pounds and feet, viewed through lenses, scanned by instruments of ingenious kind and variety, and disciplined to move with grace and speed. But my ill body is different from the bodies that others observe through the technology of medicine, employ in the service of their art, or submit to training for gain. My interest lies in *my* body, the one I live with, the one that feels ill, bent, or in pain. The space I want to illuminate is *my* space, whether it is stuffed huge with the possibilities of easy access and action or constricted for me by the very openness you may find exhilarating. The time I want to describe is *my* time, marked with duration and tempos drawn from the cacophonies of disease.

A major consequence of chronic illness is one's own body, its needs, secrets, and intimacies as well as its most private areas and boundaries, becoming subject to and the object of the min-istrations and manipulations of others. There is no other activity in which our bodies are more examined and explored than mod-ern medicine. Needles violate our skin, blood and a host of other fluids are withdrawn, tubes as well as television cameras(!) are fed down our throats or up our colons, microelectrodes are attached to muscles and nerves, and tissue of all kinds is cut, removed, replaced. Skulls are drilled, and abdomens sutured. Anesthesia renders the patient unconscious, and powerful drugs induce chills, convulsions, fevers, and fatigue as side effects. There is almost no end to the procedures that are per-formed on the ill in the medical quest for proper diagnosis and effective treatment. Frank (1991) writes, "To get medicine's help, I had to cede the territory of my body to the investigations of doctors who were as yet anonymous. I had to be colonized" (p. 51).

There is no implication here that these processes are not implemented with the good faith and best practice of physicians and other health professionals in the best interests of the patient, although the drive for status, profit, certainty, and knowledge ought not to be discounted. It is important, however, to acknowledge what a person's body—and therefore a person—may be subject to in the quest for health or, at the least, some surcease from distress. Imagine the rationalizations and fear of someone who accepts penetrations and intrusions in medical settings that he or she would never permit anywhere else. In addition, the very behaviors that characterize a "good patient"—for instance, compliance with authority—might be seen by a therapist as unhelpful to that person in any other sit-uation. Many with chronic illness can join Matisse in his protest against the continued ministrations of physicians: "I have some right to defend my own skin" (Sandblom, 1995, p. 86).

A BODY OUT OF CONTROL

The ability to manage what, when, and where material goes into and comes out of the body is one of the earliest goals of the process of socialization. Toddlers are praised for demonstrating control of bladder and bowel, as well as for spitting, burping, coughing, and holding their own spoon, fork, or cup. Most parents show concern when acquisition of these competencies seems to be delayed.

We view the loss of these capacities for body regulation among the elderly as a sure sign of aging, as a normal and somewhat inevitable prelude to dying. Nevertheless, many older persons are afraid as well as discomforted if they do have "accidents," because they may precipitate more restricted lives or institutional care.

Children who wet their pants or beds feel shame. The "pee and poop" jokes of five- and six-year-olds show the anxieties many feel about their still recent achievement of such a potent symbol of social maturity. It is a mark of personal mastery among some grownups not to give in to the promptings of nature as long as "more important" matters are at hand. In those worlds, one's duty comes before one's "doody."

For a great many individuals with chronic illness, however, the luxury of measuring one's status in such a concrete way is not available. The most embarrassing things happen. Bladders leak or overflow without warning. Sphincters don't hold and let go with a great stench. Most people have a hard time imagining such an event happening to themselves. For many individuals with chronic illness or disability, however, a lot of time, ingenuity, and money goes into guarding against such hazards. The rush of alarm at a fall or the anger that accompanies a sudden surge of pain or wave of nausea may be replaced by a guarded withdrawal from one's former pattern of living. The ability to manage one's symptoms is not the same as having a sense of control over one's body. Fears of losing control contribute to feeling-states and compensations similar to those associated with anxiety disorders. The body, after all, has a mind of its own.

It frequently takes a number of unpleasant incidents and

failed hopes before one acknowledges how unruly one's body may have become, but such acknowledgment is a first step toward maintaining composure and keeping mishaps from turning into calamities. Chronic illness relentlessly attacks, however, pushing our creatureliness right in our faces, through aches and pains, dizziness and falls, disturbances of vision, blood in the toilet bowl, weakness, fatigue—all harbingers of illness or regular accompaniments along the way. Some find it difficult to accept these random betrayals by their bodies.

Chronic pain, seizure disorders, vertigo, and similar symptoms are dreaded reminders of the body's anarchic potential. Apprehension about fainting, enduring a convulsion, or suffering nausea or dizziness in public is surely an understandable reason for many individuals with chronic conditions to restrict their activities to places where they are sure of some privacy, comfort, or relief. In her account of her life with chronic fatigue and immune dysfunction syndrome (CFIDS), Kat Duff (1993) remarks, "I have trained myself to a path of moderation, curtailing my activities to that small circle—a radius of twenty miles from my home—that I know I can comfortably inhabit" (p. 18).

The sense of a body out of control can emerge in a gradual and, at times, devastating manner. The awful effects of some cancers, diabetes, multiple sclerosis, rheumatoid arthritis, AIDS, emphysema, and other chronic illnesses commonly occur in a progressive manner. Individuals become more and more incapacitated, with fewer and fewer physical resources to draw on. Horror, despair, and resignation may seize and settle upon those who are aware of the apparently inevitable falling apart of their bodies.

Many people with illness live with a chronic panic about the soft underbelly of our psychic life, the undeniable bond between creatureliness and death. We employ a host of strategies to avoid this basic suffering, ranging from individual defense mechanisms and security operations to family scapegoating and secrets. Chronic illness, however, erupts into lives with a perverse disregard for persona, status, or plans. It threatens the bulwarks we have erected to keep existential facts and anxieties at bay. Its attacks leave us open to a return of the repressed—the felt recognition of the imminent possibility of illness or accident, pain, loss, and death, realities our culture keeps masked beneath its pride in material progress, performance, and production. Sensitive to these realities himself, Arthur Frank (1991), who experienced cancer and a heart attack by the age of forty, writes:

> In society's view of disease, when the body goes out of control, the patient is treated as if he has lost control. Being sick thus carries more than a hint of moral failure. . . . Of course the problem is not that . . . the ill person has "lost" control; the problem is that society's ideal of controlling the body is wrong in the first place. (p. 58)

The disease process is a disruption of normal organic functioning. As a result, many professionals focus on the organs or limbs that are "diseased" and fail to appreciate the subtle and often pervasive effects that bodily changes can have on the ways that patients organize their lives. What the observer may see as a minor physical discomfort can affect nearly every project and person in the life of the one with chronic illness. Once-simple choices about trips to the city or walks downtown become intensive, hypervigilant, body-scanning, problem-solving matters.

Until I became ill with multiple sclerosis, my body usually stayed out of consciousness unless I chose to bring it onstage for acts of pleasure or mastering new skills. Riding my bike to work, enjoying sex, tossing a football with my daughter or son, relishing the sensory favors of intoxicants, putting eye and ear in the service of paintings and music, were all occasions when I wanted to take some notice of how my body moved, responded, and quickened.

Now, my body, I find, has usurped authority from my self. Its demands and distractions assert themselves without concern for my desires. I don't want to have to pay attention to keeping my footing on a wet walkway. In fact, the more I focus on it, the greater the spasticity of my legs and the likelihood of losing control—too stiff to fall, too inflexible to stop. What I wish to do becomes more and more dependent on what my body permits me to do. In the presence of illness, the absence of the body can no longer be sustained. Although this constraint is in the natural order of things as we move toward old age, *it is not supposed to happen now.* I am too young for this. I want to put my body in its place and haul it out as I will. But it refuses to allow me such liberties.

Individuals with chronic illness are likely to be very ambivalent toward their bodies. On the one hand, the body is the source of the distress, threat, and loss that they have encountered. At the same time, it is through the body and its capacity to respond to the healing interventions of medicine, psychology, or faith that the ill and their families look for relief from suffering and even death.

"I remember when a friend of mine told me that the reason he continued to enjoy lifting weights was that he 'loved his tissue,'" remarked Fran. "I didn't know what he meant. In fact, I found the expression kind of odd. But once I started to work out, I understood—the sense of being at home in my body, of experiencing the gain in strength and endurance. My body image changed, my muscles were awakened. I felt more alive. I became more confident. I felt in control. I could do things in sports and just around the house I hadn't done before.

"But that was before my recent exacerbation. I get tired so quickly now. My hands are too numb to grip. My legs feel like sticks that can't bend. Just the idea of working out and the exhaustion that I'm sure will grab me afterwards keeps me from getting back to what I know I could or ought to be doing. My vision went bad for a while too. It's horrible. Friends, doctors, counselors—everybody tells me that I should be exercising more and maybe even building back the strength I had before. But it's so discouraging. I wasn't easily motivated before I got this bad. Now it's even harder. I know it sounds weird, but sometimes I think that if I didn't have a body, being sick wouldn't be so bad. No wonder an angel doesn't have a body. It would only drag her down."

Fran's quip that, if not for her body, her disabilities would be bearable is loaded with irony and can be appreciated as such. It certainly reveals her frustration in finding that something that used to be a means toward fulfillment now obstructs her pursuit of that end. More important, Fran's jest underscores the degree to which she would like to believe, and act as if, she were free from vulnerability and death. She hungers, as do many of us, for a self unanchored by the pull of the earth and of aging, a self bounded only by the expansiveness of visions, dreams, and desires.

A clinician might be concerned that Fran is headed for an emotional fall as the reality of her vulnerable embodiment hits home. Feelings and thoughts of shame and self-alienation would not be unlikely, even with no objective change in her medical status. The way we approach life emerges to a great degree out of the passing judgments we make of our bodies' ability to fulfill our most basic needs and cherished ideals.

The contradiction inherent in maintaining the fitness to compensate for the loss of strength, endurance, and flexibility that accompanies many chronic illnesses is all too evident to those who suffer. The effort involved in building up muscles already weakened by disease and disuse can leave one fatigued and, over the short term, less able to perform the tasks for which exercise was undertaken in the first place. Although a workout program can be very helpful and is frequently recommended, it may not be carried out. Like anyone else, people with illness often need to see quick, concrete benefits to a prescribed regimen. The need to conserve energy may take a higher priority than its expenditure when the immediate cost is worse than the status quo. "Why should I push my body," asked one patient, "when all I'll get out of it *tomorrow* is more pain than I feel today? Sure, if I start working out, it could be next week that I hurt less than I do right now. But why should I put myself through hell now for a maybe later on?"

THE ENEMY IS ME

Thinking of the world as filled with opposites such as sickness and health, body and mind, many people, whether afflicted by illness or not, divide the organism itself into "good" cells and "bad" cells. Illness and its symptoms, causes, and processes are singled out as "the enemy." Some individuals identify with the medical ideology of "fighting" disease and feel empowered to join battle against, for example, their cancer. There are those who see their illness as something to be defeated or who struggle to subjugate the immune, digestive, coronary, or respiratory system gone wrong. Is it not possible, however, that such "splitting" between different aspects of one's body can be as problematic in the long term as the splitting that can occur in one's internal psychological world?

When a chronic illness identified as a genetic disorder is diagnosed in a family, attitudes toward one's self and one's body can vary widely. Individuals who have inherited a genetic anomaly—such as that associated with Huntington's chorea—but have not yet displayed symptoms may imagine their bodies as a kind of fifth columnist, primed at any moment to initiate attacks on their health. They may live under a cloud of what Rolland (1994) calls "anticipatory loss." Such individuals and their families might structure their lives in a way that reveals an orientation toward the body as a source of harm and a destroyer of lives and goals, rather than as a bearer of possibilities for pleasure or accomplishment. Holding such a fearful attitude toward oneself, toward one's body, can, of course, be profoundly alienating.

Some people respond to genetic testing and results in unexpected ways. "I remember when I tested negative for Huntington's chorea," Marcia remembers. "I was relieved to some extent to get verification that what I had feared, but planned for, was unlikely. I frankly don't know how I would have felt if I had tested positive, since the way I handled my life was based on the likelihood I would get ill. For the longest time I felt that I had this little time bomb in my body that I might have planted in my kids. Why couldn't I have given them good genes? And although I know it's irrational, I think that maybe because I tested negative, my sister will be more likely to test positive. Now I find myself watching my sister more closely than I ever did before, and if she gets a headache or anything, I worry about her."

Parents whose children live with illness that may be the result of what they believe to be predisposing genes—which can include emphysema, mental illness, juvenile diabetes, and some types of cancer—may unfairly blame themselves for the presence or possibility of disease. A parent, for example, may identify his or her body as a source of contamination, a lethal biochemical weapon aimed and perhaps tragically fired at a child. Jesse's son Roy was diagnosed with a form of leukemia. Since several members of Jesse's family had been diagnosed with and died from cancer, Jesse blamed himself for Roy's illness. The hardships Jesse's family experienced during the cruel seasons of Roy's diagnosis and treatment were made more difficult by Jesse's self-recrimination and guilt. Unable to do anything for his son except remain by his side during all the treatments and hospitalizations, Jesse displaced his feelings of shame and helplessness onto his wife and argued that she didn't care enough about Roy when she took time for herself to recover from the terrible illness of their child. Jesse withdrew from intimacy during this time; not only was he upset by his son's misfortune, but he questioned whether anyone, including his wife, could find his own body, which he viewed as a genetic enemy, attractive.

Feelings of hopelessness and helplessness about one's body and oneself are common after being diagnosed with an infectious disease such as AIDS. Men and women in long-term partnerships who are told they have AIDS may inaccurately conclude that they have nothing to lose by continuing to engage in unsafe sexual practices. People may blame and hate themselves for unknowingly transmitting a virus to others, particularly children. They may withdraw from caring for their young ones, believing that their own lack of worth is as infectious as the disease with which they live.

THE BODY POLITIC

The fields of social medicine and medical anthropology have described how "symptoms of hunger . . . , whether among the North American poor or the impoverished cane cutters of Brazil, are often medicalized, treated as a condition of individual bodies—'diarrhea,' 'TB,' 'nerves,' or 'stress'—rather than as a collective social and political concern" (Good, 1994, pp. 57–58). The anthropological view also suggests that powerlessness and somatization are linked. The distress that accompanies chronic illness may undergo "somatic amplification" (Kleinman & Kleinman, 1985, p. 476), particularly when resources to provide care and companionship are not easily accessible. Explanations for why someone becomes ill typically do not go beyond the most proximate cause. One's tuberculosis is due to infection from certain bacilli; it is not described as a result of poverty and political neglect.

Lung, heart, and other diseases attributable to smoking are often viewed within the framework of individual responsibility, with no acknowledgment of the powerful advertising incentives that contribute to the maintenance of a biopsychosocial addiction. Claims that some diseases and disabilities are occupationally linked—such as the deleterious effects of exposure to asbestos or the harm to farmworkers from pesticides and other environmental toxins—are met with great opposition. It usually takes enormous courage and perseverance to redefine the injury to one's body as a by-product of economic interests rather than of the failure of one's own immune system or of bad personal choices. One's body becomes an exhibit for both plaintiff and defense, figuratively and in fact, when illness is unclaimed territory in political war.

The health care, pharmaceutical, biogenetic, biotechnology, diet, and other industries perceive the body, ill or well, as a source of continued profit. They engage in a kind of biological and emotional strip-mining as "risk factors" are turned into illnesses and the hope for cure becomes an opportunity for gain. At the same time, corporations want to make their services or products most available to the people who have the greatest ability to pay for them. In the current insurance industry environment, individuals and families, frightened that illness may disqualify them from further coverage, may postpone visits to the physician even after diagnosis is made. The complaints of the body and definitions of illness are also subject to intense negotiation when disability status is being adjudicated. These are just a few of the ways in which the body is perceived as an object to be fought over by various political and social interests.

THE THICKNESS OF SPACE

Space, for those with chronic illness, is dense. Just as illness gives the body a new solidity and weight, space, once "transparent" in relation to the simplest objectives, is now an obstacle to those aims. The mechanics of body and space are much more a matter of conscious concern. As with athletes and dancers in particular, space, as well as the body, becomes something to be manipulated, handled, and dealt with. Ironically, many who are not sick are unaware of the physicality of illness beyond the specific symptoms that may be associated with a particular diagnosis. For instance, distances that are inconsequential to my friends are a challenge for me to overcome. I visualize a huge pulley, like that found on the end of a rope tow or chair lift at a ski slope. I imagine a rope connected at one end to the pulley wheel, and at the other end attached to me. Exhausted as I am, limping along and dragging my legs, I keep a single focus on my goal. The phantom rope pulls me there.

The need to engage in the continual processing of the physical world can be both exhilarating—as when one notices features that others neglect—and, more often, fatiguing. Running through water or walking against a strong wind are examples that convey the concreteness of the medium through which we make our way. The "thereness" of the environment is also experienced by those with illness with a fascinating degree of perceptual specificity. Those with vision difficulties may pick up sounds to which most of us are insensitive. People whose balance is impaired or whose mobility has been lessened notice the rise and fall of streets and the angle of sidewalks.

But it's usually not fun. Walking or rolling through a city, I must continually judge the height of curbing, the composition of walkways, the layout of buildings, the size and manners of crowds, the location of sun and shading. People in wheelchairs or with illnesses that affect locomotion are acutely aware of the tilts of floors, the heights of sinks and steps, the shapes of handles and drawers. Our annoyance at not being able to help out or pitch in with even simple kitchen or household tasks is not to be lightly dismissed. Donald Moss (1978) describes the " 'lived-

space' about a body disposed to possible actions [as] an organized network of routes, pathways and obstacles to those
actions . . . [as] a human space full of hospitable oases and dangers to be circumvented; of familiar settings and alien territory;
and of points of departure and destination" (p. 85).

Space, no longer a more or less empty container in which
things are done, is solid and concrete. It is defined, not by measure of meter or rod, but by what one's aims and projects
within it may be. It is a thing-in-itself to be wrestled with and
managed.

EMOTIONS

The changes wrought by illness in a person's habitual movements and sensations affect, of course, not only the emotions
experienced but the manner of their expression as well. It is difficult for a person in a wheelchair to stomp off in rage or, conversely, to get away quickly to cool off. Many of the symptoms
of a variety of chronic illnesses include physiologic responses
that in our culture we have learned to read as signs of emotional
upset or stress. Headaches, diarrhea, skin rashes, and fatigue,
for example, are all popularly associated with feeling upset.

Many of the most psychologically minded among us use
these symptoms as clues: we track them back to their source in
some personal difficulty or concern. Those with chronic illness
who come to identify such somatic complaints as manifestations
of illness, on the other hand, may have to create a new geography by which feelings are located and alternative routes by
which emotions are tracked and articulated. Ironically, it is a
deaf poet, Donald Wright (1990), who has spelled out how much
we take for granted the interweaving of body, thought, emotion,
communication, and sociability, a web of connections that in his
case was not as impaired as it might be with others:

> The deaf man can, if he knows his friend intimately, make a good
> guess at the identity of the caller at the other end of the wire. He
> will do this by noting his friend's expression, or the tempo of ani-
> mation in his countenance; the posture of his body (relaxed or

tensed); and what his hands are doing. . . . Few, apart from professional actors, realize just how much stance and carriage of the body reveal of mood and emotion. (p. 112)

"I think what many people without illness cannot understand is how the changes in my body affect the way I feel and, in turn, who I feel I am," remarks one especially articulate person who suffers with emphysema. "I smile and laugh, I get very excited when I'm happy. Feeling the smile on my face, hearing myself laugh, and talking with my hands is a feedback process that contributes to both my experience of pleasure and my idea of myself as a happy sort of person. Wanting to jump or yell or swing my arms are all things I did before because I felt good doing it, and it was a way of signaling to others that that's what I feel as well. People thought of me as I thought of myself—a warm and demonstrative person.

"Now I've got emphysema, and I'm tied to this oxygen. I get breathless so easily. It's very scary. So I'm very careful about how happy or excited I get. Being demonstrative has become more difficult, and it's harder to show warmth. I've become more irritable. The back-and-forth of feeling, action, and me that I was accustomed to was disturbed, and I'm disturbed because of it. My body doesn't feel like me, and so I don't feel like me either. I'm a stranger to my body, and I'm not sure there is a 'me' that's not my body too."

It is possible that much of what is diagnosed as depression among some with chronic illness is a function of a shift, whether dramatic or more subtle, in the body's emotional communications process. Work in the area of trauma has demonstrated that catastrophic events have major effects on a wide array of cognitive, emotional, and physical functions. Postures and gestures are all means by which a person expresses and exists for himself or herself and others. The changes in postures and gestures resulting from illness, accident, imprisonment, or some other unwelcome event must surely have great impact on a person's sense of body and, therefore, of self.

The anthropologist Robert Murphy (1990), who lived and wrote about his experience of quadriplegia, confirms and extends my patient's poignant account:

As my condition has deteriorated, I have come increasingly to look upon my body as a faulty life-support system, the only function of which is to sustain my head. . . . The quadriplegic's body can no longer speak a "silent language" in the expression of emotions or concepts too elusive for ordinary speech, for the delicate feedback loops between thought and movement have been broken. Proximity, gesture and body set have been muted, and the body's ability to articulate thought has been stilled. (p. 101)

One of the tasks and mercies of therapist and family is to listen for the "silent language" that the ill body speaks.

CHAPTER 4

Time Out of Joint

Nothing endures but change.
                                    Heraclitus

TIME AND ILLNESS have been kind to me. Since my diagnosis of multiple sclerosis in 1982, I walk unaided in my office and home, use a cane on short walks (no more than twenty-five or fifty yards without fatigue and wobbling), and travel in a wheelchair in airports, malls, and warehouse stores. I drive with hand controls because of my inability to safely coordinate my feet.

Fortunately, my family and I have been able to meet our personal and cultural markers of life stages and successes mostly unhindered by illness, and as a result, I think of my MS as stable. If I worked in an occupation that required physical strength, if I had not been blessed with a wife able to offer both moral and financial support, or if my children's interests had been in some way harmed by my illness, I probably would perceive my situation differently.

My wife thinks I am "in denial" as I stumble or trip about the house or crawl from barbecue grill to shade on a hot July day. My neurologist writes of my condition: "Over the past year, his disability (attributable to his stepwise, progressive form of multiple sclerosis) has shown some progressive change, and he has a spastic-ataxic and weakened gait with poor balance. He can only walk for four to five minutes without a rest period of about five minutes before proceeding."

More importantly to me, my illness, along with my marriage, my family, and my profession, has become a means through which I have attempted to work through and live out the values and virtues that constitute my version of "the good life." I tap my own lived experience, my memories of my family's episodes of illness and loss, my encounters with physicians and hospitals, and my attempts to cope with insecurities about money, job, appearances. I shuttle back and forth between my world and my patients' worlds, hoping to create, at least for a brief but fruitful time, our world. Then we can hear each other's voices in good faith.

Each life-world has its own sense of time. In the dreamer's world, as in the world of the theater, the novel, and the arts, time is extraordinarily plastic. The impossible and the improbable occur side by side with the mundane. For the physician, the fifteen-minute appointment, the forty-eight- or seventy-two-hour grippe, distinctions between acute and chronic illness, and post-operative recovery time are all salient. The fifty-minute hour, the six- to eight-session therapy limit, the childhood years no matter how long past, are just a few of the crucial time dimensions of the psychotherapist. In the everyday life through which all these worlds intertwine, the rhythms of waking and sleep, the workdays and weekends, the life trajectories that match the social expectations of individual and family life cycles—all contribute to the meanings the world and self possess for each person. We move through time as we travel through space, giving it little thought beyond noticing how it helps or hinders our immediate projects. We take our sense of time as a given, unaware of how much its perception is influenced by habitual personal, familial, social, and cultural practices and beliefs.

When people take time differently than we do, surprisingly strong emotions can be generated, even around what might be quite small time differences. We get angry and impatient with a husband, wife, child, or friend who's "always late," "never ready on time," or "keeps showing up early." We are concerned when the people we care about "act younger than their age," or "don't realize time is passing" and fail to get on with their lives within a time frame we think appropriate. Yet when we express our anxieties or frustration, others may tell us, "Relax," "People move at their own pace," "It's only been a half-hour" (or "six months" or "three years"). Our time orientations are idiosyncratic and deeply embedded. They are a crucial constituent of the worlds we inhabit. One might say our sense of time is even more a part of us than our arm or leg. If it begins to unravel, twist, or turn, the fabric of one's identity may threaten to come apart.

Time is an inseparable thread of the web of experience that illness easily tears, wreaking havoc with the lives of the people who suffer from its lash. The flow, meaning, and value of time are altered by the working and worrying of chronic illness. Attitudes toward past, present, and future are changed. For some, the past, once a source of enriching memory, becomes instead a pool of regrets and absent pleasures. The present, filled at one time with ordinary trials and complaints, is now the place of "a million annoyances." The future that held hope and promise is now a tunnel at the end of which is a brightening light that could as well be an oncoming locomotive as a sign of darkness's end.

"It's funny," Mary Beth says. "Now that I've been diagnosed with Hodgkin's, I feel that I ought to make firmer plans for the future. My parents seem really worried, and they keep pushing me to take the kind of job where there's probably more job security and definitely better benefits than what I'm doing now as a television producer. But I love this work. I figure that if I get sicker or can't do some of the things I've always dreamed of in the future, I might as well stick with where my heart is as long as I can. I swing back and forth between living for today and preparing for tomorrow. One day I'm the grasshopper, and the next I'm the ant. Because the future's more scary than it used to be, right now seems even more important. But I know that the future could be even worse if I don't do something about it. I really feel caught in a terrible pickle that has knocked what sense of goals and future I did have out of whack."

Memories are shaped by the nature of our present hopes and

fears for the future as much as by events in the past. They are not like prehistoric animals preserved intact through the passage of years; they are better compared to fragments of bone, skin, and fur whose true nature, use, or meaning can only be guessed at. Another scrap is found, and all must be rethought or reconfigured. A betrayal comes to light, and yesterday's stories darken.

So it is with the mixing of illness and memory. The scenes from years gone by that once appeared to the mind's eye in a certain hue change color when mixed with the gray tint of melancholy, the red stain of anger, the blue of hope, or the purple and black of mourning. Some people living with illness look back with regret at opportunities missed or absent pleasures. They feel waylaid by their illness upon a road once taken with another destination in mind. Others regard the past as a paradise remembered and use reminiscences of people loved and adventures enjoyed as a consolation for their sufferings. There are also those who can recall occasions when they met and overcame challenges and trials, and who use such images to maintain morale and fashion a vision of faith for the hard days to come.

Attempting to understand how both individuals and families hold the past is especially important. One of the great values of religious, cultural, or longtime family myths and stories is that the listener does not need to prove their veracity or to have "been there" to identify with their narratives, morals, characters, and heroes. There is, of course, a great danger when people are overwhelmed by the force of collective memories, as can occur under the spell of nationalism, fascism, or racism. In proper perspective, however, one can draw on the power of stories and symbols to hold up ideals, whether of overcoming affliction, accepting fate, or bearing faithful witness to suffering and pain.

Our links to multigenerational family histories and other traditions are increasingly tenuous in contemporary society. Individuals and couples from different backgrounds and communities are assimilated into the dominant culture, and the refashioning of the past into nostalgia products for commercial exploitation goes on. One consequence of these forces is that a person's memory store is increasingly stocked with individual recollections of discrete events within his or her own life span. The support that common reminiscences about the past, whether real or imagined, might provide to individuals and families is undermined. One patient, diagnosed at midlife with amyotrophic lateral sclerosis (ALS), told me that the divorce and moving apart of his parents when he was ten left him feeling like "the seed of a dandelion, blowing in the wind, never finding anyplace to settle in and take root." Although he had a loving family around him as his illness progressed and he was not a "religious man," he was often troubled by "strange thoughts . . . that I wouldn't know with which parent I'll stay in heaven when I get there." He had no family legacy to dip into for sustaining imagery.

It is easy to speculate that a person with a richer heritage of shared memory would not be as concerned with finding a place in line with those who preceded him in death. Although he lives alone and has had little contact with his family since his childhood, Lawrence, ill with AIDS, thought of what he had learned of his family history from other relations, stories of aunts and uncles and of towns and farms where they lived, as "a safety net with plenty of strong ropes that will catch me whenever I start to fall into depression. They were good people, powerful people, and right now I've got the time to think back about them. They give me a lot of good feeling."

Nowhere is the mercurial aspect of time more evident than in that passage of experience we refer to as "the present." Time seems to have an existence of its own independent of whatever attempts we may make to contain its movement. On occasions of great joy, who among us has not wished that the moment could be captured and kept forever? And as danger or grief approaches, who has not wanted to be a Joshua stopping the transit of the sun? Although we may not by definition rule out miracles, time, at least within our modern culture, seems to be little subject to plea or prayer. Whether we are asleep or awake, ill or physically robust, the river of time does meander or rush on.

For individuals and families living with chronic illness, the experience of the present is likely to acquire a texture much different from what prevailed before diagnosis. Illness disrupts the large and small tides and rhythms that people hold onto amid the flux of their lives. Lifelong patterns of sleeping, waking, eating, and defecation are often disturbed. This is no minor matter. Moods and emotions, fatigue and morale are closely linked to the assurance of the regular satisfaction of our most basic needs. Interrogation and torture, or periods of battle or natural disaster that interrupt, threaten, or deprive individuals of their accustomed schedules, often produce powerful and lasting effects. Indeed, as many critics of modern medical practice have argued and as patients have long complained, the strict routines of waking, feeding, and temperature-taking in many hospitals is designed to produce, even if not intentionally, a state of passivity and dependency in the patient. Yet little thought is given to the acute and cumulative effects of temporal disruption upon those with illness.

The structure of time within which a family lives may be rendered uninhabitable by chronic illness. No longer does the expected follow the anticipated, as it did before illness arrived on the scene. And when the rhythm of one's life is altered, the very nature of one's existence can become problematic. The "I" of "Who am I?" is no longer the same. The activities during which time passed quickly and through which aspects of one's identity were affirmed—a favorite hobby, the play of sex, cooking for a party—now take "forever," if they are enjoyed at all. Not only may the people identified as ill suffer from the stretching of time, but those with whom they shared their pleasures are often deprived as well. People of all ages may be called upon to rise to the occasion or to take on certain roles before they ordinarily would have been expected to—or after.

Most of us also take for granted a normal progression of the life cycle. One expects that increasing accomplishments and engagements in the world will gradually give way, over some seventy or eighty years, to lessening involvement with its desires and demands and a coming to terms with death. As John Rolland (1994) points out, this dimension of time in relation to the illness experiences of individuals and families has been overlooked. As a consequence of illness, the timelines for meeting the challenges or confronting the crises that characterize personal, family, and cultural stages and cycles of all kinds are frequently extended, compromised, neglected, or seen as completely unattainable. Rolland has devised a psychosocial typology that locates an illness according to its onset, course, outcome, kind and degree of impairment, and uncertainty of knowledge about these variables for individuals and families. The phases that are part of the profile of an illness experience—crisis, chronic, terminal—vary in nature from one case to another. Rolland makes a strong argument that an integrative treatment model that takes longitudinal, life-cycle, and illness phase issues into significant account is often of greater utility than a clinical approach oriented toward the traditional biological criteria.

"How has my illness affected me time-wise? I never *thought* much about time until I got sick," says Bill, age forty-three. "It seems like I have both more and less time. It takes me more time to get simple things done, and I feel like I probably have less time to do what I really care about, because this illness is progressive. And one hell of a nuisance. I wake up when everyone else is sleeping, and I'm just so exhausted when the rest of the family is ready to go. My body's getting worse, and I have more time to think about it. There are fewer places where I can go, because it takes me longer to get there. I once had goals, a plan. And I was proud of that fact. I wasn't just a guy who did stuff on the spur of the moment. I did it because it made sense in terms of what I wanted to accomplish for my family and for myself. But without those goals, or at least the possibility of getting them, I'm not sure who I am or who I'm supposed to be."

The time frame in which one lives is wrenched out of shape. What is included on the canvas of the present changes. The future may lap at the margin of the next twenty-four hours, or even closer, whereas before illness brushed one's life it could extend out some months or even years away.

"What's the point of it all?" Louis wants to know. He is sixty years old, blessed with grown children and a wonderful wife. "Why do I have to burden her with my care? I have diabetes. I have to go get hooked up to that damned dialysis machine all the time, it seems. She has to take me to the hospital, and she sits around all day. What kind of life is that for her? Why should I go on? I've done what a man's supposed to do. Why keep my wife a slave to my illness? I think maybe my dying would be a bigger gift to her than my keeping alive. Really, what's the point?"

Faced with what Miguel Unamuno (Zaner, 1982, p. 46) defined as the "too long life," and Renee Fox (Zaner, 1982, p. 47) calls a "chronic way of dying," Louis no longer finds value in his life. Rather than striding through his older years toward different, but still worthwhile, pleasures, he is crawling on a treadmill to which he is tethered with no promise of relief but death. Visions of the netherworld are filled with people in perpetual motion, fated to reach for goods without satisfaction, to desire without consummation. What is it like to live with the possibility of death presenting itself every day, kept at bay only by a treatment that seems worse than the death it prevents? It sounds like war. It sounds like hell.

The attempt to live "one day at a time" serves different motives and different functions as illness and circumstances change. For the same individual and family, it can be either a defense against ongoing discomfort or a style of coping that momentarily relieves suffering. At other times, it may help deflect thoughts about anticipated losses or inspire people to focus on using the present moment as richly as possible. The clinician who advocates the motto as a therapeutic goal needs to be sensitive to how it will be taken. For one individual, "I take it one day at a time" is a proud announcement. For someone else, it is a weary sigh of resignation.

Even the feelings of relief that may come with periods of remission can be tainted by the shadow of relapse. "Any suggestions on what to do with all of this incredible 'I will beat cancer' intensity that's still in my system?" asks Judy. "I'm having a difficult time pulling things together after being declared in remission. They don't give you the answers to 'What do you do with your life after remission?' You're not supposed to worry about relapse, but that's a moot point. I think I've completely forgotten how to relax. Is there a balance?"

Imagining the future is central to human existence. The angels in Wim Wenders's extraordinary films *Wings of Desire* (1987) and *Far Away, So Close* (1993) reside in eternity. Their one wish is to know what it is to be human. The wish cannot be granted unless they fall into time and subject themselves to the possibility of unfulfilled desire or the yearning passion for again or more. It is only because we are mortal that we are obliged to imagine the future. We are faced with the impossibility of a limitless horizon and so must choose. Central to the argument of the critic Harold Bloom (1994) for the importance of a literary canon is the fact of our passing from this world in three score and ten years. Had we double that time to read, he suggests, there would be less of an imperative to mark out those masterpieces that one *must* read.

The ability to defer present and immediate gratification for future satisfactions is typically considered a significant measure of maturity. The person who makes a prudent decision on behalf of children or grandchildren whom he or she may never see is proud and admired. One of the pleasures a parent takes is daydreaming with children, partners, or friends about what lies ahead in time to come. We fantasize about how we will be as parents, what our children will look like, the kinds of lives they will lead. Indeed, we conceive our offspring imaginatively before we conceive them in flesh.

The approach to the future of people living with illness is a makeshift process that reflects the uncertainty and changes in conditions, diagnoses, resources, and support that cannot be avoided. Most individuals make ongoing adjustments during their lives and attempt to plan for that which might or might not come to pass. They hold on as long as possible to the fundamental assumptions that undergird their confidence or fears about what is to come. Events that do overthrow bedrock beliefs about time are experienced as calamitous. Judith Herman (1992) reminds us that, for war captives,

> thinking of the future stores up such intense yearning and hope that prisoners find it unbearable; they quickly learn that these emotions make them vulnerable to disappointment and that disappointment will make them desperate. They therefore consciously narrow their attention, focusing on extremely limited goals. The future is reduced to a matter of hours or days. (p. 89)

Who has not been behind the wheel of a car at the peak of a hill beyond which the road is not visible? Who has failed to playfully imagine the terrifying prospect that there is nothing on the other side? For those with chronic illness, however, faced with the possibilities of exacerbations and progression along a trajectory of unknown direction and drift, such dread reveries become commonplace. The present is different because the future is no longer the same.

CHAPTER 5

A Catalog of Losses

Each substance of a grief hath twenty shadows.
Shakespeare, *King Richard II* (II.ii.14)

I NDIVIDUALS AND FAMILIES living with a progressive illness do not receive the closure that people who suffer with an acute illness are permitted. Indeed, one loss may not only make way for but bring on another. If my multiple sclerosis worsens so that I am unable to walk, my loss of mobility, as bad as it is in itself, is not my loss alone. Additional significant burdens will accrue to my wife. She will suffer new restrictions and injuries as well. I will not argue that my losses—really *our* losses—are good for her or for me. But loss is inevitable, and there is something to be made out of it.

The experience of loss, after all, is at the core of being human. Gods take what they want from mortals and then leave them— abandoned, broken, sometimes ecstatic, always changed. Asked who his masters were, Freud answered: "The Greek tragedies." We often forget that Oedipus's story was one of exile and abandonment from beginning to end. The central myth of classical culture may be that of the maiden Persephone, abducted into the underworld by Hades. As grief fills Persephone's abandoned mother, the goddess Demeter, the earth dries up, unable to bear a harvest. Humankind itself is threatened with disaster. Although Zeus prevails upon his brother Hades to release her daughter, Demeter is unable to feel joy. Persephone must return to the underworld for a full season each year. The meetings of god and man are often followed by separation. The anticipation and reality of loss is bred in our bones.

"We have to find ways to handle the experience of perpetually grieving, of never being out of grief," commented one psychotherapist who works with HIV groups. Perhaps those who live with or alongside life-threatening illness are not so different from others, for all of us, whether conscious of it or not, *are* surrounded by sorrow. Are many of the signs of physical distress characterized as illness—somatization, anxiety, depression, and so on—expressions of that sorrow? Is illness itself a form of grieving?

It might be said that the world is drenched in loss. There are the obvious losses of death, illness, and dislocation. Divorce, abandonment, separation, and leave-taking between couples and within families are all loss experiences, as are the psychic losses that may occur from a lack of empathy between parent and child. Traumas—whether intentional or accidental, the result of physical assault or emotional abuse, an "act of God" or the consequence of a force of nature—leave losses, wounding, and grieving in their wake. Where there is life, there is loss.

Ross was an outstanding and hardworking surgeon who prided himself on his tireless energy, laserlike concentration, precise handwork, and command of any medical situation. His wife and children complained to each other of his neglect. They joked that Ross's real family were his colleagues at the hospital. Ross denied their charges, but he knew in his heart that there were times he would sooner lose a family than lose a patient.

Ross dismissed the first symptom of his illness, the tremor he had detected when he recorded notes after operations. He blamed them on a lack of food and exhaustion and wrote them off as signs of the overwork of a dedicated physician. Soon enough, however, he could no longer ignore the very real possibility of Parkinson's disease. He had some difficulty standing and focusing for long periods while performing procedures and occasionally needed to take a break to rest. These were particularly upsetting events, as he had prided himself on his ability to "go the limit" for hours on end.

Aware that there were other possible causes for the changes he observed, Ross sought a confidential evaluation at a major medical center in another city. He did not reveal to his wife the true reason for his trip, telling her that he was meeting there with a well-known surgeon to discuss procedural advances. Although testing ruled out many other possible diagnoses, Ross clung to the hope that his symptoms were stable. On his own, he decided to use an antihistamine to reduce his tremors. He also consulted a psychiatrist for his increasingly obvious depression while not revealing his true fear. Ross convinced him to prescribe an MAO-B inhibitor as an antidepressant that he hoped might further decrease his physical symptoms. Ross knew that if he were diagnosed with Parkinson's, his surgical career was over. The vocation that gave his life value and meaning was at risk, and his anxiety and depression worsened.

Too soon, however, the tremors and other symptoms reappeared, each time with greater effect. He was unable to share his panic with family, colleague, or psychiatrist. His life, his identity, his self were built around a lifelong dream and drive to be a great surgeon. Ross felt helpless for the first time against disease. He was one patient he could not cure, a physician who could not heal himself. One day Ross, an avid sailor, put out to sea for what he told his family was a day trip. The next day his boat was found empty, and the next day after that the body of the forty-eight-year-old surgeon was washed ashore.

Ross was seen as an extraordinarily competent and self-directed person by all those who knew him. His family found him to be lacking in intimacy, but not in what they perceived as a personal strength and capacity to sacrifice all, even them, for the good of his patients and the success of his scalpel. Yet Ross's "self" was apparently not able to survive the loss of his identity. He was not able to come up with a new personal myth, narrative, life story, for what would be left of him after Parkinson's had its way. Ross was well aware of the vulnerability of the slender filaments of nerve cells to the illness that inevitably, he believed, would demolish his most cherished ideals. He refused to become increasingly dependent on a family whom, he felt, owed him little. How are we to judge what he did?

In his classic work *Identity and the Life Cycle* (1959), Erik Erikson drew upon his work with soldiers subjected to trauma to formulate his concepts of ego identity and loss:

> [The soldiers'] ego impairment seems to have its origin in violent events, in others in the gradual grind of a million annoyances. Obviously the men are worn out by too many changes (gradual or sudden) in too many respects at once; somatic tension, social panic, and ego anxiety are always present. Above all, the men do not know who they are: there is a distinct loss of ego identity. The sense of sameness and of continuity and the belief in one's social role are gone. (p. 42)

There are significant differences, of course, between the victims of battle, battering, or rape and individuals afflicted with illness. The terror of assault may be less overwhelming, the impact and injury of the initial symptoms may be less severe, and the exposure to threat may be less immediately life-threatening. Nevertheless, individuals with chronic illness are commonly subject to lifelong uncertainty about the cumulative effects of a progressively incapacitating process. The "gradual grind of a million annoyances" and "too many changes . . . in too many respects" is characteristic of the illness experiences of many people. Their possible losses are so extensive that one can empathize with one active young man who received a letter from an extraordinarily insensitive neurologist confirming a diagnosis of multiple sclerosis and who was prepared to take his own life rather than suffer, as he put it, the "death of a thousand cuts."

Each person and family suffer, survive, or surmount the experience of chronic illness in their own way. It is vital, of course, to respect the particularity of the losses with which people are afflicted. Each grief is entitled to a name and identity of its own. It is not possible, however, to memorialize the sufferings of each person or family living with illness. Approaching loss from a variety of angles and viewing it through a thicket of meanings can serve as a reminder of how far, wide, and deep the damage may spread. Like the waters of a flood, the illness can penetrate everywhere, leaving little untouched and rendering much unrecoverable. How is it possible, one may ask as the toll mounts, that any lives can go on as before? And yet they do.

The catalog of losses commonly associated with chronic illness seems overwhelming. Although few individuals struggle with all these hardships at any one time, it is not unusual for many to be present at least some of the time during the course of an illness: decreased mobility, loss of certain kinds of emotional range and display, increased vulnerability to additional illnesses from a compromised immune system, greater potential for injury from decreased coordination and strength, increased spasticity and fatigue, loss of independence associated with deteriorating mobility and control, decline of a sense of physical well-being and self-assurance, fear of pain, loss of physical attractiveness, loss of forms of sexual expression, inability to eat and drink as one pleases, difficulty falling and staying asleep, fewer opportunities to participate in activities for pleasure's sake—sports, walking, drawing, playing piano, reading without visual difficulties, writing, rocking a baby, wrestling with a child, dancing.

Additional losses and problems include weakening of more "mature" ego defenses, difficulties with concentration and memory, obsessing about current and future difficulties, decline of problem-solving abilities, increased distractibility, loss of privacy, and feelings of irritability, anxiety, depression, and sadness. One distinction that a therapist may find helpful is between losses that limit what people living with illness can achieve and those that remove protection from some indignity. The former result in a diminished capacity *to do*, to perform once simple tasks such as shopping in the mall, throwing a football, driving a car, cooking a meal. The ability to carry out more long-range projects—keeping one's job, raising children, maintaining a certain lifestyle, retiring with financial security—is also threatened or eliminated by chronic illness. The second type of loss comes in the form of the absence of freedom *from* something, as one is no longer free from pain, from certain kinds of anxieties and concerns, from having one's body subject to medical diagnosis and treatment, from the responsibilities and obligations of caretaking, or from making hard moral decisions.

Still another way of thinking about loss is from the angle of whether and how much it affects one's self-esteem, self-respect, or self-concept. I find it helpful to differentiate between the three. *Self-esteem* refers to one's basic sense of trust and well-being in one's body and the world. Positive self-esteem might be described as a core feeling of, and belief in, the fundamental all-rightness of the universe. Someone with high self-esteem is less easily threatened by ill fortune or loss. *Self-respect* is closer to what could be referred to as feeling secure in one's identity. Personal commitments, relationships, and projects are valued by oneself as well as by significant others. Self-respect provides a firm means and direction with which to move along in life. Losses that inhibit one's ability to develop and sustain important relationships and projects can put one's self-respect at risk. Losses that are uncomfortable or painful but not as crucial to these meaningful endeavors are less costly.

Finally, one's *self-concept* comprises those mental images or feelings we have about ourselves that may be more transient and situational than those associated with self-esteem and self-respect. The self-concept of a person who can no longer imagine himself or herself as physically competent as a result of a medical condition is set back and altered, but his or her self-esteem and self-respect can hold.

Suffering is a word rarely used in either medicine or psychology, except in connection with the specific sensation of pain. It is possible, however, to experience little suffering in the presence of pain, as many women report during childbirth and as we are told by soldiers wounded in battle. The knowledge that pain will end and that it can be controlled, and the meaning one attaches to it, can distinguish pain itself from suffering. As with pain, so with loss. For one person, a loss may be an opportunity for growth. For another, it is the end of the road.

People with chronic illness may suffer from their illness even in the absence of the disease or its symptoms. Treatments for cancer, for example, that result in successful "cures" or remissions may leave a person suffering more than when the disease was present. The distress that results from hair loss is often greater than the immediate effects of a disease. The financial burdens that pile up while families are utilizing the health care system regularly create more difficulties than did the disease for which expenses were incurred.

The words *patient, pathology,* and *passion* are related to the Greek term *pathos,* to suffer. In many medical and therapeutic settings, however, both the patient and his or her pathology are lifted out of the context of suffering. Within psychotherapy, one could argue that the medicalization of the concept of depression has placed the experience of suffering on the margins. Nevertheless, the willingness to encounter affliction, whether or not it is diagnosable as a disease or a disorder, is the moral obligation of any physician or therapist.

It is important to think about the effect and meaning of loss, as well as its isolation within a narrower descriptive or causal framework. Many losses are aspects of other privations. They cannot be separated out from the rich context of the selves and souls that make up the personal worlds of illness any more than labeling a disease can tell us something about the patient. One might assume that a particular symptom has similar consequences for one person or family and another, all other things being equal—which, of course, they rarely are. The symptom that seems like a minor nuisance to some people may be crushing to others, for reasons that may be not at all apparent at first glance. The availability of resources, the environment in which the illness event occurs, the meanings that individuals and families bring to their encounters with illness, are just a few of the factors that determine the outcome of loss over the short and long term. It is never easy to foresee how far any particular individual and family will travel along the road toward maintaining, losing, or remaking their world.

The intricately interlaced worlds of embodiment, consciousness, and time, and individual, family, society, culture, and environment, are pulled here and there by the hand of fate. Illness disrupts the trajectory and context of our imagined lives, and its course and reach may be radically changed. The language and grammar of illness as lived by the patient is often quite different from that of the physician or those who remain untouched. Thus, the sense of shared meaning that contributes to a familiar experience of the self cannot be easily nurtured.

I have earlier described some of the ways in which the life-world falls apart. The ordinary experience of time is disrupted. The present often seems choppy and disjointed or long and drawn out. Chronic uncertainty and the strict measure of temporal templates can make the realization of personal and family goals conspicuously unpredictable. Relationships with others are altered. Many with illness, facing a greater risk of social hostility, discredit, or isolation, are more dependent on others for care and in greater debt to them as well. They are also vulnerable to the intrusion of agents and instruments of medical, political, and corporate interests into their bodies and lives if they are to receive the benefits and care they need and to which they are entitled.

The body for individuals with illness, previously in the background of experience and the instrument of their ends, becomes more dominant in the everyday landscape, an obstacle to carrying out both spontaneous action and long-range goals. Its presence in consciousness is a threat to self-image and effective performance. The plausibility of the world has been damaged. The realities of death, embodiment, luck, and limits, as well as problems of meaning, loss, and moral ambiguity and choice, confront those living with illness in direct and unavoidable ways.

A HIERARCHY OF LOSS

I have found it useful to construct a "hierarchy of loss" to describe loss by the degree of injury or harm it causes to a person or family. Individuals living with chronic illness undergo (1) a variety of physical, emotional, and cognitive losses that (2) may dramatically limit their ability to carry out or express important projects, aims, values, or roles, the effect of which may be (3) to undermine a personal and family identity, narrative, or life story that, if grave enough, may (4) culminate in a loss of self, severe moral injury (including loss of autonomy, honor, moral innocence, and good character), or the elimination of any possibility of a good life. To the degree that the experience of loss moves one along this path, the greater the suffering.

Figure 5.1

Hierarchy of Loss

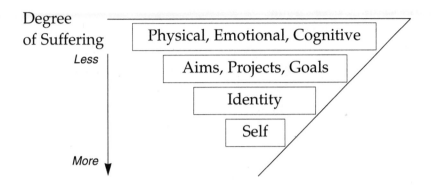

Living in the Archetypes of Loss

It is through imagery that patient, family, and clinician can often begin to tackle the range of pain and suffering that afflictions such as illness or disability may bring. Metaphors express common ways in which individuals live through illness. They capture psychic configurations that possess and animate individual lives for a while and then move on. They are not meant to be taken literally or as "types." To do so would be to repeat the error of the physician or psychotherapist who mistakes the reality of a person who suffers for the utility of diagnostic nomenclature.

The Exile

Home and its attachments suggest a familiar embrace. The term "home" connotes safety and shelter. The complex feelings we may have about our own particular home pale beside the rich and resonant meaning of wished-for, and somehow expected, support that the simple four-letter word implies. As a rule, those symbolic connections, whatever our actual experience, are expected to be positive. We sense that something is awry if they are not so for another or ourselves. For most people, for example, the invitation to "make yourself at home" evokes feelings of ease and relaxation. One is offered the opportunity to enter into an atmosphere of familiarity and comfort.

Whether or not one's actual home was or is a source of well-being, the phrase is understood by all to be a gracious gesture, bringing with it the possibility of intimacy and an unreflective loosening of constraint.

A sense of place and of home is deeply rooted in our personal, social, cultural, and, indeed, animal histories. In the autumn, we look up at the millions of migratory birds managing by some little-grasped means to return to their nesting sites of previous years. We can find something to identify with in that instinctive behavior. It is soon after, at Thanksgiving time, that "homeward-bound" humans fill the skies as well.

The situation of many newly diagnosed with chronic illness is well illustrated by Alfred Schutz (1945/1970) in his essay "The Homecomer." The stranger who arrives in a different land "knows that he will find himself in an unfamiliar world, differently organized than that from which he comes, full of pitfalls and hard to master" (pp. 294–295). The homecomer, on the other hand, expects to return to a setting both intimate and familiar. If he discovers that his anticipations are in error, his mind may easily travel to thoughts of disaster or betrayal. Imagine the surprise and shock of those patients and families with chronic illness when they discover that many of the most routine actions and habitual expectations by which home life has been defined can no longer be carried out with the ease of prior times, if at all. We take for granted the layout of our home's interior, the arrangement of furniture, the operation of the infrastructure of plumbing, heating, electricity. The comings and goings of our home's inhabitants become routine. We pay attention only when changes are negotiated, before a welcome regularity is once again restored. Some of the same process is at work with chronic illness, but the stakes and the costs of variation are usually much higher.

Lucy compares the impact on her life of a newly diagnosed chronic illness to the uncertain fate of an apparently secure home built along the shore of an inlet to the sea. One day an unexpected storm descends upon the bay. The sky, shortly before filled with sun and an occasional cloud or shower, now becomes an ominous black. Winds, pushing huge, fury-foamed breakers, howl around the house as shingles fly and walls shake. The water, once a benign provider of refreshment and sport, now slaps threateningly at the front porch and door, demanding admittance.

Fortunately, the tempest passes, leaving behind only a few broken panes, a flooded cellar, and a dock, bereft of all but a few pilings, with nothing else left to support. The storm-driven waves, however, have gnawed away at the beach. A lesser storm than this one, even a few higher than usual moon-pulled tides, may lead to greater losses. The house, despite its firm structure and its history of safe shelter, is left more vulnerable than before.

What these striking words convey is a recurring theme in the experience of chronic illness. Lucy's extended metaphors, powerful and generative, are packed with rich stores of imagery and feeling that arise out of our most basic needs. Some, like Tom and Ross, already see their lives as broken worlds filled with shattered glass and wounded souls. Lucy is apprehensive, her home threatened, subject to the ungracious whim of wind and waters. She does not know whether the illness now shadowing her will suddenly splinter her life or, just as painfully, more gradually, yet inexorably, erode her powers.

Primal and well-founded fears pull at Lucy. Loss, after all, creates in many people a profound sense of dislocation, disorientation, and unease. The dread with which one views the destruction of a home by wind, earthquake, water, or fire parallels the potentially catastrophic losses that many of those with chronic illness undergo. To be homeless has always struck humans as a great misery or tragic fate. In 1688, Johannes Hofer first described a medical condition he called "nostalgia," the pain that arises from separation from one's fatherland (Abt, 1989). A portion of the distress that those with chronic illness and their families experience is a consequence of their status as refugees. They have been expelled from their old worlds of interconnecting habits of body, mind, feelings, and relationships.

It is not uncommon for a person coping with chronic illness to feel like a stranger in a strange land, searching and yearning for home. What one knew is gone; what one has found is either not known or too terribly familiar. "I have never been anywhere but sick," wrote Flannery O'Connor (1979). "In a sense, sickness is a place, more instructive than a long trip to Europe, and it is always a place where there's no company, where nobody can follow. . . . The wolf, I am afraid, is inside, tearing up the place."

The homecomer's fate is often one of exile, the calamitous curse that Oedipus unwittingly called down upon himself. The image of the exile is one that resonates with the experience of many with chronic illness. One is cast out from the world of ordinary experience to which one once belonged. The exile is forced to go from one tentative identity to another, chased on by exacerbations and accumulating losses, until he or she settles into a new world that can contain some of the comforts of the old. Some people with illness define themselves in large measure by their diagnosis. It is from the exile's association with those similarly afflicted that he or she can find and build community. The exile is sometimes an angry partisan in battles against what he or she perceives as the uncaring and unenlightened forces of the medical establishment. Exiles can be characterized by their foes as hostile or oppositional, but their complaints and demands to be recognized and heard make professionals pay attention to the individual human suffering masked by the operational accounts of disease.

The Victim

For the victim, the experience of chronic illness is one of total catastrophe. The losses and suffering are so overwhelming that more than one's identity is at risk. The self or "I" that is able to reflect upon or construct a life story or narrative faces obliteration. In response to the question, "Who are you?" the victim answers, "I am nothing, worthless, without hope." Pain, sheer, awful physical pain, can leave no room for a new story to be told or an old one reworked. Paralysis also can so dominate the field of being that the body of the victim cannot yield to the play of imagination and conceive a future despite immobility. The dishonor that marks one's failure to fulfill an important and obligatory role within certain communities can also lead to feelings of shame so powerful that no self in such a social order can survive. The actual or emotional suicide of the victim is often disparaged in our culture. In other ages and traditions, however, the ability to choose one's own death when the goods of life are destroyed has been a mark of virtue rather than a fault.

Estelle created a story for herself that enabled her to get

through many years in which she had little opportunity to enjoy her anticipated pleasures. She worked hard for most of her adult years, raising children and then helping out to make money for the family. It was not easy, but Estelle didn't feel sorry for herself because she knew the life she wanted when she didn't have to work so hard anymore. She saw herself gardening and taking watercolor lessons. If anyone were to ask her, "Who are you?" she would say, "I'm a gardener," or, "I'm a painter," because that's who she felt she really was. She went to flower shows, read gardening magazines, and always thought about how she'd love to paint the flowers she grew. When she'd practice by closing her eyes and moving her hands with an invisible paintbrush, she could see the colors of the blooms and leaves as if they were real. Meanwhile, she had to work as a secretary until she had a chance to be the "real" Estelle.

Now Estelle has the opportunity to become the gardener she always dreamed she was. She has the talent, the income, and the leisure to satisfy her wish to cultivate beauty. In the last five years, however, she has been ill with Parkinson's and has been unwilling to spend any time doing what she dreamed she would most enjoy. "I'm not a gardener anymore," she says. "I was once, but now I can't even poke a few holes in the ground to put in a tray of annuals. I'm just someone who's sick with nothing to do. I'd feel like I was not being honest if I thought of myself as a gardener." Despite her many years of interest, Estelle discounts her identity as a gardener. Unable to participate in the creation of beauty in the manner she imagined, she is possessed by her sense of victimization and betrayal by her own body. She feels like a flower past its bloom.

Estelle recalled that when she was first diagnosed with her illness, she often thought of an old woman who lived on her block when she was a child. The old woman hobbled around with two canes, all bent over. Estelle recounts that the woman often seemed angry but acknowledges that her expression may well have been the mask of her disease. Estelle has a very hard time not seeing herself as a poor, crippled old lady instead of as a gardener or painter. She feels as if "there are these big, empty spaces in my mind where my dreams used to be."

Estelle has lost the future she imagined she had and, as a consequence, she has lost a significant portion of her identity. Much of it was set not in the life she lived everyday, a life of toil, but in the much more pleasant years to come. Estelle had always assumed that in her middle years she would be able to be the kind of person life's realities had not allowed her to be when she was younger. Now she feels twice robbed. It is as if a baby were snatched from her arms, a baby she had conceived, to be replaced by nothing but a sadness that fills her whole heart.

The Invalid

The invalid is another common figure. With no expectation of cure, he lives with few needs and believes that he makes minimal claims on others. The invalid is content to see the skull beneath the skin. The intimations of his own mortality give him, he believes, greater insight into the valley and shadow of limits and death in which we all walk. In a world of transient pleasures and questionable goods, the invalid chooses to bear his suffering with the "patience of Job." His sense of irony can be quite magnificent, and the detachment he has achieved by wanting very little enables him to be kind to others who are struggling for health or success. His illness complaints are not expressed through verbal insults against body, physicians, or fate, but by an unwillingness to move beyond his self-imposed boundaries of possibility and motion. Labeling him as "depressed" not only is wrong but discredits his world and what it offers us. The melancholic soul of Ecclesiastes, for example, judges the worth of the things of the world better than most others do.

Walter suffers with chronic pain. He is unable to participate in most of the activities he enjoyed before his condition worsened. Even when he experiences some relief, he is wary of working and playing as he did before, lest his anguish return. Although he maintains the same capacity to reflect upon his situation and make what most would agree are rational decisions, he thinks of himself as a man deprived of liberty, a prisoner of his own body, enslaved by his physical suffering.

Walter's family is saddened that Walter lives in such constant distress. He encourages them to enjoy their own lives, to go places and do things without him. They are very reluctant to do so. He has always provided for them, and they feel that to go on with their lives as before would be to abandon him.

One could suggest that Walter and his family are less differentiated than many others, but that would tell us very little about what they undergo. His family is unable and unwilling to follow Walter's directive, "Enjoy yourself, don't worry about me." They feel, on the one hand, less autonomous and less capable of taking action than they did before his pain became chronic and severe. On the other hand, they accept the obligation and expect to do the right thing by Walter, as others will do by them. The members of Walter's family believe they have gained something of great value—a pride in doing what is right—that is worth more than the goods or pleasures they have forfeited.

Sisyphus

The Sisyphean figure has great dignity. She never stops searching or hoping for improvement or healing. In the face of medical pessimism or the doubts of family and friends, she follows all kinds of trails and clues in pursuit of a remedy for her ills. She credits personal tales of dramatic improvement as much as the more constrained testimony of scientific journals. No matter how absurd or foolish her quest appears to others, the Sisyphean perseveres. She believes it is better to do something than nothing. She has great faith in the power of her own faith and attracts others who want to be empowered by her hope. She avoids bitterness so as not to undermine both the energy she needs to endure in her adventure and the most likely source of healing—her own hopeful spirit. Some might characterize the Sisyphean as in denial, or even manic. To do so would miss the nobility and courage with which she carries on in the face of great odds and frequent disappointment. And miracles do occur.

Thirty years after her recovery from polio, Pam, now forty-five years old, started losing strength in her legs. She experienced pain and muscle cramps as well. She told herself they were symptoms of aging to which she would easily adapt. But incidents of numbness in her arms and legs, mood swings, back pain, painful headaches, and overwhelming fatigue finally drove her to a physician. For several years, as her symptoms continued and new ones emerged, Pamela was given one diagnosis after another—menopause, multiple sclerosis, neurofibromyalgia, chronic fatigue syndrome, hypochondria. After researching the illnesses as much as any layperson could, she rejected each one.

She finally encountered a physician who described the symptoms and course of post-polio syndrome. Although she accepted the diagnosis, Pamela was unwilling to agree with the doctor's prognosis that the tissue and strength of her legs would deteriorate profoundly. Despite her doctor's raised eyebrows, she used acupuncture, vitamin combinations, changes in diet, and almost any other alternative therapy she could find to retain her mobility. She was determined that her battle with post-polio syndrome would end in a repeat of the victory she had won at the end of what she called her first world war.

The Hero

The hero accepts and employs his illness as a way to bring meaning and satisfaction to himself and others. Whether it is through wheelchair athletics, professional activities, or voluntarism, the hero is proud that he has snatched something worthwhile out of freakish ill fortune. He frequently presents himself, in his own mind or more directly to others, as an example of the use of illness itself as a journey toward healing and can offer many suggestions to both acquaintances and strangers on how to cope well with sickness. His rightful pride of accomplishment, however, can be wounded by an unexpected blow from chance. The hero is often upheld as a cultural ideal, the model of successful adaptation to disability or disease. A danger is that he may tarry too often or too long among the ill and not commit to relationships or satisfactions outside of that world. If his condition worsens and his accustomed way out of pain is blocked, he might be left with little to hold onto.

Carla has suffered many physical and emotional losses, but her identity and ability to nourish and fulfill important relationships and projects remain intact. Carla's experience with chronic illness began some twelve years ago. She was hospitalized following her reports of a variety of symptoms and was discharged with a diagnosis of spinal myelitis. Carla continued to cope with "slamming" fatigue that made her feel as though "every bone in my body died and forgot to tell me." Three years later her vision became blurry, and a neurologist confirmed the presence of multiple sclerosis.

Her illness continues to evoke in her sadness and grief for new deficits or for old ones that worsen. She feels disappointment when the limits it imposes rob her of being able to do what she wants. "Rage is also a primary feeling," she says. "If I'm alone, I'll scream, punch pillows, throw things—it can be quite cathartic." She gets along pretty well at home using a chair lift for stairs. When she's outside the home, she uses a cane if she has someone's arm to hold onto, or a walker or collapsible wheelchair when that is not possible. The chronic pain she experiences with MS disrupts many of her plans, and her neurogenic bladder requires her to self-catheterize four times daily and wake during the night to use a commode at her bedside. Carla also has to moisten food to swallow without respirating.

Despite all this, Carla reports that "my MS is manageable for me." She works with clients who have chronic illness and chronic pain. She also acknowledges experiencing many positive emotions during her years of living with MS, and she prides herself on her ability to call upon techniques such as visualization, relaxation, TM, and yoga when her MS flares up. Carla also feels proud of how well she and her husband have coped with her illness, and she loves the celebrations they have when a bad exacerbation ends and her neurologist "tells us the good news that I'm back to baseline." She does fear that some recent cognitive symptoms may keep her from continuing at her work as before. Carla remains, nevertheless, an example of someone who, with good fortune and resourcefulness, has contained the impact of her losses so that neither her identity nor her sense of self are threatened.

To grasp how individuals and families respond to loss is crucial to creating a constructive engagement with them during experiences of illness. Within any person, family, or therapeutic situation, certain voices are less likely to be raised or heard than others, especially during the often hurried encounters within the medical setting. A therapist, on the other hand, is obliged to listen to others' complaints, as well as to what remains unmentionable or is only suggested. Someone who feels ashamed that he or she grieves for the loss of a special "little" pleasure, or guilty about how minor that loss seems compared to the burden it places on others, may, as a result, never speak of it. Family members may naturally not tell of the losses they incur. They may feel obliged to surrender their claims of pain in recognition of what they perceive as the greater suffering of the ill. Unfortunately, therapists, in the interests of time, technique, or self-protection, may be inattentive to the kinds and context of loss for each individual and family. When illness arrives on the scene, the possibility of psychological cacophony is quite high as inner and outer voices struggle to be heard and others search for silence and hiding. One job of the therapist is to create a therapeutic space, analogous to individual and family interior spaces, in which those mocked or dispossessed voices may be heard.

It is a form of hubris for one untouched by harm to speak of the opportunity for growth that suffering and pain may bring. A therapist must be wary of heroic fantasies of rescuing the ill and leading them to health. It is essential to be able to accept and acknowledge the personal and social worth of the victim, the refugee, the infirm, the discredited, the ill, the poor, the least of us. When we lose touch with the distinct suffering of the souls of individuals and families, we run the risk of being swallowed by the values and ideology of the collective.

The good that may come from some calamities is often what is most difficult to perceive. People who identify blessings amid ill fortune may be dismissed as abruptly as those who want to speak of what has been lost. After the diagnosis, prognosis, and treatments have been given, the therapist who is willing to look into, listen with, and speak from the heart, does have a chance to be a midwife of meaning, hope, and life.

CHAPTER 6

Physicians, Patients, and Families

May I never see in my patient anything else than a fellow creature in pain.
　　　　　　Maimonides (1135–1204), physician and sage

F OR NEARLY one hundred years, the socially sanctioned way to grapple with the experience of chronic illness has been through the science, vocabulary, and values of biomedicine. As the worlds of those living with chronic illness begin to strain or come apart, the physician and the hospital have served as containers for the suffering that such afflictions bring. Ideally, the good doctor and the worthwhile hospital stay offer time, solace, and treatment to patients and families. Medicine, before the arrival of the "health care system," was perceived as a safe harbor from the pressures of profit and the market. During uncertain phases of chronic illness, the doctor's medical constructs could give some coherence to what was often a confusing and frightening experience. The physician's role and identity seemed secure to the patient and family, who in turn felt they were in good hands.

The physician has interpreted and commanded the ground

upon which the definitions, diagnosis, and treatment of sickness take place. This order, however, is rapidly changing. The consequences of the approaching transformation for individuals and families living with illness and for physicians and others who offer healing will be great. Before detailing those consequences, however, I would offer a summary of the significance and power of the physician in our culture, as well as a brief history of the physician's former status and rise to dominance. This overview will hint at the significance of what is being lost, whether for good or ill, and enable us to reflect upon the meaning of contemporary changes for those living and working with illness.

A BRIEF HISTORY OF THE PHYSICIAN

Acting as the carrier of the archetypal image of the healer may well be the most important role that a physician provides for a patient with chronic illness. Even specific pharmaceutical and technological interventions owe much of their ability to treat effectively to the power of this archetype. The presence or absence of symptoms in chronic illness are frequently due as much to the healing forces represented by the physician and other health care personnel as to any other definable medical agent. This is as true in contemporary Western medicine as in older, more traditional practices and ways of dealing with enduring illness and suffering. The importance and meaning of the healer archetype go beyond what is meant by a placebo effect.

Archetypes, in the simplest sense, are images and symbols that provide links between the psychologies of individuals, families, and the outer world. We are able to enjoy and find meaning in classical mythology and drama, for example, because the behaviors and situations of gods and humans are recognizable within our own lives and times. Homer's *Iliad*, Virgil's *Aeneid*, and Dante's *Inferno* include characters, passions, and moral complexities present in both art and real life. Motion pictures and their sequels draw upon certain stock types that can be counted on to evoke powerful bonds and reactions in viewers.

Everyone can easily think of actors whose screen personas or roles embody the archetypal figures of the lone hero, the beautiful siren, the wanderer, the rebel, the witch, the confused or cruel old king. Our emotional responses to these cinema images can be quite strong, as Hitler and the Nazi propagandists knew.

Common political archetypes include the leader and the fallen leader; the son who lusts for or fears the removal of his father from office; the faithful political wife who, like Penelope, dutifully awaits her husband's return; the powerful woman, such as Margaret Thatcher or Hillary Clinton, who raises the specter of Lady Macbeth in the fearful imaginations of those who oppose her policies. Cultural archetypes or icons are the Dionysiac singer who sends women into frenzies, the business mogul whose Midas touch turns everything to gold, and the scientist whose discoveries and technologies seem to venture onto Promethean turf, challenging the gods and their powers.

Among the reasons professionals have the status they do—and may be met by scorn when they fall short—is that, whether they wish to or not, they represent ideal types whom people expect to fulfill common and basic human needs. The lawyer ought to both serve and exemplify justice, the soldier display courage, the minister model faith and caring, and the scholar embody wisdom. The physician carries the gift and burden of the healer archetype. Archetypal physicians include Asklepios, tutored by Chiron the centaur; Jesus, the physician of the soul; St. Francis, kissing and healing lepers; and the knight Parsifal, whose quest for and offering of a sip from the Holy Grail brought new life to a king dying of spiritual thirst. A more secular depiction of the healer can be seen in Norman Rockwell's painting of the kindly doctor and his apprehensive but trusting young patient.

In fact, only recently has the physician become the container for the archetype of the healer. Practitioners of the medical arts were formerly suspect and guilty of quackery and incompetence, and their visits seen as a last resort. Although the effectiveness of both local and itinerant healers as setters of broken limbs was sometimes acknowledged, this was a skill demonstrated by those who tended horses as well. Preparing potions for pain and other maladies, applying herbal remedies, assisting in child-

birth, and giving comfort to the elderly or dying were roles typically filled by women of the community. The archetype of the
healer might be projected onto a wise woman, a good king, a
local priest, or, ultimately, God, Jesus, or Mary in Christian communities. Previously, resort to a doctor was evidence of a lack of
faith in God. "To cure the sharpe accidents of disease," wrote
John Donne in the seventeenth century, "is a great worke; to
cure the disease itself is greater; but to cure the body, the root,
the occasion of diseases, is a worke reserved for the great Phisit-
ian." Gradually over the past one hundred years, however, the
practice of medicine has acquired a higher status and recognition than it ever had before.

Public health measures introduced in the eighteenth and
nineteenth centuries led to a reduction in the number and viru-
lence of outbreaks of infectious diseases. The prevention of
some diseases through inoculation and quarantine also heightened popular belief in the ability of science and scientists to
reduce certain kinds of human suffering. None of this progress
was yet linked to the person or profession of the physician. For
most individual ills, science and medicine still had little to offer.
Indeed, the presence of a doctor often brought more fear than
hope. The cures he did attempt usually gave little relief, prolonged pain, and lightened the wallets of the afflicted family. As
a result, practitioners of all kinds—chiropractors, homeopaths,
allopaths, neuropaths—competed for patients with different
theories and treatments for disease.

But with the discovery of bacteria, the introduction of antibiotics, and the growth of the general hospital and its attendant
admitting privileges, the allopathic physician, or M.D., swept
the field of rival healers. The physician's place at the apex of the
health care pyramid was cemented by state licensing boards.
The right to prescribe drugs and to enter, examine, and cut the
body was reserved for the M.D. The money for research projects,
the training of physicians through the presentation of patients,
and the use of human subjects was linked to the university hospital, reinforcing the monopoly and prestige of the physician.
The escalating costs of hospital procedures, the rise of health
insurance companies, and the increased demand for ever more
technologically advanced interventions for diagnosis and treat-

ment further empowered the doctor and the hospital. Although the individual doctor's practice was as often as not grounded in the empirical evidence of his own experience with individual cases, the medical community claimed access to and use of a large body of scientific methods for the relief of a wide variety of ills.

As medical explanations of individual distress supplanted more traditional ones, the doctor took on the mantle of the priest. He (usually) was present at the sacred moments of birth and death, even though, for the most part, his services were not required at either. The physician also became for many people the individual who stood closest in their lives to the splendid discoveries and achievements of the life sciences, which seemed to promise an abatement of the claims of aging and death. The longing for immortality began to be focused away from the priest and onto the doctor. The sip of medicine and the tablets of aspirin, the neurologist's instructions to extend arms and touch nose, and the confidentiality of the consulting room became psychically indistinguishable from the Eucharist, the sign of the cross, and the confession. Both priest and physician took to carrying their implements in black bags. Both gained almost unlimited and unquestioned access to hospital rooms and patients. The APGAR and the baptism, the last rites and the death certificate—the parallels go on at risk of overstating the case.

The physician judged whether an individual was sick, and what the family's role, if any, was to be in caring for him or her. The hospital became a total institution where the particulars of daily life, including diet, eating schedules, privacy, and access to patients through "visiting hours" and "doctor's orders," were determined and controlled by medical personnel. Few patients or families complained of being examined by anyone at any hour for the benefit of "rounds." People were encouraged to perceive the hospital with all the awe reserved for a holy place and to be comforted by the sight of the white coats and skirts of doctors and nurses. Doctors were regarded with the same respect accorded to ministers of faith. In fact, often they were accorded more because they conveyed the practical and evident blessings of the miracles of science. It was easy to have confidence in the doctor to do the right thing.

Typically, for most of this century, one family member, most often a woman, was delegated as the major contact with the physician. The doctor was familiar with the family and the cases the delegate had presented to him in the past. Immediately after the presentation, a sense of reassurance was provided; the illness was now "in the doctor's hands." Many patients and families still yearn for this idyllic feature of midcentury American life. Stereotypical and paternalistic as he may have been, the family doctor was nonetheless a reality devoutly wished for by a great number of people—whatever his personal or moral failures might have been. Like the excesses of the whiskey priest, the doctor's personal habits were not generally used as a measure of his devotion to his calling.

For the Smith family, some years ago, the wait for the pediatrician, Dr. Harold, when a child was ill was filled with a mixture of mild apprehension and great expectation of relief. Doctors made house calls in those days. Mrs. Smith's well children did not need to be bundled up to make the trip to the medical building to sit in a crowded waiting room, as she has often had to do to help out her now-grown children. An unfamiliar nurse or physician's assistant did not beckon her and the ill one to come into an examining room while the others sat amid more colds and coughs. Mrs. Smith and her children had loved, admired, and respected Dr. Harold as he helped each of them make their way through all the sniffles, scrapes, grippes, and bone breaks until they were through with college and on their own. The few times Mrs. Smith had been sick, she too had called the pediatrician, and Dr. Harold had been more than willing to suggest a remedy or prescribe some medicine that soon took care of whatever she had caught.

Now, in the 1990s, Mrs. Smith was very uncomfortable calling the health plan, for she knew that she would probably be asked to come in to be seen. Her physician there was a nice woman, but Dr. Hancock rarely had more than a few minutes to offer her, and Mrs. Smith had already told her complaint to the nurse. A conversation with Dr. Hancock only seemed repetitive. Why, she had already told it three times—once on the phone, then to the nurse (if that's what he was), and a third time to the doctor. Her daughter told her she was spoiled if she expected house calls like Dr. Harold had made. Maybe she was. But now that she was older, stiff with arthritis, and ill more often, like her husband, she thought she would feel much better if she knew that Dr. Harold could be at the plan to at least answer the phone when she called, without having to talk with somebody else, unknown to her, who could not be counted on to tell her what to do.

For close to a century, the physician has served as the one figure in our society in whom most people have placed faith and trust. The fact that the health and longevity of populations is more a result of nutrition, sanitation, environmental well-being, and preventative health measures, for example, rather than of specific medical interventions, has been little noticed. Most people are healthy because they have not become ill to begin with. Those who do become sick generally recover on their own without the help of diagnosis, over-the-counter or prescribed medications, or any treatment at all. Nevertheless, the faith of patients and families in the beneficent healing power of the physician remains an important part of popular culture. Films and television shows frequently portray the selfless heroism of the doctor. Even more recent TV series in our time of disillusionment have shown physicians whose devotion to their patients is unquestioned, though their motives or personal lives are not quite so pure. The physician's authority, competence, and integrity have, in general, been acknowledged by Americans of different religious, social class, and ethnic backgrounds. Even within those communities where other healing traditions have validity and respect, the medical doctor is still accepted as a legitimate source of knowledge and cure for acute and emergency care.

THE PHYSICIAN TODAY

That picture, once so familiar, is now all changed. As the physician becomes increasingly unable to fulfill the former, idealized role, and the meaning of the physician within the culture is transformed, the view and very character of illness will be different as well. An item from a chronic illness folder on the Internet suggests what has occurred: "A good joke helps along the way—How can you tell the difference between a doctor and God? God knows he/she is not a doctor." The nature and quality of interactions in the physician-patient-family triad influence the experiences of illness and healing, and the consequences of these shifting attitudes toward medical care are significant, multiple, ongoing, and still to be sorted out.

The public's belief in physicians' commitment and autonomy to practice in the best interests of their patients is undermined by their employment by HMOs, ownership of diagnostic laboratories, and need to undergo utilization review and selection for "preferred provider" panels. Sensational media reports of physician wrongdoing and denigration of their competency by interests seeking to limit the cost of and access to medical care have also contributed to a lowering of the esteem in which the profession had been held.

The movement for patients' rights led to certain reforms, including the need for physicians to obtain informed consent from patients and to show greater respect for their autonomy. Direct marketing to "health care consumers" of prescription drugs, hospital services, and physician groups, as well as more restrictive insurance plans, have forced individuals and families to become "informed advocates" for care in the "new health care environment" and "medical marketplace." The appearance of self-help groups and message boards and conferences on the Internet and increased coverage of medical news give many people access to information and opinions beyond those available in their local medical environment.

The crumbling of the employer-paid insurance system and the end of the long-term employment contract that existed between many American families and their employer are developments that also have major consequences for those living with illness. Families face tremendous financial and emotional burdens as their ill members are more quickly discharged from hospitals, the costs of care accumulate rapidly, treatment options proliferate, and the potential confusion from multiple "patient advocates" within the same family grows. At a time of great individual and family distress, the confidence that many people once had in their physician has been eroded.

For thousands of years, people have sought out the ministrations of healers for the relief of their suffering. Those with a prolonged affliction might travel to the relics of saints, places of miracle, or sacred groves. Changes of diet, the use of baths or herbs, or exercises of body, thought, or prayer might be prescribed. The physician and his office, his medicines and their prescribed use, the hospital and its labs where blood, urine, and stools are collected, may often serve the same purpose—giving people something to do while the malady moves toward its own likely resolution of a return to health, even though the experience of illness may persist.

The loss of faith in the ability of the physician to heal delivers a strong blow to many people's sense of well-being, the effect of which ought not to be underestimated. The practice of medicine takes place within a field of moral reciprocities. Most people acknowledge its limits. If they are literally to put their bodies and lives in medical hands, however, they expect to be treated in ways commensurate with the social trust they confer upon physicians. The betrayal of that reciprocity through insensitive or inadequate care or an unwillingness to engage in dialogue can hurt deeply. One's physician may be discarded before faith in modern medicine is undermined. Individuals and their families may go "doctor-shopping," searching for a physician or someone from outside the dominant health care system who will provide them with the time and willingness to listen and to heal.

WHAT PEOPLE WANT, WHAT DOCTORS NEED TO DO

"We need to demonstrate more effectively our dedication to caring for the whole patient—worries, quirks, and all," argues an editorial writer in the *New England Journal of Medicine* (Campion, 1993, p. 246), responding to a survey reporting that one-third of American adults use alternative or nonconventional medical approaches. As long as the concerns of the "whole patient" are described (dismissed) by medical doctors as "worries, quirks, and all," it is little wonder that so many people visit nonmedical practitioners.

In the context of chronic illness, most physicians have four primary functions:

1. Serving, consciously or not, as the personification of the healer archetype that is activated at a time of distress and suffering
2. Making a diagnosis, delivering a prognosis, and prescribing treatments
3. Acting as the gatekeeper who facilitates entrance into the biomedical system
4. Legitimizing and collaborating with nonmedical professionals and other caregivers to provide for those with illness

If a physician can, at a minimum, perform these roles effectively, the patient and family will be well served.

When the worlds of patients, families, and physicians meet, however, the results can be collaboration, collision, or indifference. The expectations and activities of each are often at cross purposes. People in physical distress, for example, may be looking for professional confirmation of what they already know or suspect. Families may be seeking specific suggestions to manage the symptoms that are already present. Physicians are frequently limited to getting the information they need for diagnosis and medical treatment.

In addition, the lack of a change in the status of a disease commonly ends a physician-patient encounter and signals to the doctor that there is no need for additional action. For those individuals and families living with chronic illness, on the other hand, the absence of improvement can be a spur toward exploring other possibilities of healing or cure. As a result, the physician often becomes increasingly peripheral to the day-to-day lives of those with illness and their ongoing attempts to make sense of and cope with the illness experience.

The physician can compromise his or her ability to be a significant presence in the lives of those with chronic illness by:

1. Failing to appreciate the archetypal nature and power of the healer
2. Misunderstanding the relation between illness, disease, and suffering

3. Not grasping the importance of the *process* of diagnosis to the patient and family
4. Being unwilling to recognize that individuals and families have the same needs for autonomy, participation, and respect within the medical milieu as professionals expect for themselves

Adults do not first visit a physician because they are sick. Most people go to a doctor because they don't feel well. Others encounter a physician when someone has noticed enough of a change in their behavior or appearance to raise concern. There is often a long waiting period to see whether the change persists or worsens before a first appointment is made. Friends and family members are consulted as to whether they have had similar occurrences and what they did as a result. People turn to medical self-help books and may question acquaintances associated in some way with health care. They may be encouraged to try out nontraditional practitioners, who are sometimes helpful. Finally, if symptoms continue, this extensive, often anecdotal, information-gathering process may culminate in a request for an appointment with a doctor.

Victims of crimes frequently feel peripheral to what has happened to them after they report the crime. Their experience is taken over, managed, used, or discarded by police, prosecutors, and attorneys in their pursuit and trial of the perpetrator. Victims are told what statements to make and to whom to speak. They have a big stake but little say in how the process goes forward or in determining the fate of the perpetrator. Helpless and powerless, they are traumatized a second time through, at best, a benign neglect.

Individuals and families are often treated similarly once they enter the medical system. Their descriptions of their illness, their beliefs about its origins and what has brought it on at this particular time, are typically neglected or abbreviated in favor of a medical account shaped by the doctor's beliefs and experiences more than their own. It is not that the physician's hypothesis of etiology or diagnosis is inaccurate. It is too thin. A richer description would include the individual's and family's hypotheses as well, for that is where clues to easing the suffering, if not curing the disease, are likely to be found. A patient's search for cure is also a journey to find people willing to listen to or test out new hypotheses. The attempt to discover an etiology that leads to a treatment that works is also a pursuit of meanings and explanations that cohere and bring some relief.

Rarely does a medical account of an illness tell more than the barest facts. The degree and extent of a person's or family's feelings and fears, resilience and helplessness, can nowhere be found in the medical record. How can the absence of the human details be justified? It is well established that these factors are often as important, if not more so, than any pharmacological aid to a person's ability to recover from or survive illness despite the accumulating losses that illness may bring. It seems to me that a chart or a clinical conference that does not mention the costs and the meanings that individuals and families make of their encounter with illness is an incomplete one. As Kathryn Hunter (1991) points out: "Among the most valuable strategies for patient-centered interviewing are questions about motivation and meaning. . . . George Engel's questions—"Who is there at home?" and "How is that for you?"—are excellent keys to a patient's life situation . . . acknowledg[ing] courage, loneliness, anger, alienation, fear of death" (p. 168).

The official account of an illness experience typically begins at a point that is well into the individual's and family's process of upset, illness, coping, and difficulties. Any professional who gathers a history of illness complaint without asking for the whole story of how the patient came to be in the office or clinic is likely to be missing out on a great deal of important information. Without the opportunity to talk and listen, many patients and their families will neither follow up their first visits with any kind of regularity nor keep up with prescribed regimens. Health care professionals have become sensitized to the need to provide continuing compassion and support for those who have suffered the violence of trauma. They recognize the need for therapeutic approaches oriented to the particular sufferings of such patients. Those who work with people with chronic illness need to show the same concern. Frequently people receive diagnoses with no supportive family or friends present to help them process the information and receive the empathic responses that can be so crucial at such a moment.

Many individuals with chronic illness comment that their initial encounters with the medical system, oriented as it is toward acute care, influenced their subsequent attitudes, often negatively, toward physicians and the illness itself. Yet even sensitive medical observers have suggested that during the first or acute phase of an illness or disability, the technical priorities set by a physician are most important. Patients and families are expected to be primarily passive, reinforcing the doctor's orders. Far too often it is assumed that coping with illness consists primarily of complying with medication orders or other medical regimens. Studies show, however, that many individuals with chronic illness fail to follow through with treatment or rehabilitative recommendations. Far too often physicians assume that when symptoms are under control or in remission, the illness is no longer in need of their attention. But it is the psychosocial costs and consequences of illness that leave individuals and families vulnerable to ever greater distress. Far too often treatment is focused on the patient's disease rather than on his or her losses and suffering. It is vital for providers of care to explore, as Kleinman (1988b) puts it, "the nature of meaning within the experience of illness and the trajectory of care" (p. 162).

One study, for example, indicates that the disappearance of symptoms presented to physicians is correlated much more highly with the patient's perception that the doctor acknowledged the soundness of the patient's evaluation of his or her problem than it is with the accuracy of diagnosis or the sophistication of treatment (Brody, 1992). Unfortunately, medical professionals often assume that individuals are not aware of the actual or potential psychosocial origins of their discomfort. It is more likely that many people do not disclose what they believe to be the nonorganic sources of their distress because they are aware that their chances for care would be diminished without a "real" disease. Even when disease is present, those living with illness may fear that the presentation of other problems may be seen as a distraction from the more important focus on the signs and symptoms the doctor looks for and sees. Therapists are often the professionals who, with the family, must witness and attempt to care for all the "stuff" that precedes and falls out from the process of diagnosis, treatment, and care.

The diagnosis of a chronic illness brings an end to uncertainty for the physician, the satisfaction of solving an intellectual and professional challenge, and, sometimes, the opportunity to relieve someone's fear or discomfort. For an individual and family puzzled by symptoms, on the other hand, the naming of an illness is a more ambivalent affair. There is some relief in "knowing what we're dealing with" and, more hopefully, in the idea that "at least it's not as bad as it sounds." Simply knowing that an illness is real, not imagined, might be enough. Complaints are validated. By gaining a legitimated and widely used currency of language and meaning with which to discuss and describe their distress, patients enter into a world of shared anecdote, vocabulary, social groupings, and associations. Naming their illness places them in a world with which many are already acquainted—the world of illness, doctors, medicine, and science. Diagnostic labeling also provides many individuals and families with what they believe to be an initial framework for meaning and action. It is important for therapists to recognize what these gains contribute to the healing. The sense of coherence that can come from full participation in the diagnostic process is often as beneficial, if not more, and possibly less dangerous, than the medical plans presented following diagnosis.

Caught between the need to know and the fear of knowing, some individuals are relieved to have a diagnosis, no matter how grave, because it brings some closure to cognitive and emotional uncertainty. Others are frustrated and disappointed with the reductive effect that an explanation for their illness has on their suffering. They do not want the book closed, the case solved. As with many doctors, the diagnostic puzzle is sometimes more engaging than its completion. Mystery novels and police and medical dramas are always popular. It is only natural that patients and families, as well as physicians, would be engrossed in their own story, looking and guessing at different possibilities, digging for information, following hunches. Physicians and therapists can encourage patient collaboration by asking for and taking seriously patients' hypotheses and assuming that patients' logic and common sense, if not expert knowledge, are as good as their own. Most people, however, have never been asked by a physician why *they* think they are ill. Some of the anger that those living with illness may direct toward physicians arises from the gradual recognition that, unlike the diagnosis of most acute medical problems, the diagnosis of chronic illness is not followed by treatment and cure.

People want to know that their opinions and concerns are worthy of interest and response. They wish for information, not necessarily to evaluate options or to contradict their doctor's diagnosis or recommendations, but because being given information is a sign of respect. Once individuals and families enter into a medical setting, they are subject to invasive procedures, whether by questionnaire, probing finger, or placement within a tube for electromagnetic imaging. No one likes to be fully known by another. We attempt to hang onto some personal, undisclosed part of ourselves. In return for giving up the privacy of our bodies and the exposure of our fears, we ask for something in return. From a lover, it is commitment and fidelity. From the doctor, it is knowledge, dialogue, and the right to withhold or give consent.

When the physician or therapist nails down the diagnosis, the sound of his mental hammer can keep him or her from listening. The physician now knows, and the patient's voice goes unheard. The passion or movement of suffering has become fixed. One physician, committed to collaborative treatment and oriented toward family systems thinking, hypothesized that an individual's chronic back pain was no longer due to pinched nerves, muscle spasms, or slipped disks. Now, according to the doctor, it was a result of certain dysfunctional patterns of family interaction. One causal explanation replaced another. Psychological or systems explanations can certainly be as limiting as biomedical ones. On the other hand, the fact that the physician obviously cared enough to spend the time to converse with the patient, trying to understand the life and world of the person in pain, could well contribute to the latter's experience of healing and relief.

COMPLIANCE

A diagnosis of chronic illness usually marks the beginning of a lifetime of great uncertainty. The willingness of individuals and families to follow up, or comply, with the treatment recommendations of medical professionals is highly variable. The likelihood that people for whom treatment does not offer immediate relief from pain or distress, and whose illness is not directly life-threatening, will go along with suggested regimens is quite low. If medication is prescribed and its cost and side effects are minimal, the chances of its continued use are much better than if expense or discomfort are present. Exercise or physical therapy is unlikely to be pursued if financial strain, transportation, child care, or other logistical barriers exist.

A person's illness does not exist in a social vacuum. Individuals, whether afflicted by illness or acting as caregivers, have multiple roles, and their role related to sickness is one among many. For most people, the social, time, financial, energy, and other costs of pursuing recovery or delaying progression are weighed against their probable occurrence. The range of treatment and compliance choices can be pictured as a simple matrix like the one in figure 6.1, with numerical values affixed to costs, probabilities, and benefits. From this model, the individual,

FIGURE 6.1

Benefits/Compliance Ratios

High Costs of Compliance— Low Probability of Benefit **A**	High Costs of Compliance— High Probability of Benefit **B**
Low Costs of Compliance— Low Probability of Benefit **D**	Low Costs of Compliance— High Probability of Benefit **C**

family, therapist, or physician could make rational computations to arrive at decisions. The need to be in intimate conversation might be alleviated, and we could assume that compliance or adherence would easily follow.

To more adequately represent the variables people consider when making their choices, we would have to add the additional factor of how costs and benefits play out over time. A short-term high cost of compliance is different from a long-term one, just as a low probability of benefit over the short term does not necessarily predict benefit over the long term. Thus, using s to refer to the short term and l the long term, we would now have this matrix:

FIGURE 6.2

Benefits/Compliance/Time Ratios

High Costs of Compliance Over Short Term— Low Probability of Benefit **As**	High Costs of Compliance Over Long Term— Low Probability of Benefit **Al**	High Costs of Compliance Over Short Term— High Probability of Benefit **Bs**	High Costs of Compliance Over Long Term— High Probability of Benefit **Bl**
Low Costs of Compliance Over Short Term— Low Probability of Benefit **Ds**	Low Costs of Compliance Over Long Term— Low Probability of Benefit **Dl**	Low Costs of Compliance Over Short Term— High Probability of Benefit **Cs**	Low Costs of Compliance Over Long Term— High Probability of Benefit **Cl**

It is easy to imagine a matrix of rapidly increasing complexity, the cells doubling with every additional factor. Given that the context of choice is crucially important, the factors to be weighed would proliferate dramatically. Individuals and families think differently about medical situations involving an elderly person or a child. The confidence they have in their medical care is important as well. What is considered costly or beneficial also depends on available resources and cultural, family, and personal values.

Consider the dilemmas and difficulties of policy makers such as the board in Oregon that constructed measures for the allocation of health care funds. Therapists and physicians are confronted by the particular souls of the individuals and families before them. It is likely that much noncompliance is an oppositional expression of an individual's wish to be consulted and heard. How often do physicians or therapists check in to see whether their recommendations are being followed? To see if help is needed to adhere to a regimen? To ask about any remaining or unsatisfied doubts about an agreed-upon course of action? There is no decision-making technology that can make choices for people. Respect for the rights and autonomy of patients does not mean silence on the part of the professional. Individuals and families deserve and have the right to be challenged. It is in dialogue and conversation that meanings and values emerge and are reshaped. People do not want to be patronized. Besides pronouncements on studies, probabilities, and chances, they want to know what the professional thinks *and feels*.

The physician who abandons patients emotionally is more likely to receive projections of unrealistic hope and anger. Physicians who believe that patients expect too much of them have usually expected too little of themselves when it comes to learning how to ask about and be attentive to the spoken and silent yearnings of individuals to be treated as persons with dignity in a time of great need.

Sara, ill with cancer and the side effects of powerful chemotherapy, wanted to be treated as a patient when she was sickest. She did not want to get involved in a lot of decision-making about future measures when she was most nauseous and fatigued. She was being overwhelmed by respect for her autonomy and the need for her informed consent. It was when she felt weakest that she wanted to be able to rely on her physician's judgments. She complained to her therapist about the physician's failures to take the time to meet with her during her better periods. Involving her family at her times of greatest illness was also not helpful.

Physicians and therapists need to remember that people are different. Many individuals and families with chronic illness have more in common with others with different diagnoses than they do with those with whom they may be grouped by physician, code, or organization. People who have a variety of diseases but are ambulatory might have more to offer each other than do those whose diseases are identical but whose degrees of disability profoundly differ. Many newly diagnosed individuals and families back off from participation in some groups, at a time when they could use support, because the presence of those whose disease has progressed further may be quite frightening. Yet most physicians continue to approach people from the point of view of the illness with which their patient has been diagnosed.

INDIVIDUAL CARE

Medicine has been modern culture's way of explaining and relieving suffering. The physician has played the central role in this domain. It is a great burden to carry, and the risk for patient, family, and physician can be great. Whether described as transference, mana, or charisma, the perceptions and expectations of those who suffer toward those who are believed to heal can lead to anger, disappointment, and more suffering. They can also influence interactions in a positive manner, as placebo research indicates.

Many physicians also have needs that they expect their patients to fulfill. They anticipate that those who come to them with illness complaints will respect their authority; call on them for additional advice or reassurance only at times of urgent need; not question their competency or the basis upon which they make their judgments; comply with office procedures about when to undress, what to wear, and when to speak; accept their excuses or rationales about lateness; hear and understand what they say and know the difference between important and unimportant comments; and not expect too much in terms of their abilities. These expectations constitute the "demand" characteristics of the situation in which individuals and families with illness often find themselves. Medical professionals continue to act in ways that compel people to conform to these dependent roles.

Patients in even the most prestigious of HMOs are still addressed on a first-name basis by personnel who introduce themselves with their professional titles; are asked to sit disrobed in examining rooms with doors closed for long periods of time without being informed of the realistic length of wait; are rarely, if ever, asked their opinions on etiology, diagnosis, prognosis, or likelihood of compliance; and are never asked directly for feedback on the physician's manner. I recall one time when a young physician approached me in the examining room and said, "Hello, Robert. I'm Dr. Smith."

"Hello," I said. "I'm Dr. Shuman."

"Yes, hello," he said. "I'm Ken." Was an introductory minuet of this sort necessary? If I had been addressed simply as Mr. Shuman, I would have felt no need to fill the absence of what the Tibetan physician Lobsang Rapgay calls "a warm quality of presence" with at least a small shock of fresh air and mutual professional respect (Cohn & Rapgay, 1994).

A medical doctor may not be the best professional to take responsibility for the care of someone with chronic illness. Unable to provide a remedy and displaced from his or her role as the symbol of medicine's power to cure or relieve suffering, there is little the doctor can do, besides diagnose, that others cannot do as well. Currently, in most managed-care settings, the primary care physician serves as the gatekeeper into the medical system. It is he or she who is responsible for the initial diagnostic decisions that determine whether an individual has further access to care and reimbursement. Unfortunately, even the primary care physician is increasingly distanced from patient care. Many initial contacts with the health care system are with non-physician professionals, and even meetings with physicians may be constrained by the corporate norms of the managed practice.

The "therapeutic triangle in medicine" (Doherty & Baird, 1983) of patient-family-physician is being rendered obsolete. In some places, it is being replaced by the new nontherapeutic triangle of corporation-physician-patient and family. The individual and family find themselves in alliance with the physician as they cooperate with or confront medical decisions made by individuals at a distance from themselves. One double-edged feature of the standardization of medical care is the use of "best practice" protocols for specific diagnoses. It is likely that their utilization as a measure of physician effectiveness will decrease the amount of time doctors spend with each patient. Unfortunately, primary care physicians will be able to give fewer individuals and families the respectful hearing that people who suffer need. What remains of the role of the physician in the new world of health care when his or her ability to treat, refer, and hospitalize becomes ever more constrained? Physicians become technical specialists, including those in primary care who are deprived of the time to listen and the freedom to proceed as they see fit.

As physicians are deidealized and more information, autonomy, and choice become available to the individual in the immediate physician-patient encounter, the power differential between the two is not as great as it once was. A competence gap continues, however. Many people wish to have greater personal reciprocity with their doctors or therapists, to make a humanizing gesture toward them. "I would also like," the writer Anatole Broyard (1992), ill with cancer, perceptively noted, "a doctor who enjoyed me. I want to be a good story for him, to give him some of my art in exchange for his" (p. 45). Unable to give physicians gifts or payment in goods, as in the romanticized past, we want to give a good doctor or therapist something of ourselves in return. Although such "gifts" are frowned on in traditional practice—for good reasons as well as possibly bad ones—the professional caregiver who can show genuine warmth and delight in the personalities of those in his or her care and express something of his or her own personality is engaging in good practice.

It is inevitable in our culture, with its emphasis on individual responsibility, that the sources of illness, suffering, and healing are located in individuals. The power of the transference onto the physician, whether it results from early childhood dependencies or from more archetypal processes, is both a source of potential healing and a useful target of anger over continued illness. Therapists and physicians can make effective use of the transference phenomenon if they express attitudes and behaviors consistent with respect toward and trust in the individuals and families living with illness. Discussions about roles, expectations, and values model a way of adult functioning that offers all involved—professional, patient, and family members—both autonomy and empathy. The exploration of fears, hopes, limits, and skills builds people's confidence in the physician and other providers as people who are competent *and* who care.

It appears that a majority of encounters with physicians, if not most of them, are motivated by "causes" other than detectable organic disease. Diagnosable psychiatric disorders, particularly depression and anxiety, account for at least 11 percent of visits to doctors (Eisenberg, 1992). Feelings of malaise, fatigue, chronic back pain, headache, and other complaints that may be construed as somatization constitute up to three-fourths of primary care physician visits in the United States and the United Kingdom (Kleinman & Kleinman, 1985). In our culture, the psychosociobiological distress that most people experience is defined, diagnosed, and treated within a medical framework. The primary care physician's training, in the best of cases, does emphasize a biopsychosocial approach to illness.

"The primary-care physician," according to Howard Brody (1992) "must work within the patient's definition of the problem until either the problem goes away, according to the patient's own report, or the physician succeeds, through a process of open negotiation, to get the patient freely to accept a relabeling of the problem" (p. 59). Indeed, Brody also states, "it may be argued that the ongoing personal relationship with each patient is the . . . tool of the trade for the primary-care physician. *The primary care physician's approach to the patient's problem is grounded in the way the patient himself defines the problem* [italics in original]" (pp. 38–39). The primary care physician ought to be sensitive to this fact.

It certainly happens sometimes that sudden, dramatic, and potentially life-threatening illnesses—such as heart attacks, seizures, or spiking fevers—bring people into the established health care system immediately and extensive negotiations are unwarranted and unlikely. But most individuals, even those who may be suspected of or diagnosed with a chronic illness, are ambulatory at their first doctor's appointments.

The "rationalization" of the health care industry and the accompanying changes in the physician's role—in relation to the archetype of healing, in the use of best practice protocols in diagnosis and treatment, in patients' more difficult access to medical care, and in the physician's decreasing ability to make independent judgments about referrals—might, contrary to many observers' expectations, further contribute to the demedicalization of suffering. If nonphysician professionals can resist the temptation simply to substitute themselves for the doctor within the biomedical framework, then the sources of human suffering might be better addressed. A role that medical providers often fail to fulfill is one that therapists can provide. As short-term, solution-oriented, therapeutic technologies become more popular, however, we risk the further deterioration of the role of the therapist and the acceleration of the subordination and replacement of psychotherapy by the biomedical professions. Rather than the psychologizing of medicine, we see the medicalization of the psyche. New "holding environments" will need to be created to contain the distress that accompanies and exacerbates illness and disease. The attitudes of professional caregivers and their ability to collaborate with each other in ways that make a difference to patients and families will go a long way in determining whether what is lost by the disappearance of the physician can be restored by the informed caring of "the team."

There is by now a well-established distinction in theory, although not often in process and practice, between illness and disease. Disease usually refers to the observable damage or malfunctioning of organs, tissues, or systems of the body. Textbooks refer to the typical and recognizable symptoms and course of a disease. Whatever its theoretical validity, characterizing a form of bodily suffering as a disease, from the biomedical point of view, makes diagnosis, prognosis, treatment, referral, reimbursement, and research possible. Disease can exist with no previous signs of illness, and some of its features are unique. Illness, on the other hand, captures the meanings and biopsychosocial outcomes of an anticipated or identified disease. People may feel ill even when no disease is present in their bodies, just as some apparent symptoms of their disease may be due to the distress they experience as a result of their illness. Illness may linger once disease is gone. Since most chronic conditions are not curable and their symptoms and course fluctuate, it is very difficult to distinguish between disease and illness.

Bill, for example, has experienced no major or obvious exacerbations during the ten years since being diagnosed with multiple sclerosis, but it appears to others as well as to himself that his legs are weaker, his balance more tentative, his muscles more easily fatigued. Are these symptoms attributable to a progression of the disease? Or does he stumble more often because his initial MS symptoms led him to not use his legs as much and adopt a more sedentary lifestyle to cope with his illness, leading to further deterioration of his muscles? Does it matter? Well, it might. If his symptoms are due to disease, then he may be a candidate for certain medications, and regular contact with his neurologist may be more important. If not, then facing the issues involved in exercise, feelings of powerlessness, and coping styles could be helpful for Bill and his family. It seems that a collaborative family or individual approach coordinated by a therapist, making appropriate referrals to medical specialists, might provide better care than disease-oriented interventions with an exclusively medical focus.

When people judge themselves or their loved ones to be ill enough to seek medical advice, they are usually prepared to place themselves in the hands of another to receive care and be relieved of what worries and ails them. The illness experience awakens feelings and wishes associated with childhood dependency. Doctors who provide neither a cure nor any comfort are often the targets of the anger of the individuals and families who anticipated some remedy. The fault often lies with neither the frustrated patient and family nor with the doctor. To some degree, simply by virtue of being a practitioner of the medical arts, a person of high status and income, and the locus of cultural themes of suffering, the doctor is going to be on the receiving end of emotional expressions of unrelieved human distress.

Who or what will replace the power of the art of medicine and faith in the physician is yet to be seen. Some have suggested that the proliferation of twelve-step programs is one sign of people's need to find new ways of explaining and healing their distress; another sign, of course, is the increased use of alternative healing practices. It would be unfortunate if the lack of personal and long-term connections between physicians, therapists, patients, and families within the medical system kept people with diseases from receiving care and comfort for their illness.

THE GOOD-ENOUGH PROFESSIONAL

What are the characteristics that the "good-enough" professional caregiver will need to act effectively for patients and families as the delivery of health care services becomes increasingly rationalized?

1. *Understanding the existence, power, and importance of the archetype of the healer.* As the belief in the curative powers of the archetypal physician is shaken, the concerned person who seems to care and truly wants to listen to what is wrong may be handed the healer's robe. The best of the television or radio talk-show hosts are aware of the power to offer meaning and relief from distress with which the public credits them. The worst of them exploit that trust for purposes of profit or politics.

2. *Recognizing that illness is a form of suffering that touches many dimensions of the human spirit and individual and family lives.* Today a narrow focus on any one aspect of chronic illness can leave many individuals and families without the shelter that either religion or medicine have provided in the past. As Sullivan (1994) notes, "So many religious traditions have found sickness and healing—and the impulse to care—to be the paradigm of the human condition in the world" (p. xii).

3. *Accepting the inextricable connections between disease, illness, and suffering.* It is the task of those who are oriented toward healing as well as cure to help patients and families understand that symptoms of disease, of illness, and of suffering are often indistinguishable from each other.

4. *Acknowledging that biomedical treatment is only one of many forms through which care can be offered and that it can support other sources of care.* The professional caregiver must help people learn methods and employ meanings that can prevent or lessen distress, whatever their source.

5. *Collaborating with those who have the skill and patience to listen and discuss as well as with those who know how to wield a scalpel or read a scan.* The doctor who cannot share his or her diminished authority will be left with less. The doctor who is able to do so will gain. The therapist needs the physician to treat the disease. The physician needs the therapist to engage with people and their illness.

6. *Ensuring that patients experience some regularity and stability in those who provide care.* Some people experience an anonymous reciprocity of devotion, loyalty, commitment, and obligation through their faith and their church; others find it in, for example, Alcoholics Anonymous. Unfortunately, few HMOs or other health plans have demonstrated their ability to provide such reciprocity over any prolonged period of time.

7. *Creating an environment and context for listening and care that makes it easy for individuals and families to express distress and receive solace when they feel the need for it.* Much of the effectiveness of traditional religious institutions, as well as the twelve-step programs, comes from their accessibility. When that disappears, comfort is diminished.

8. *Encouraging and respecting people's own interpretations of the cause of their suffering and the means through which they might get some relief.*

9. *Appreciating the threats that illness brings to individual and family roles, activities, relationships, identities, and selves.* Four levels of loss and suffering were described in chapter 5. Most physicians or medical teams intervene primarily at the first level, where illness is construed chiefly as the loss of particular abilities or functions unrelated for the most part to an individual's or family's larger life projects.

10. *Accepting the responsibility of being invited into and learning from the worlds of those who live with chronic illness, however painful, unchanging, or challenging those worlds seem to be.*

Both illness and disease are forms of suffering. In many social and cultural traditions, a person's affliction, whether from illness, injury, the death of a loved one, or some other calamity, is viewed from a perspective that transcends the biological, personal, or psychological. The loss may be an opportunity to participate in communal rituals that touch and embrace natural and supernatural dimensions. Disease and illness may not be carved out as misfortunes that are fundamentally different from other forms of affliction. In Marxist ideology, it is the alienating influence of capitalism and class structure that is responsible for much individual misery. Among Buddhists, the karma of generations past may create the pain that one experiences today. In more traditional cultures, something may have gone astray or needs to be set right in the village, environment, or cosmos.

Too much has been expected of the physician and of medicine in the past. Too little will be available from them in the future. Although medicine can bring great cures and relief from much of the suffering that illness inflicts, it cannot do it all, and often medicine has little to offer for what has been so easily diagnosed but so painfully borne. Once the doctor has answered the questions of the name, seriousness, and remedies for chronic illness, a large part of his or her unique role is done. The importance of this role ought not to be denied. Identifying a disease as a cause of suffering is a very powerful act, but other ways of looking at suffering exist. I predict that in our culture chronic illness will increasingly be addressed through frameworks that confront and struggle with the meaning and facts of human suffering. It is only through patients, families, and professionals working together with patience, respect, and compassion that the archetype of healing, with nowhere else to go, will find its place in the authentic encounter between humans who suffer and humans who care.

Freidson (1988) describes the specific world physicians inhabit. It is maintained, like other professions, by professional training, peer pressures and collegiality, economic rewards, social status, jargons, governmental licensing, beliefs, attitudes, ethics, and an assortment of other practices and controls—all of which leads to effective practices of a certain kind. Medical training and successes also reinforce for the patient, family, colleagues, and physician the role assignments, limits of affection and camaraderie, and approaches to treatment to which the physician is committed.

The "clinical mind" of the physician, concludes Freidson, is characterized by a preference for action over knowledge; faith in his or her own work; a confidence that what she or he is doing is for the good of the patient; a pragmatic attitude focused on the facts at hand and a willingness to "tinker" (within the biomedical paradigm) rather than a commitment to particular medical theories; belief in the value of his or her store of firsthand experience (even if limited to one or two cases); and a recognition of the amount of uncertainty and ambiguity at play in her or his work. In all these respects, with the possible exception of a commitment to a biomedical model of pathology, the clinical mind of the physician is very similar to that of the psychologist.

CHAPTER 7

Wealth, Home Care, and Diversity

Inasmuch as ye have done it unto one of the least of these my brethren, ye have done it unto me.

Matthew 25:40

The family is the unit of illness because it is the unit of living.

Henry Richardson (1989)

PROFESSIONALS WHO EXPRESS CONCERNS about the ethical and moral dimensions of living with chronic illness cannot avoid taking into account the gross disparities of income, the inequities that restrict access to medical and psychosocial resources, the distortions of good practice and care by clinicians in medical, pharmaceutical, and associated industries driven and shaped by marketplace forces, and the political judgments that define and limit the resources available to individuals with chronic illness and their families. Discussions of limiting coverage or managing care based upon "medical necessity" are not morally sound as long as the rationing and allocation of resources takes place in an environment of nonuniversal coverage and nonprogressive taxation for programs such as Medicare and Medicaid.

Those who voice concerns about diversity, relative to illness, and focus on cultural and social differences, gender identity, sexual orientation, and racial, ethnic, religious, and other distinctions and groupings too numerous to mention, are missing the point, and dangerously so, unless their concern includes an acknowledgment that the economics of health care access and use are extremely important. The pernicious effects of for-profit "health care" and "home care" companies and their not-for-profit bureaucratic cousins on the health of individuals and families and their ability to provide care are many.

We ought not to allow the marketplace to determine the terms of our care or frame our debate, for several reasons. First, a large and growing number of individuals either have no health insurance or are inadequately covered. Even people with "full" insurance coverage face increasing out-of-pocket, copayment, and deductible charges. To avoid the cost of treatment, many people avoid medical care until their condition has worsened.

Second, most home care for individuals, with or without insurance, is provided by family members, who are not compensated for either their time or the income they forgo to provide care and assistance. In addition, owing primarily to the economic leverage of managed care, more medical procedures are performed on an outpatient basis, and hospital stays, when allowed, are of much shorter duration. Unfortunately, not only are fewer nurses available in hospital and other medical settings, but fewer are able to come to the homes of people with illness to teach and assist family members in performing medical and nursing tasks. Family members are expected to organize their time and logistics to respond to illness and care needs, demands, and expectations, apparently without regard to their resources or competing obligations. Social critics have warned of the medicalization of human suffering, that is, characterizing more and more social problems or personal difficulties as medical phenomena. Thus, alcoholism, drug addiction, mental illness, and other chronic problems have become subject to medical diagnosis and intervention. What is germane to this discussion is that, in the long run, the burden of care for those with these problems is shifted onto the family rather than addressed through the use of social and political resources.

Third, these events are taking place in a demographic environment in which an aging population that is living longer will contribute to a growth in the number of individuals with chronic illness. Medical care is still organized on an acute illness model that emphasizes short-term intervention, restoration of the patient to the level of functioning that existed prior to the illness event, and an emphasis on patient autonomy, identity, and rights. Each of these priorities conflicts with the reality of chronic illness. Care for the chronically ill is usually long-term or intermittent, the ill person's ability to maintain previous levels of performance usually fluctuates or deteriorates, and family members are typically affected much more strongly than they are in cases of acute illness.

THE HOSPITAL IN THE HOME

Much is made of the technological revolution in medicine and the impersonal nature of most hospital-based medical treatment. The fact is, however, that our society is undergoing an enormous shift in the way technology is used to care for those with chronic illness. Homes and families are expected to function like medical settings at the same time that hospitals are attempting to bring the family into hospital care. One study (Arno, Bonuck, & Padgug, 1994) showed that the ratio of expenditures for hospital care to those for home care diminished from 279:1 in 1970 to 29:1 in 1991.

Even when done with the best of intentions and love, people are often unprepared for some of the physical, emotional, and financial consequences of providing extensive, as well as intensive, care at home for those with chronic illness. The movement of health care for the chronically, seriously, or terminally ill person into the home can be a form of exploitation and unexpected hardship, playing upon the desire of a family or individual to give comfort to the ill loved one within the intimacy and security of the home for as long as possible. At the same time that they must continue to cope with the ordinary and often stressful tasks of everyday life, family members have to perform complex, frightening, intrusive, and painful procedures on child, spouse, partner, or parent. Such medical interventions formerly were either not available or done in medical settings only. It is one thing to change soiled bedsheets or assist someone in the bathroom. It is another to replace a tracheotomy tube in the throat of a child who is dependent on a ventilator for life support or to supervise the use of an infusion pump for a parent's cancer.

What is the "carrying capacity" of the home environment? How much of a load can primary caregivers and individual family members bear? Time, a limited resource, is especially inelastic to those who must carry out all the tasks of caregiving as well as other daily roles. Taking care of individuals with illness at home has never been easy, but it is made even more difficult when expectations change about who will provide treatment and how. When the goal of home care was primarily palliative, aimed at reducing the immediate suffering of someone who was ill, the "treatment" was usually an extension of what was already within the home—cooking, laundering, companionship, helping out with small chores, occasional trips out to the doctor, the hairdresser, or visits with family and friends.

This is the orientation toward care of most traditional cultures. It takes place under the nurturing eye of Hestia, goddess of the hearth and domesticity. Traditional home care reflects the unity of family, neighborhood, parish, and other voluntary associations ensuring some degree of mutual support in times of need. Unarguably, it has long been assumed that mothers or daughters would bear the burden of giving care. The assumption that hands-on care is within a woman's sphere has long been accompanied by the expectation, often unmet, that husbands and sons bear the financial obligation to keep the household functioning and to maintain insurance or reserves to meet medical costs.

Unfortunately, the plight of many women caring for those with chronic illness has worsened during the last twenty-five years. Although Medicare and Medicaid have relieved some of the financial burden that chronic illness delivers upon a household, nearly forty million Americans are un- or underinsured.

Most families cannot live safely on a single income. Single parents are largely women trying to meet the multiple responsibilities that the role brings. The term "sandwich generation" refers to those individuals—again, primarily women—who have responsibility for the care of children and elder parents simultaneously. With respectful irony, I use the term "club sandwich generation" for women who give care to children, elderly parents, and spouses or others with chronic illness. Many suffer from "caregiver's syndrome" as their health deteriorates under the strain of providing physical care to adults.

THE HOME AT RISK

The home is at risk of becoming a place of treatment, rather than of refuge, for both the family and the ill. It is important to distinguish between the services provided by those in the home—cleaning, cooking, and personal care—and home health care, which is the delivery of medical services by nurses or other ancillary medical providers. The former, so often identified as "women's work," is done at some emotional, physical, and/or economic cost to a member of the household. The latter, offered theoretically in the best interests of those with illness and their families, often leads to more work, greater suffering, and higher real costs.

As painful as such decisions might be, if there were no alternatives available, families and individuals would acknowledge the need for out-of-home care for those with severe, progressive, or incapacitating illnesses and conditions such as amyotrophic lateral sclerosis, late multiple sclerosis, Parkinson's disease, stroke, Alzheimer's disease, AIDS, and ventilator-dependent quadriplegia. The fact that technologies, medications, personnel, and procedures are available increases the moral pressures on people to maintain an incapacitated person at home.

The initial appeal of home care to families is undeniable. It seems to offer the ill person more personal and humane care in familiar surroundings. Family members do not need to travel as often to be with the one who suffers. The bureaucratic authority of the medical establishment is replaced by the willing care of intimates. The shame of abandoning a loved one is avoided. The cost appears to be less than what hospitalization or institutionalization would entail. And mastering equipment and skills that were once reserved to the awesome province of the physician can be exciting.

The downsides, however, are discovered soon enough. Children compete for the time and attention of parents, who may resent the hugely disproportionate energy and resources they must direct toward the person with illness, and all feel guilty. The ill person, in turn, may want to relinquish his or her claims on family resources, feeling ashamed to have needs that receive considerations perhaps better directed toward those younger or more able.

Family members are not able to employ the defense of detachment that health care professionals use to avoid being overwhelmed by the suffering around them. They cannot turn their attention toward another patient with a better prognosis, join a debate about the choice or quality of a technology or drug, discuss research protocol or results. They cannot even think about what they will do when they get away from the office, the lab, or the hospital because, of course, *they are already at home.* Much like the person with chronic illness, who cannot easily escape from his or her own body, families with a seriously incapacitated individual at home cannot avoid the presence of that person's body.

Those who are not at home are more easily touched by guilt as well. Betsy Lewis, a college student, felt badly about going off to school, leaving her mother and brother behind to care for her father, whose illness required extensive support to get through his daily hygiene and dressing routines. Mr. Lewis pleaded with his family to put him in a long-term care facility when Betsy left. He believed that what his wife and two children had barely been able to accomplish for him would be too much for only two helpers. In addition, he was becoming fatigued by the frequent visits of his devoted friends and feared that they would volunteer to share in some of his care. Even if only his wife and son were to provide intimate care, he dreaded having the smells and sights of his uncontrollable body become more noticeable after Betsy's departure because they would not be able to respond to his needs as quickly. He dreamed of the benign indifference of the institutional staff and the removal of self-imposed constraints, such as trying not to cry out for help at night for fear of disturbing his sleeping family. He wanted to use his "exit right" to remove himself from the current constitution of his family, as Betsy had done by going to college. He had no desire to commit suicide or to cease seeing family or friends and enjoying their visits. He simply wanted, as William Ruddick (1994) describes it, to enter the "shrunken, self-absorbed world of illness," to become his "sick self," and to allow his family their own lives once again (p. S12).

So the decision was made that Mr. Lewis would go to a care facility. Then Mrs. Lewis was informed by her physician that her HMO had recommended the less costly alternative of home care. The HMO would be willing to provide home aides, "durable medical equipment," and other kinds of assistance; she, her husband, and her family could reap the benefits of knowing that Mr. Lewis was getting the care he needed from the people he loved most, in the place he loved best. Mrs. Lewis and her son agreed to this change in plans despite Mr. Lewis's protests. The idea of "putting away" their father and husband was intolerable to them when an alternative was presented.

When Betsy was informed of the change in plans, she was devastated by powerful feelings of anger, guilt, and helplessness. She felt "like a sparrow in the kitchen," vainly trying to fly toward the tree outside and smashing into a window. She had been as relieved as her dad when they were looking forward to their mutual departures. Now, she believed, she was abandoning her whole family, leaving them to manage a responsibility she equally shared. Home would not be the place of refuge she had hoped it would become, nor would her dad find the refuge he sought in a care facility.

Bill and Tracy's situation is different. Tracy is quite ill with AIDS and frightened at the prospect of entering a hospital or hospice for terminal care. He and his partner have created a warm and welcoming home, and they have arranged rooms and spaces to make Tracy's care as easy as possible. Bill, however, is weary. He has to work twice as many hours to generate the income that both brought in before Tracy's illness, and he gives Tracy as much care as he is able. There are limits on what they can do because of the inadequacy of their insurance coverage, as a result of Tracy's diagnosis and their lack of marital status. Bill is fearful that his continued obligation to care for Tracy will bankrupt them emotionally as well as financially. Tracy says he could understand Bill's position if there were no possibility of getting medical care at home. The development of infusion devices, however, makes it possible to use medications as safely, routinely, and effectively as in a hospital setting. Bill and Tracy are at a crossroads in their relationship at the worst possible time—one that for better or for worse might not have occurred without the benefits and unanticipated costs of home health care.

Both Mr. Lewis and Tracy have a sense of themselves, of who they are and what they want from their lives while existing under the punishing regimes of their illnesses. Each is a person who is deprived of some function and limited in significant ways by his illness, but making choices and decisions about how to go on with his life. Yet it is probable that we, the readers, feel differently about what each is doing with the life that remains for him. We also may make different judgments of those in close relationships with them than they do of themselves. Our evaluations may revolve around how we grapple with words and phrases like *identity*, *person*, *self*, and "the good life." Intuitively, many would consider Mr. Lewis's behavior mature and healthy, indicative perhaps of some wisdom attained. Some might empathize less with Tracy's decisions.

SUFFERING AND COMMON GROUND

Issues of diversity and ethical concerns are linked by common experiences of suffering and the wish to be healed. All forms of social identity, whether defined by gender, epidermis, or culture, have a conception of justice, caring, the good person, and the good life. Attempts by therapists and physicians to understand the illness beliefs, clinical practices, and ethical claims of others, as well as their sensitivity to the contexts of institutional, familial, marital, and personal power in which dialogue and action take place, can go a long way toward touching, if not grasping, others' moral worlds.

How to find common moral ground in a pluralistic culture like our own is a topic that has interested philosophers. In the context of illness, however, it is an exaggerated concern. The simple fact that people are engaged in a medical or therapeutic encounter already demonstrates some shared values: that talk is more helpful than force; that something called "health" is desirable; that some individuals (therapists, physicians, healers) are better able to help people understand and transform suffering. Because some individuals and families do not find value in or receive comfort from the style or approach of particular therapists or physicians does not demonstrate cultural incompatibility.

Groups of people are profoundly different in how they experience, and give meaning to, sickness, disability, healing practices, death, and every other element that goes into making a way of life. In many cultures, for example, the concept of disability does not exist (Whyte & Ingstad, 1995). People are blind, deaf, or crippled. The specific limitations each category places on individuals are recognized, but even that meaning may have secondary importance compared with *how* the affliction (if it is so interpreted) came about. These cultures would generally not find it useful to assign individuals with a variety of sicknesses or "handicaps" to the general category "the disabled."

Not only do cultural variables influence how disease and suffering are construed by those who live with illness, but they also affect how professionals perceive and respond to others' complaints and attempts to give aid. Even within the more developed countries, where biomedicine has established professional hegemony, there are significant contrasts in when and how different groups of people feel and interpret distress and from whom they seek explanation and relief. There is evidence, for example, of significant bias in the diagnosis, treatment, and hospitalization of individuals with major mental illness on the basis of race and ethnic group (Good, 1992/3). Even in areas of limited size or heterogeneity, wide variations in rates of surgery and hospitalization continue, determined primarily by the "local-practice cultures" of physicians. These practices in turn are affected by significant differences in demand for services by individuals and groups of varying incomes and medical outlooks, rather than by an objective determination of need (Gesler, 1991).

It is also true, however, that if there is to be any collaboration between people living with illness and the professionals with whom they have contact, willingly or not, there must be meanings and events that both patient and clinician cherish and fear. Any appreciation of diversity is founded on a respect for significant local differences *and* an implicit agreement on some shared values. If nothing could be agreed to, not even the process by which to find some common ground, on what moral basis could care be provided? Examples of immoral—or questionably moral—care include the physician or therapist who insists upon treatment either by force of arms or terror, as in Nazi Germany and the psychiatric wards of the Soviet Union, or by force of law, as in the United States in cases involving Christian Scientists or those individuals diagnosed with severe mental illness.

It is unusual for therapists, or physicians for that matter, to find themselves in situations that involve beliefs so divergent from their own. Even in these cases, however, professionals and families share a wish to promote the well-being of a child, although there may be profound disagreement about the best means to attain that end. In the interests of the child, it ought to be possible for both biomedically oriented physicians and religiously committed parents to listen with humility and good faith to the concerns and anxieties of other parties. If a professional cannot establish a helpful rapport with individuals and families, owing to his or her difficulty with the intensity or nature of their religious practices or beliefs, it is wise to refer them to therapists or physicians who may be more knowledgeable or tolerant. Many care providers who do not imagine themselves to be biased or discriminatory make stereotypical judgments about the political beliefs and attitudes toward therapy, gender, and family roles of those who hold beliefs different—usually more orthodox or fundamentalist—from their own.

At times, the involvement of clergy can serve as a useful bridge through which secular professionals or those of different faiths can work effectively and empathically with people of strong religious belief. Again, I find some knowledge of the stories and parables of the Old and New Testaments to be helpful. It establishes me with patients as someone who takes religious views seriously, whether or not I agree with the particular beliefs of another. Once I have established religious faith as an area they need not be reluctant to share, I often ask individuals or families who are strongly religious how they make sense of their illness and the burdens of caregiving it may require. I find that a great deal more energy and questioning arises from discussion of the latter than of the former. Hearing from different religious traditions can also enlarge the perspective of the professional. Both therapist and physician may be viewed as largely peripheral to the reality of the suffering person and the hopeful and helpful family. Sometimes the best thing either can do is to suggest that a person become involved, or reinvolved, in a community of faith as a way to receive additional human and divine solace and aid.

Jane grew up in a home where religious faith was emphasized through the practice of good works and caring. As an adult, she was very willing to lend a hand and give comfort to friends and neighbors in need or members of her religious community who were alone in illness or aging. When her mother-in-law died, she thought it was her moral obligation to take her elderly father-in-law into her home, despite her husband's sincere assertions that it was neither her responsibility nor his wish to do so. His relationship with his father, as both a child and an adult, had not been close, and he was able in good conscience to suggest a care facility as an alternative.

Jane could not live with herself, however, if she did not provide the care of which she felt capable. At no time did I suggest that her belief in the obligation to care for others was not justified from a religious point of view. Both she and I were concerned, however, that her involvement with her father-in-law would allow her little time for her own interests and little respite from the labor of caregiving, both being important to maintain the commitment and energy to give care. Our problem was how to help Jane satisfy these personal needs while maintaining a sense of identity and integrity consistent with her past values of self-sacrifice and devotion.

Fortunately, Jane was always thinking of ways she could help people. She remarked one day that she felt badly that her father-in-law, as well as other elderly or ill people, could not participate in their local community affairs. I suggested that she use the equipment of the local community college to record older individuals at the nursing facilities and at home. Jane was enthusiastic about the idea with people at the college. Soon she was attending classes in oral histories and volunteering as a historian for other community events. Her feeling of well-being increased as she was able to integrate her need to offer service, her involvement in community, her wish to develop new competencies, and her need to spend time away from her caregiving tasks at home.

Professionals in our pluralistic society are likely to encounter less problematic cross-cultural situations when the life of the ill person is not believed to be at risk. Nevertheless, religious and cultural beliefs about how to make sense of the experience of chronic illness, what constitutes good care, and how best to provide it can often create serious disagreements between professionals, families, and individuals. Some traditions emphasize the role of the extended family and devalue involvement with physicians when medical treatments can provide no cure. Others stress the importance of controlling the information the patient receives in the belief that bad news can adversely affect his or her health. Western professional assumptions about patient autonomy, disclosure, and confidentiality may be iatrogenic in such contexts.

I remember viewing a television series about health care practices throughout the world. One segment showed an apparently typical meeting between a Japanese physician and a husband and wife following a breast examination and biopsy. After explaining the treatment he recommended, the physician asked the wife to wait outside his office so that he might report the full finding and prognosis to the husband. We would find such a practice intolerable in our culture.

A second segment portrayed a physician attempting to present his findings in a more open, Western manner. Following a young woman's mastectomy, the doctor entered a room where the patient's husband and three sisters sat. The physician described the operation in detail and drew diagrams of the breast with appropriate measurements in centimeters on the blackboard as the husband took careful notes. At the conclusion of his presentation, he picked up a box from the table in front of him and, with no apparent preparation, opened it, exposing the breast and its connective tissue to the silent family. A moment later, the doctor closed the box and, with a brief shaking of hands, left the room.

The two episodes serve to illustrate several points of which a professional ought to be aware. First is the danger of professionals promoting cultural values, no matter how well intentioned, that may diverge from those of the people with whom they work. Second is confusing the goals and means of medicine and therapy. The central goal of each is to relieve suffering. That goal, it seems to me, underlies the principles of patient autonomy, confidentiality, and disclosure. When these patients' rights become ends in themselves, however, both the therapist and the physician run the risk of rigidly insisting on principle over person. Third, it should be acknowledged that sometimes the professional's behavior and beliefs are at odds with the cultural mainstream. In such situations, professionals may have to make judgments about the degree to which they can comply with local conduct and when such compliance would not be consistent with personal goals or those of the profession to which they belong.

The case of a Navajo woman, Mrs. Tsosie, illuminates such a dilemma (Jecker, Carrese, & Pearlman, 1995). The sixty-five-year-old woman was brought to the hospital by her daughters with a variety of symptoms that indicated the possibility of meningitis as a cause of her delirium. A lumbar puncture was suggested for diagnostic purposes. Mrs. Tsosie held traditional Navajo views on illness and healing and had refused most invasive procedures during previous hospital admissions for rheumatic heart disease. Her preference, strongly communicated to her daughters upon this and other occasions, was to participate in a traditional Navajo healing ceremony if the medicine man did not judge her to be too sick to do so. Although the physician and other professionals with whom she consulted perceived the medical risk to be greater, and potentially fatal, if the lumbar puncture was not performed, Mrs. Tsosie and her daughters' wishes were respected, and she left the hospital to join in traditional rituals of healing.

The cross-cultural conflict in this situation was resolved to the satisfaction of all. Her daughters helped Mrs. Tsosie receive care consistent with her own wishes and her deeply held values. The physician acted with what she believed to be professional integrity, recognizing that

> Mrs. Tsosie stands to benefit by placing matters in the daughters' hands. Understood in this light, the subject of medicine becomes the suffering patient, and the injunction to benefit the patient does not necessarily require producing certain physiological effects on the body, but requires instead caring for the patient and producing outcomes that patients themselves can appreciate. (p. 12)

Cultural constructs of illness are "not in fact simple structures with clean lines and clear functions. . . . Rather, they are home-made jerry-built affairs made of available materials and subject to remodeling by worried parents, curious neighbors, and heal-ers, both traditional and untraditional. . . . People are actors within social contexts, not prisoners of a fixed cultural construc-tion" (Whyte, 1995, p. 241). As mentioned earlier, all forms of social identity have conceptions of justice, caring, the good per-son, and the good life, spelled out in text, myth, folk wisdom, and common sense. Overwhelmingly, however, issues of diver-sity and ethical concerns in relation to illness are linked more by the common experiences of suffering and the wish to be healed. Even as certain cultural and social constraints upon belief and behavior exist, human agency and individual imagination find room for novel acts.

Richard Katz (1993) suggests three "commitments" to be hon-ored by professionals who participate in the lives of people from cultures other than their own:

1. "To engage in respectful inquiry"—suspending one's own judgments and listening with patience and care
2. "To recognize and value experiences of vulnerability"—"a radical questioning of one's worldview ... [and] assumptions as to what is 'valid,' 'correct,' 'obvious,' and 'common practice'"
3. "To activate an exchange, giving something meaningful back to those with whom [one works]" (pp. 356–371)

CHAPTER 8

Families, Ethics, and Illness

Nobody who has not been in the interior of a family
can say what the difficulties of any individual of that
family may be.

Jane Austen, *Emma* (1815)

THE EVERYDAY ETHICS of living with chronic illness are different from those ordinarily addressed by physicians and the professional bioethics community. Jennings, Callahan, and Caplan (1988) acknowledge the special ethical challenges of chronic illness and identify three in particular that call for closer study. Chronic illness, they conclude:

poses a challenge to our understanding of the ends of medicine, the nature of the physician-patient relationship, and the ethical principles and standards governing health care decision-making;

challenges the normal moral boundaries of caring and conventional expectations about the caregiving duties of the family in relation to the social welfare obligations of the state;

challenges our understanding of social justice and community, as these ideals are reflected in society's response to different kinds of health care and social service needs. (p. 4)

118

The moral challenges associated with chronic illness extend beyond the person diagnosed and the immediate caregivers to encompass the larger field of families, friends, even community. Siblings may compete for parental time and attention. Elderly parents of adults with illness may relinquish their claims on family resources or experience guilt if their needs seem to conflict with the care needs of the younger members of the family. When holiday gatherings are postponed, changed, or go on without one or another family member present, holes may be torn in the family tapestry that are not easily patched. Other family members may experience "survivor's guilt" or feel shame for taking pleasure in the ill fortune of another who had been favored by the gods.

There is no moral hub as far as illness and families are concerned. Every person is a potential center of pathos, movement, passion, and suffering. Our luck in the world is no more fixed or certain than are the ways people respond to the accidents of fate. Therapists can help in such circumstances by offering broad contexts in which to search the sky or plumb the depths for meanings that give some solace. The communal rituals that take place at the times of entry or departure from life or certain changes in status are not available at the time of diagnosis or during periods of exacerbation. At one time the hospital visit, marked by a mixture of solemnity and sociability, was one such rite, but as schedules have become busier and hospital stays shorter, even that rite is passing.

We live in a time, the philosopher Agnes Heller (1988) points out, when one asks not only whether a behavior is good or right or just but whether the norms or rules by which behavior is judged are good or right or just. Public and private ethics are inseparable. Moral pressure may be applied to the therapist in situations where the experiences, evaluations, wishes, and needs of individuals and families engaged in psychotherapy may be in conflict with those of other health care providers or with the settings of which they may be a part. What do people mean to each other? How do they define family and obligations? Who do they *want* to care for? Who is financially responsible? How are spending decisions made? How much knowledge do people within the family have of medical treatment, illness, and home care? Who is responsible for decision-making? Who are the primary caregivers? What do they give up to fulfill that role? If a parent·is ill, do other people step in to give children the attention they may need? Who is sensitive to the suffering of others in the family and, in particular, to the emotional needs of the primary caregiver?

The assignment, maintenance, and reallocation of the roles associated with chronic illness are areas loaded with ethical concerns. Prior to illness, agreements as to who is the primary provider of financial resources, who takes on child-rearing and house care, who is responsible for initiating emotional and sexual intimacy, who functions as the social planner, who makes medical, financial, and other major choices about how individual and family time and money are to be spent, who sets family rules and boundaries—all these questions are often settled by tradition, gender, negotiation, power, and circumstance. One family member's difficulty in fulfilling an expected role can lead not only to feelings of inadequacy but guilt on the part of others who may empathize with his or her shame. The need to give up, switch, or take on existing roles can place overwhelming demands on the resources of individuals and families.

The vignettes I present in this chapter are knitted with moral knots and tangles. I do not presume to suggest how any person living amid such circumstances of suffering and loss should solve his or her moral dilemmas. The purpose of presenting these stories is to encourage therapists and physicians to appreciate how much of what their patients and families face is a matter of luck and, as Martha Nussbaum (1986) eloquently points out, how vulnerable and fragile both the good life and goodness itself are: "Central human values [justice, courage, generosity, temperance] . . . cannot be found in a life without shortage, risk, need, and limitation. . . . What we find valuable depends essentially on what we need and how we are limited" (pp. 341–342). With the arrival of chronic illness comes need of all kinds, confronting us with our own limits.

It is difficult to predict how the individuals who make up a family will respond to chronic illness. The person who is perceived as the family "star" may not act as other family members assumed he or she would. James Hillman (1989) mentions the two family clichés, "No one knows you better than your family," and "My family doesn't know me at all" (p. 202). There is no more likely time when the truth of these statements will be tested than when calamity knocks at the door. So much great art and wisdom testifies to the charity of the weak, the victim, the poor. Why would it not be so in the lives of the families of the chronically ill? Often those whom the therapist perceived as anxious, depressed, or disordered reveal themselves to be capable of doing what needs to be done with dignity and grace. This is not to romanticize the family but simply to suggest that one cannot easily predict how people will react when conditions turn stormy.

How can one imagine that any particular kind of response is going to be helpful to all members of a family? Who can say what may be the actual costs and benefits to a family and its members, each with his or her own needs and wishes, of one or another way of meeting the challenges that illness, loss, and suffering present? Each path taken leads to different people and other paths. The pattern of any life is not visible until the carpet is fully woven.

WHO IS FAMILY?

Many burdens fall upon families who live with chronic illness, aside from the obvious ones of increased demands upon resources of money, time, and physical energy. An unexpected stress is the issue raised by chronic illness of family membership and participation. Questions of who is in or out are more important than they seem at first glance. When I ask people whom they consider to be family, the common response is, "It depends." In a conversation with my wife, I gave a quick definition of family as "people whom I particularly care about and toward whom I feel greater obligation than others." I added that I am more intimate with many friends than I am with some family members, but that I am likely to assume greater responsibility for the latter in times of crisis or need. My wife, on the other hand, stressed qualities of interdependence and intimacy in characterizing family. She was put off by my term "obligation" because it implies acting from a sense of duty rather than out of what she called a "wish."

Discussions about who is a member of the family are not of minor importance: they can influence in crucial ways both the nature of the illness experience of the person diagnosed and the possibility of illness among others as well. Many people consider certain individuals who are related by neither blood nor marriage to be family and expect from them a reciprocity of feelings and responsibilities. Godparents and unofficial uncles and aunts quite often have this status. A woman, for example, may consider her children to be family but not her husband, and particularly not his family, whom she may expect are not likely to remain constant (and familiar) in her life.

In Walter's family, for example, Walter alone is acknowledged as suffering. His wife works outside of the home, but she assumes full responsibility for her husband's care. Only immediate blood relatives, none of whom live nearby or have the time or flexibility to offer much assistance, are allowed to play a helping role. Everyone else, including some friends and one or two relatives by marriage, is dismissed as less capable than she. "It wouldn't be right," she says.

Walter's wife is fearful that any stress will worsen Walter's pain, so she makes more and more household and medical decisions. She believes that she is living up to her ideal of the good wife. She pursues fewer and fewer of her own interests and aims. She and her immediate "blood" family, who object very little to her approach and to Walter's withdrawal from an active life, talk about a sense of commitment and pride in "doing what we have to do." Family "by marriage" and friends are concerned about the cost to her of such a commitment. She starts to have headaches, gets out of breath more quickly, and complains of soreness in her back and joints. Nonetheless, she doesn't take the concerns of others about her health seriously because they're "not blood."

The fluid nature of who is in or out of a family, and who are the friends and support networks to be relied on, can be illustrated and explored by a simple exercise. Take overhead transparencies, and on each draw a circle. Label one "Intimacy," another "Responsibilities," a third "Blood and Marriage Relation." In each circle, place the names of individuals with whom you associate those areas, ranking by proximity to the center. Now play around with these diagrams, seeing where there is union or junction, and where there is none. Take another transparency and label it "Chronic Illness Care." Move the transparencies around, and see where there are intersections between this last transparency and the others. It's possible in this way to identify new sources of assistance or to understand having been disappointed by some people from whom aid was expected.

Rosenblatt (1994) describes many of the ways in which the language that therapists use to talk about families and family systems and behaviors obscures as much as it illuminates the people with whom we work. Thinking of a family as an entity hides its diversity and flexibility and the ways in which family members function within and between networks. Systemic metaphors play down individual differences within a family—as well as the rich connections that many people have with a number of different families—and impose on it concepts that often do not resonate with the ways in which its members make sense of how they live.

I find the concrete images and metaphors of braids, ladders, tapestries, and gardens helpful in working with individuals, couples, and families. Since most people are as familiar with the terms as I am, they are able to use, refuse, or expand upon them as much as they wish and sometimes find entirely new insights or fantasies to share. Questions about current and older friendships and acquaintances are often as helpful as ones about family of origin, particularly when families must identify potential sources of short- and long-term support. Relatives frequently give enormous help in times of acute crisis, but their visits may be intermittent if they live far away. Families may want and need to use friends who are more nearby. Creating what I call a *philogram,* which combines the features of genograms and sociograms, can be very useful. To think that families are only what we as therapists imagine them to be is a mistake.

Hillman (1989) points out that to the Romans of classical times, *familia* referred to the "'house and all belonging to it.' . . . Neither parentage nor descent . . . [but] living together in familiarity as a psychoeconomic organism" was the factor that determined family (p. 202). Just as many families do today, Roman families also considered domesticated animals to be a part of the family. Relationships between children and their dogs, cats, or horses, and memories of those ties, can easily generate more emotion and meaning than the connections between siblings. Animals can play many roles in helping people live with chronic illness. They provide exercise, companionship, entertainment, distraction, security, and opportunities for individuals who are ill to give back the care they receive from others. Given the decrease in physical and social activity that often accompanies illness, a pet is usually a wonderful addition to the family.

SPEAKING OF VIRTUES AND VALUES

Families have always engaged in moral discourse when confronted by the challenges of chronic illness. They cannot avoid addressing the ethical and moral judgments and dilemmas that are such an important dimension of the illness experience. Individual and family questions about who is responsible for whom, for example, go to the heart of defining a family's ethos. Its everyday moral vocabulary includes *should* and *ought, commitment* and *responsibility, owing, shame, tragedy,* and *pity.*

Families not only join together in moral "polylogues," with all the passion and pain that situations that really matter evoke. They also demonstrate in a mostly unheralded way the four classical virtues of courage, phronesis, temperance, and justice. Individuals show courage as they accept and withstand the losses and suffering that are common companions to illness. They exhibit a sense of justice when they make the inevitable choices about the allocation of resources, whether of time, money, or attention. People struck by misfortune are commonly forced to select among incommensurable goods as they attempt to salvage something from their previous lives. How can one quantify who is more deserving of this or that support, aid, or companionship? Family members demonstrate phronesis—practical wisdom—when they decide whom to include in their conversations about proper care and how to develop and follow through on a sound course of action. Temperance is the virtue on display when individuals and families attempt to balance all these concerns and share the weight of their burdens.

The language of virtues is a lovely one with which to reflect upon and discuss how people attempt to solve the difficult problems in their lives. For instance, rather than approach her with a vocabulary of pathology or system dynamics, I would suggest to Walter's wife that she was not tempering her undoubted courage and personal sense of what was right and just with a more prudent concern for her own well-being. Such phrasing could open a dialogue that this strong and intelligent woman might be willing to enter.

"What is the right thing to do?" and, "What kind of person (father, mother, son, daughter) do I wish to be?" are moral questions. In the course of everyday life, our behavior implicitly poses such questions, with little reflection on our part. It is through the answers we receive, from others as well as ourselves, that our character, self, and family are formed.

In Erikson's psychosocial view (1959), for example, identity formation is at bottom a process of building character. The ability of a family and community to help individuals make their way through developmental crises lays the foundation for the emergence, as one ages, of the virtues of hope, will, purpose, competence, fidelity, love, care, and wisdom. The family, then, is a moral and ethical milieu in several ways.

It is a social space in which individuals learn and practice ways of caring, making sense of what is worthy of honor, and confronting shame. People learn from each other a sense of fairness, reciprocity, generosity, and commitment. In the family, however it is defined, the first moral prototypes (Johnson, 1993)—the cognitive structures through which we recognize the kind of ethical situation we face—are formed. Is this a question of fairness? Do these circumstances call out for justice or for mercy?

In most people's encounters with chronic illness, making moral judgments is not an abstract process. Prototypical situations are those that professionals who develop ethical policies are most likely to identify and debate. The arguments that break out between family members, between friends, and even within oneself, however, are usually ambiguous and more crucial to living through the illness experience than the thinner cases discussed in medical and ethical journals.

In the family, decisions are made and actions taken that are not in the best economic interests of either individual family members or the family as a whole. Parents willingly make monetary sacrifices for the sake of their children. Many family members give up their own needs for individual achievement or remain in difficult relationships for the sake of more vulnerable others. There may be different perceptions about whether someone deserves or is responsible for what has befallen him or her. There are disputes about the degree of harm or significance of a loss. And many individuals do not believe they might someday encounter similar calamities of their own. Some refuse to acknowledge that smokers who suffer from emphysema, drug users ill with AIDS, or those who abuse alcohol are worthy of pity. The effects of these moral judgments are not inconsequential. They determine how much care, attention, support, and resources family members may offer each other, and how much social institutions are willing or able to provide.

People find themselves in families, whether one or many, bound by ties of kinship, marriage, intimacy, and responsibility. Receiving life, care, and opportunity from one's parents, participating in the give and take of family life, expressing vows of marriage and fidelity, bringing children into the world, initiating and sustaining friendships and drawing new people into the web of family relations—these are among the many events that confer ethical obligations upon oneself and others.

The Smiths are a professional couple, a physician and a psychologist. They have two children who do well in school and are involved in youth sports and other activities. The Smiths donate money to political and social causes, attend cultural events, and enjoy an active and fulfilling social life with a group of intimate friends. When the emphysema of Mr. Smith's father, who lives alone some twelve hundred miles away, worsens, the couple and family are faced with a decision about whether to bring him to their home for care.

Although the Smiths have both the living space and the financial resources to provide for him, husband, wife, and children are upset by the potential impact the older man will have on their lifestyles. The members of the Smith family give each other a lot of leeway and support to pursue their own interests. These decent people feel a great deal of happiness will be sucked out of their lives if they have to reorient their family and individual activities around the illness of the grandfather. They decide to search for an assisted living residence for him near where they live, although they know in their hearts he would prefer to be with them. All dread the interruptions and obligations that his move and illness will impose upon them.

This is a common situation for many families living with chronic illness. When families like the Smiths turn to therapists for support or guidance, a focus on family dynamics might not be as helpful as approaching their concerns from an ethical slant. Few professionals are better prepared than therapists to help families explore such choices, but therapists must be aware of their own biases, which may influence their perceptions and ways of dealing with such matters. A therapist who enters discussions looking to maximize the best interests of the child in a family where illness is present will usually need to consider the interests of additional children and the parents' interests as well.

As moral philosophers have pointed out, the attempt by a clinician to arrive at a legitimate conclusion as to what constitutes a person's or family's best interests is profoundly difficult. People have multiple interests that are often in conflict with each other. The interest of one person's health may collide with the family's financial interests. The obligations toward one child may interfere with what is due another. There is no way a physician can know which alternatives or choices are likely to serve the best interests of patient or family, even if such interests and how they are weighed are known.

The family is an important source of meaning, value, and identity for many people. It also provides resources and a means of support to individuals coping with the loss and suffering of chronic illness, which weighs down a lattice of interlacing roles and obligations with additional moral strains and pressures. Harm can be done if the ethical questions that good people ask are turned into a hunt for pathology, cause, and blame. Therapists sensitive to the moral resonance of family strategies to cope and survive make it easier for them to bear up under the burdens of illness and care.

What, I might ask each of the Smiths, is your idea of "the good life?" What are the traits of your ideal "good person?" I want to elicit discussions about values and meaning. I give particular attention to the voices of Mr. and Mrs. Smith. He is son, father, husband. The meaning parenthood provides him is often independent of whether or not his children are a source of personal happiness at any given moment in his life. At the same time, Mr. Smith cares for and respects his father, although he does not particularly like him or enjoy his company. He thinks, however, that it may be an important life lesson for his children to see him exercise his filial duties within the home.

I want to be sure that Mrs. Smith is heard. Although she has insisted that the moral weight of the decision about her father-in-law's care falls upon her husband's shoulders, she recognizes that actual caretaking often falls to the woman of a family. It is important that the demands of illness and the giving of care are understood as much as possible. The couple's ability to communicate in good faith about these issues is important, for only through dialogue can moral concerns be resolved in a reasonably satisfying way.

I am in favor of therapists revealing their values in an open and inviting way. Silence can signify assent as well as disapproval. If therapists disclose their values, their clients have the opportunity to judge for themselves whether those values, if in conflict with their own, are worthy of consideration. Therapists are not experts in ethics, and most individuals and families do not perceive them as such. What therapists can do is model ethical conversations. They can present moral fables, traditional proverbs, folk sayings. The Bible and other sacred works are, needless to say, rich with material to provoke thought that does not require belief in or allegiance to any particular theology. Yet few therapists have even a small knowledge of what wealth such material offers. The therapist can be a moral *bricoleur*—someone who gathers and works with bits and pieces of moral meanings from which families in ethical quandaries can pick and choose to make their own arrangements.

It is helpful for therapists to share their own moral dilemmas in respectful and sensitive ways and to elicit and listen to those of others. The people I work with affirm the value of hearing and commenting upon my stories. Moral deliberation is more often social than solitary, a matter of dialogue rather than of decree, a process rather than a precept.

Can a therapist approach the issue of Grandfather Smith's care without a moral vocabulary and imagination? Will the moral burden or guilt that the Smiths may feel after the passing of the older man reverberate through generations to come? Is it bizarre to speak of the Smiths' failure to bring the grandfather into the home and family as a moral insult? What are the consequences of failing to do what it is possible for a family of the Smiths' means to do?

Therapists who prefer ethical dilemmas that are neat and righteous may feel emotionally and intellectually vulnerable when they are caught in the currents of their clients' tragedies and choices. However objective he or she may appear to be, the therapist or physician, by presence alone, influences the process and the result. Professionals bear some responsibility for the decisions made by family members, and for others they avoid making. "Uncertainty," Arthur Kleinman (1988a) suggests, "must be as central to the experience of the practitioner as it is to the patient" (p. 228). To stay with families and individuals as they struggle with ethical problems and allow doubts, hesitations, and objections to find their own ways to resolution can be wearying. There is a temptation to get it over with and cut to the chase. It is not easy to stay alert and listen to the whispers and shouts of others and to give sympathetic attention to the prompting of one's own heart.

Difficult as such moral grappling may be, it is through confronting painful questions, working through differences of opinions and values, engaging in dialogue with those who make alternative moral claims, and reflecting and acting upon one's own moral debts and duties that dignity, caring, respect, and hope can be nurtured and sustained. "There is no overriding reason," the moral philosopher Stuart Hampshire (1983) writes, "why we should look for simplicity, clarity, and exactness in the conduct of life. . . . Our need is rather to maintain and construct a way of life of which we are not ashamed and which, we shall not, on reflection, regret, or despise" (p. 168).

Despite admirable efforts, researchers cannot yet identify or predict the relationships between family patterns and behavior and the course of chronic illness; nor can they say which families will be most successful in helping the member living with illness cope with his or her many difficulties (Ramsey, 1989). Just as there is no generic cancer patient, there is no ideal family that responds effectively to illness. Family therapists build models and describe certain recurring features of family life, although such fantasies are defeated again and again by the realities of human imagination, quirkiness, intelligence, and desire. Disease and illness dynamics, the larger social and cultural milieu, available resources, are just a few of the many forces at play. The outcomes along the way cannot be easily foreseen.

Therapists must always remember, respectfully, that in every person there is something that does not wish to be seen, that shies away from being fully known. The short-term responses of most people to experimental situations or therapeutic encounters do not predict the decisions they will make when immersed in specific and personally meaningful ethical challenges. There are many ways of being and doing good. And good deeds are sometimes done by those of whom we would not think it likely.

NOT THE BEST OF ALL POSSIBLE WORLDS

The concept of functional and dysfunctional families has probably contributed little to the practice of good therapy. It has substituted cliché for close listening, thoughtful reflection, and sensitive conversation. Just as in discussions of "best interest," assessing family function cannot be done from the vantage point of only one member. Who decides which goals are healthy, and for whom?

A determined drive to build security and accumulate wealth is common among many first-generation immigrant families. Marital dissatisfaction may be high, loyalty to the family may be demanded, one or both parents and children may experience very little closeness, and the need for intimacy may be very low on the family's list of priorities. The financial foundation thus established, however, gives children and grandchildren access to education and health care. As Owen Flanagan (1991) demonstrates: "This is not the best of all possible worlds. Happiness, goodness, and psychological health are not inexorably linked. . . . There may be trade-offs—possibly only at the extremes— among the demands of a stark and complete authenticity about oneself and the ways of the world and happiness" (p. 332).

Imagine the case of Mr. Jones. He puts in long hours working for a small company as a machine tool operator and has a second job as a clerk in a package store. He thinks of himself as a "player," always willing to give 110 percent to any task he takes on. He prides himself on his attention to detail, his perfectionism, and his willingness and ability to do "whatever it takes" to design and cut a quality part on time. Few people find Mr. Jones to be warm, but all acknowledge his integrity and mechanical abilities. His only joke is the wry comment that "people want Van Gogh on their walls, but nobody wants him at their home."

Mr. Jones is deeply committed to what he perceives to be the welfare of his family. His wife and children seem to be satisfied with the kind of person he is, and the lives they lead are filled with interests and activities of their own. Mrs. Jones has never been employed outside of the home, but since her children reached adolescence she has been more involved in community and church work. There is no question that Mr. Jones dominates his household, although he does listen carefully to his wife when she describes some of the ways in which she wishes they had a different life together.

When his mother becomes ill, Mr. Jones is deeply upset by her suffering and does everything possible to ensure that she gets the best care and is as comfortable as possible. He speaks with the doctors and makes the arrangements for his mother's physician visits, in the expectation that his wife will provide transportation. He also gives his mother a substantial amount of his time and attention, despite the long hours he works. He insists that she live in his home, and he selects the nursing staff. Once again, he expects his wife to be responsible for managing the aides, but she asserts that she expects and accepts the role. All members of his immediate and extended families, as well as his coworkers, know that they could expect the same consideration from Mr. Jones if illness or tragedy were to befall them. The importance of honor, loyalty, and family to Mr. Jones cannot be overestimated. He knows that others think of him as an old-fashioned man, including his children when he closely monitors their dating and indicates his disapproval of their plans to live away at college. He says his strictness is a sign of caring.

The Smiths, described above, would be acknowledged as decent people by all who know them. They seem to fit most criteria for well-functioning families. They respond to most crises quite flexibly and are pretty adept at negotiating and taking on new roles. Their psychological health certainly seems to be "superior" to that of Mr. Jones, whose behavioral patterns include a number of obsessive and narcissistic characteristics. Their response to Grandfather Smith, however, is quite different from Mr. Jones's to his mother, and possibly less healing.

The ability of therapists to help families from diverse backgrounds and traditions to address moral issues is important. The choices and perspectives expressed by Walter's wife and the Jones family are characteristic of many traditional cultures— ones based on concepts of honor and identity linked to specific virtues and roles (Berger, Berger, & Kellner, 1973; Heller, 1988; Stout, 1988). It is a framework of conduct that differs from the ethos of modernism, with its emphasis on individuality and rights. There is agreement in honor-based societies about the obligations that people owe to one another and to the larger families and communities to which they belong. Identity, as well as one's good name and reputation, is determined by how well one measures up to established norms and ideals. Feelings of shame and loss of face are effective means of regulating conduct. Both Mr. and Mrs. Jones receive a lot of acknowledgment from the men and women in their neighborhood, workplace, and church communities as exemplars of strong "family values" and as positive role models for younger couples.

The Smith family expresses the modern ethos. Both adults and adolescents are expected to discover and maintain their true identities independent of social and institutional roles and expectations. Authenticity and self-creation are significant values (Feinberg, 1989). "A person" in this tradition "is authentic to the extent that he can and does alter his convictions for reasons of his own, and does this *without guilt or anxiety* [italics added]. ... Self-creation in the authentic person must be a process of self-re-creation" (pp. 32–34). These are notions that Mr. Jones would find difficult to believe have moral weight. The Smiths, on the other hand, would see the Jones's moral code as sexist, rigid, and out-of-date.

Mr. Smith and his family place great emphasis on giving their children the best opportunities to "make the most of their lives." Most of the arguments Mr. and Mrs. Smith make against taking in Grandfather Smith center on their concern that his presence would affect the children negatively because they would not be able to be as involved as they believe they ought to be in their children's extracurricular lives ("getting to their games"). Like many parents, they invest a great deal in their children, both emotionally and financially, so that their children will also be successful enough to choose to make lives of their own away from their family. The Smiths are an example of "the only family form in history whose very essence required disloyalty" (Luepnitz, 1988, p. 135). Now it turns out that much of Mr. Smith's self-respect is rooted in how well he performs his familial roles and lives up to each of his ideals. Almost despite himself, he feels his conscience squeezed.

Certain tensions at the core of American life and values are strikingly illuminated by the strains that chronic illness places on individuals and families—the pulls between agency and communion, getting along and getting ahead, autonomy and homogeneity, intimacy and power, cooperation and competition, separation and attachment, enmeshment and differentiation. Americans cherish pioneer images of the self-reliant frontiersman even as we fondly recollect the more communal ideals symbolized by barn-raising and quilting bees. Our culture pays homage to the ideal of marriage and family, yet most social and economic policies make it difficult for one or both parents to give a good portion of their time and energy to child care or to helping elderly parents.

Psychotherapists can make significant contributions to healing by encouraging people to come to grips with questions of value. It is also important to help them honor the decisions they come to after unraveling tangled knots of loyalties and commitments. Therapy is, among other things, an emotionally engaged and reflective inquiry into what it means to be a good parent, person, friend, spouse, or partner.

What are the moral complications when one fails to press one's own interests in the face of the suffering of another? Self-respect, after all, is no less a requirement of virtue than self-sacrifice. Individuals have projects, activities, interests, long-term plans, and important relationships that do not disappear when they are filling their role as a member of a family. To give up one's attachments to provide care or resources for another is itself a cause of loss and suffering. How much can one be expected to sacrifice for another? To some degree, cultural affiliations determine the duty of a sister toward a brother, of a father toward a son, of an adult child toward an elderly parent. What are one's duties to oneself? The emotional and physical distress that people experience as they face these questions can be quite wearing. Moral anguish is as real a source of illness as the disease with which another has been diagnosed.

THE WORTH OF PITY

The entrance of chronic illness into the life of a family often has a tragic dimension. Time itself seems out of joint, for example, if suffering falls upon the young. Some people are met by more losses than seem their just share. Families may have to choose which goods and goals for one member are more important or necessary than those for another. Fortune's wheel turns, and the heavy weight of necessity drops upon every person's wishes and dreams. The old possibilities for happiness may at first seem mocking and remote. Or illness may only gradually reveal the extent and cost of its claims. Painful conflicts, expressed in sounds or silence, may arise within a family. Individuals differ in their assessments of the often competing needs and interests of the person diagnosed with illness and other family members, and unfortunately, the complexity of individual emotions within a family living with illness often goes unnoticed.

Doug Allen had been unhappy with his marriage for several

years. Yet he remained at home, concerned about the impact of a separation or divorce on his younger child, Bobby, ill with cystic fibrosis. Mrs. Allen was distraught about her son's health and care. Understandably, she made his well-being her priority. Mr. Allen, however, believed that he and their daughter were not receiving a proportionate share of attention from Mrs. Allen. Both husband and wife acknowledged that their marriage was intact only because of Bobby, but Mrs. Allen affirmed that, however irrational it might seem to others, she could do no less for her son. She refused to attend counseling sessions with anyone for fear they might challenge and undermine her devotion to Bobby. Mr. Allen felt trapped and was becoming increasingly depressed. He did not know what was the right thing to do. Staying at home, he was afraid of how his visible distress was affecting both his children. If he left with his daughter, who felt neglected by Mrs. Allen, for an apartment nearby, their unhappiness would be diminished but his feelings of abandonment and guilt would become more pronounced. Either course was filled with pain for all—father, mother, daughter, and son.

The neglect of one's own moral rights is characterized by philosophers as "servility." Some are afraid to assert themselves out of an overly heroic sense of responsibility for the well-being of another. Mrs. Allen was not servile in relationship to her husband. She did appear to derive some angry pleasure from justifying her neglect of him and her daughter by presenting herself as the only person with the depth of love necessary to give adequate care to their son. That somewhat vengeful satisfaction was secondary, however, to her belief in a mother's absolute obligation to her child. If she were any less consumed by her role, she ran the risk of falling into a deep hole of despair from which she could imagine no way out. Pastoral counseling may have been of some help in freeing Mrs. Allen from the bondage of her false pride. Unwilling to trust others, her only means of emotional support was the belief that only she could give to her son what he needed.

Her rage at others and at life itself for the bad hands dealt her son and herself prevented Mrs. Allen from achieving a sadder and wiser appreciation of life. She could not tolerate the risks that came with attachments. She became obsessed with the time she spent with her son as a proof that no one cared more than she. She risked the destruction of her family for the sake of her image as the good mother, becoming more bitter in the process. She allowed herself no pity and became harder for it. Mrs. Allen could not see beyond what she felt she owed to her son. Any pleasure she experienced was a betrayal of his suffering.

Mrs. Allen had no sense of identity or tradition of principled action in which she could integrate her feelings and behavior. She and her family were subject to her own moral calculations. With no broader categories to frame her afflictions, Mrs. Allen could see only herself and her son as the victims of fate's cease-less spinning. She had no sense of a tragic story in which her husband and daughter—and in fact so many men and women— were immersed as well.

It was only when he was helped to cast his experience and dilemma into the language of tragedy and pity that Mr. Allen was able to find a bit of relief and comfort. He could see that he was a good man caught up in a world not fully of his own mak-ing. His alternatives were limited. He accepted his part in the undoing of his marriage and recognized that no sort of love might remain between his wife and him. The illness of his son, finally, prevented him from acting as many of his contempo-raries had done. He ruled out divorce, although with an ambivalence that pained him. Mr. Allen did not see himself as noble, courageous, or wise. But he did have a greater sense of the fragile contours of life and the importance of living up to his commitment as a father. He was neither right nor wrong to choose as he had, for many arguments could also be marshaled to justify separation as the best solution for all concerned. In fact, there was *no* solution. With that recognition, he was able to take some pity on himself.

Pity attends tragedy. *Pity*, like *stigma*, *victim*, and *self-sacrifice*, is a word that was once part of sacred discourse. Today, how-ever, people are speaking disparagingly of themselves or others when they say, "I pity myself," or, "Stop being so self-pitying." But to see oneself and others with a pitiful eye is to acknowledge the undeserved suffering that can befall any of us. When pity is removed from the field of worthy emotions, we try to take too much upon ourselves or expect too much of others. Most great drama is about families snared in a web of misfortune. Tragic theater reveals to the spectators that they do not suffer their personal pain entirely alone. Other humans, whether great or common, whether wise, brave, or foolish, have all been struck again and again. We feel pity for those souls who suffer before us. In turn, these creatures of the imagination offer us the opportunity to pity ourselves.

DOING UNTO OTHERS

There was a time when the ideals of martyrdom and self-sacrifice were held in high esteem. There are times even now when the person who gives up his or her life for another is acclaimed. The brave soldier, the courageous firefighter, the mother who dashes into a burning house to save a child, are all honored. It seems, however, that to give up one's identity for the sake of a spouse's or parent's interests is suspect. Within psychotherapy, the bias toward individuation and differentiation loads the therapeutic dice against those people, particularly women like Marilyn, who put aside their former interests in deference to what they perceive as the greater suffering of their spouses or parents. The unjustified social expectation that the woman of the family will assume responsibility for the care of the needy or the ill is a paradoxical burden that Marilyn must carry. It may be true that her cultural conditioning has left her with a greater sense of duty and obligation than her husband possesses.

Marilyn had been married for twenty-five years when her husband Tom became ill with multiple sclerosis. A final diagnosis followed several years of symptoms. Despite periods when he seemed to reach plateaus of hopeful stability, Tom's illness followed a progressively worsening course. His physical limitations, the severity and uncontrollability of his symptoms, and the demands he made upon others as he attempted to continue his professional work created a great deal of anger and frustration in the aides and caregivers the family employed. Three in all left, one after the other. The couple's children were grown and had established their own careers and families in distant cities. Tom's relationship with Marilyn was satisfying and important, but Tom was a doer, and there was little left that the two could enjoy together. Having endured so much suffering and loss already, Tom was determined to hold onto as much of his pre-illness world as he could. He struggled to maintain his career, perhaps the central core of his identity. To lose that was, for Tom, to risk losing his self.

Marilyn also enjoyed her work as a buyer for women's fashions, but Tom's illness and the difficulties keeping paid assistance led her to cut down on her hours a little more as each year passed. Finally, Marilyn decided to give up her career to devote full attention to meeting Tom's needs as best she could. Many of Marilyn's friends were uncomfortable with her decision. They thought she was allowing herself to be manipulated and controlled by a man who, although he was ill, insisted on having things done his way. Now Marilyn's friends, who had known her as an independent career woman and mother, saw her functioning primarily as a nurse and secretary.

Marilyn spent less and less time with others and focused her formidable energy and passion for living on Tom's well-being and care. When people with whom she was intimate encouraged her to "take some time for yourself" and blamed Tom for "expecting too much from you," she became angry with them for not recognizing that she was doing what she wished to do. Called a martyr, she accepted the term with honor despite the disapprobation with which it was offered. Marilyn believed that those who had not suffered as Tom and she had suffered could have no understanding of what they had gone through as a couple and as individuals. For her to do otherwise than devote her time and energy to caring for her husband, she believed, was to be faithless to her vows of marriage and to make a mockery of the life of integrity she had attempted to construct. Concerned with world peace, social justice, and the health of the environment, Marilyn thought of her "martyrdom" for the love of her husband as the only moral role she could, and ought, to fulfill.

Marilyn's losses were substantial. She gave up many of her former interests, projects, and activities. Her friends and colleagues strained to adjust their perception of her as an individual so different from her older roles and identity. They had a hard time acknowledging a continuity between her past commitments and her present behavior. The fact that her individuality and moral passion, previously expressed in enthusiastic and cheerful public acts, could become channeled into her private life was not seriously credited.

When people suggested that Marilyn see a therapist to help her cope with what they thought of as her unnecessary self-sacrifice, she withdrew even more. Alarmed by the sadness they saw in her, they characterized her as "depressed." They could not understand why she was not more angry, whether at Tom or his illness or their fate. Marilyn thought these others, most of whom were still blessed by the good fortune of lives untouched by great suffering, could not grasp who she was and, indeed, wondered whether they ever had. They could not see that what was essential about Marilyn was her commitment, not to causes in the abstract, but to alleviating the suffering of others, the goal of her political actions in the past. To sacrifice herself was not, in Marilyn's world, something to be despised.

To question Marilyn's choices and ideals at a time of such suffering and need runs the risk of a presumptuous and unwarranted undermining of the love that informs her attitude and acts. For Marilyn, her husband's illness and their shared and unique losses have marked a path toward a life of deeper maturity and wisdom. Her anger has been pressed into a wise sadness through the sieve of service, and her tragedy is about to become an opening toward grace. If Marilyn were to present herself to a therapist because of the urgings of her friends and their fears of depression, how sensitive might a therapist be to her silent spiritual agenda? Would a therapist characterize her marriage or family as dysfunctional? Is the language used in most clinical settings adequate to explore the intuitions, half-perceptions, and graspings for meaning that Marilyn's articulated thoughts and feelings might represent?

Individuals define themselves by their overlapping commitments. The autonomy of the self is relativized and enriched by its attachments to others. Moral problems within the context of the family and illness are as likely to occur, if not more so, when there are disagreements over obligations, responsibilities, and roles, rather than disputes about rights. The most helpful solutions are arrived at when participants take into account not only the needs of the person with illness but the contextual and narrative features of the lives of every affected individual.

The risk of sadness is present in all caring. With real sadness comes grieving, because when we cast the die of decision, when we choose to respond one way or another, there is loss—of innocence, uncertainty, and the existing field of possibilities.

Jerry, in a terminal stage of AIDS, recognizes his decreasing capacity to make judgments about himself and the manner in which he wishes to live and die. He agrees that his cognitive losses are so great that he will have to give over to his partner the authority to make immediate medical decisions, which include a firm desire to employ no extraordinary measures to prolong his life. In this sense, his autonomy continues: his partner is carrying out wishes that Jerry has conveyed. Although Jerry's legal authority is to be diminished, he will continue to be the author of his life. He will have created for his last days a life for himself of which he is no longer conscious. Although Jerry's symptoms and losses are severe and he is unable to pursue many of the activities he enjoyed prior to his illness, he indisputably remains an autonomous person, with a firm identity expressive of his sense of self, even at the moment of his death.

Jerry's partner Sam is in moral conflict. On the one hand, he believes himself to be morally bound to follow Jerry's wishes as expressed to him in the later stages of Jerry's illness, although the idea of medical action or inaction to end life before "God calls you" is morally repugnant to him. Sam has assumed the role Jerry asked him to take on because there is no other person who cares for Jerry as he does. After a long period of meditation and discussion, Sam chooses to do as Jerry desires, even if those wishes are different from the ones Sam might have had for Jerry or for himself.

Like Jerry, Sam thinks of himself as autonomous, although his ability to act is constrained. It would be difficult to say that the identity of either partner has been lost. Both Jerry and Sam continue to create personal and relational narratives consistent with the values demonstrated in their life together prior to Jerry's approaching death. Although they have some fundamental differences on particular moral issues, the openness with which they conduct their relationship allows them to respect the other's distinct voice.

MORAL INTELLIGENCE

The burden on clinicians working with people with chronic illness to exercise moral intelligence has never been greater. Among the many reasons are the increasingly complex dilemmas involving apparent differences between an individual's interests and values and those of his or her family, particularly where the distribution of resources and caregiving is concerned. To what extent can the members of a person's family be asked to sacrifice their interests for the sake of one individual? What if family and individual do not share the same values? To what degree do the claims of a suffering person deserve more consideration than the claims of others?

Cultural values and institutional norms that are at odds with the clinician's ethical stances also demand to be heard. How often does a lengthy and intrusive assessment and search for the best or most rational solution create more unnecessary pain? How often do therapists acknowledge there is no good or wise or just solution? Is it any wonder that the deep feelings that surround therapists' own experiences of loss can be stirred up and hurled into the therapeutic stew in such labyrinthine situations? A clinician's attempts to rationalize his or her role may guard against burnout or the breaching of professional neutrality but may not help the discouraged, the frightened, or the ill. Sometimes one must express a point of view, take a stand.

How does the therapist respond to demands for judgments of "medical necessity?" The practices of good medicine and sound psychotherapy may differ, for example, in relation to the relief of pain, specific interventions, or the causes of a particular individual and family's experience of illness and disease. Both medicine and psychotherapy can be construed as vital traditions and moral constructs. In circumstances where people must decide between incommensurable goods, perhaps all a helper can do is to confirm that there are better or worse ways to make tragic choices.

Moral deliberation is usually a social not a solitary process; dialogue, discussion, and reflection are themselves ethical acts. But creative ways of approaching moral issues are necessary as well, as Mark Johnson (1993) points out:

> We need self-knowledge about the imaginative structure of our moral understanding, including its values, limitations, and blind spots. We need a similar knowledge of other people, both those who share our moral tradition and those who inhabit other traditions. We need to imagine how various actions open to us might alter our self-identity, modify our commitments, change our relationships, and affect the lives of others. We need to explore imaginatively what it might mean, in terms of possibilities for enhanced meaning and relationships, for us to perform this or that action. We need the ability to imagine and to enact transformations of our moral understanding, our character, and our behavior. (p. 187)

When people face adversity and the hard judgments that may be required by ill fortune, to whom are they to turn to examine, whether in leisure or in despairing haste, the most perplexing of questions and poignant of answers? Friends and family, religious figures, persons in authority, skillful writers of self-help books, can all contribute to an individual's attempts to sort out some meaning from abrupt catastrophe or to weather with dignity the ruinous accumulation of smaller miseries or grinding pain. But for many people in our culture, where religion and ritual once were, there the therapist now is. The "sacred canopy," in Peter Berger's (1967) phrase, that covered people in traditional cultures has become reduced for some individuals to an armchair or a couch. It is possible that the role once reserved for the practical philosophers of old—the doctor concerned for the well-being of the individual soul—falls to those willing to listen, to ask, to speak, to care. It may well be that providing such service is too great or grandiose or presumptuous a task for many therapists to take on. But then what shall those therapists do for individuals and families who ask that their hunger for meaning and their thirst for something beyond suffering be acknowledged and respected?

As therapists, we have little say in the biological processes or other natural or social circumstances that are defined or diagnosed as a chronic illness. We may have some influence, but usually not too much, in making resources available to help individuals and families manage illness and its effects. But we ought to be able to fulfill, in both small and large ways, and despite pressures of all sorts, the essential tasks of our profession: to affirm and witness with compassion the afflictions and suffering of our patients and to help them to find meaning, morale, and healing amid the possibilities of disability, meaninglessness, isolation, and death that chronic illnesses may inflict. I agree with James Hillman (1976) that "by paying careful attention to and devotedly caring for the psyche, the analyst translates into life the meaning of the word 'psychotherapy.' The psychotherapist is literally the *attendant of the soul*" (p. 116).

CHAPTER 9

The Therapist Near and Far

In the practice of psychotherapy, what is required is a perpetual, critical analysis of the situation and the ability to decide minute by minute, case by case, on the action to be taken.

Aldo Carotenuto, *The Difficult Art* (1992)

TRANSFERENCE IS CLASSICALLY DEFINED as an intense emotional attachment on the part of the patient toward the therapist that cannot be accounted for by the realities of the therapeutic encounter. It was assumed that these deep and irrational feelings projected by the patient onto the blank screen of an impassive therapist had their source in the patient's early relationship with his or her parents. A significant part of the psychoanalytic project was to analyze and interpret the transference. Indeed, the inability of an analysand to make a transference to the analyst called into question his suitability as a patient.

The concept of transference is used much more loosely now. Some nonanalytic therapists take its existence for granted and use the term to refer to almost any feelings a patient may have toward them, independent of their source or appropriateness. Many others ignore its operation in the therapeutic situation

144

and as a result pay little attention to how their own attitudes, words, and behavior specifically influence each client. When dealing with issues as grave as chronic illness, however, it is important for therapists to be mindful of the existence and power of transference. Recent controversy around issues of repressed memory, emotional trauma, and childhood, as well as concerns about the sexual exploitation of patients by a few therapists, point to how easily the pervasive influence of transference feelings between patient and therapist can be ignored or mishandled.

When there is a differential in power, status, or need, transference feelings are heightened. The very fact that individuals comply with physician requests to disrobe and allow their bodies to be examined suggests great trust in the doctor's superior knowledge, ability to heal, and, most important, honorable intentions. No matter how often a person with chronic illness has been disappointed by medical treatments or other doctors, he or she approaches each new clinical encounter with the hope that this time will be different.

When an individual is ill, the wish to be taken care of and feelings of dependency are heightened. The ill may expect more of health professionals than is truly warranted. Both physicians and therapists heighten unrealistic expectations. They may not want to give false hope, but they are afraid of giving no promise at all. The consequences for the patient of the clinician not acknowledging the cycle of hope and disillusionment are feelings of loss, anger, and despair.

The clinician's failure to adequately face transference issues leads to apparent agreement and assumed compliance on the part of individuals and families to treatment recommendations they may not fully understand. Patients routinely feel too anxious or pressed for time to properly reflect on medical or therapeutic suggestions. Many physician visits are no longer than ten minutes and include a physical examination, orders for lab work, and checking the patient's history.

One consequence for therapists working with individuals and families living with chronic illness is that the therapist must deal with transference issues related not only to the therapeutic session but to the strong feelings associated with medical encounters. Individuals may, on the one hand, express what to the therapist sounds like unrealistic hope or infatuation with the health provider and, on the other hand, describe anger and disappointment that seems unfounded. It is difficult to know how to respond to some expressions of an individual's or family's distress or delight with a medical professional. It is especially difficult when the therapist is unsure about the accuracy of the account and about whether the actual care and recommendations make sense in light of the client's medical, social, and economic circumstances.

Gloria was diagnosed with a kind of lung cancer that was quite difficult to treat with conventional procedures. She put all her hope and faith in her oncologist, Dr. White, whom she admired, respected, and trusted. She went along with his recommendation that she undergo intensive chemotherapy with very powerful drugs that left her enormously fatigued and debilitated for weeks during and after treatment. Gloria's husband was very supportive of her at this time, although she was angry at him for the unsatisfactory quality of their marriage before she became ill. She disparaged him in equal measure to the curious blend of dread and excitement with which she approached her hospital visits.

Before each new course of chemotherapy, Gloria's oncologist gave her the choice of waiting for fuller recovery from the previous one, but she always opted to keep going at full throttle. When I suggested she might want to take some time to heal from treatment, rather than subject herself again to chemotherapy so quickly, and use her greater energy to engage in some activities her husband might enjoy, she refused. She was a patient, she proclaimed, of Dr. White, and if he thought that she was able to benefit from treatment, then she would follow his recommendations without pause. Gloria discouraged my contact with Dr. White because, she said, we served two different purposes for her. He was the medical person who would cure her, and I was the therapist to whom she could speak of her fears and ask for reassurance.

After two years of intensive chemotherapy for lung cancer, Gloria died from an inoperable tumor in her brain. I saw little of her in the final month of her life. I believe that her unquestioning confidence in Dr. White gave her the courage to go on with enormously distressing treatments but also kept her from raising with him the kinds of concerns and fears she shared with me. By not permitting Dr. White and me to communicate with each other, Gloria made sure that the spheres of healing in which each of us operated remained separate. By not allowing her husband to participate in sessions with us, she minimized the emotional upheaval she might feel during a time of weakness. She also kept her husband available as someone upon whom she could project her fears and anger while continuing to idealize Dr. White and me.

Gloria's ability to keep significant figures apart during the course of her illness gave her a sense of control when she had so little over the illness itself. Without the transference made possible by Gloria's experience of the kindness and concern of Dr. White, I don't know if she could have survived the degree of nausea and pain she forced herself to undergo. I am unsure that she would have maintained such a tenacious grip on life until the end if this powerful transference had not taken place.

WANTING TO KNOW AND THE FEAR OF ASKING

The physician is often unable or reluctant to take the time to respond to the therapist's requests for information or discussion. The therapist, conducting hourlong sessions, may find it difficult to take calls from or initiate calls back to the physician at times that both find workable, particularly if the therapist is not part of the physician's referral network or medical group. In the case of newly diagnosed chronic illnesses, individuals also do not have the ongoing relationship with a physician that can sometimes facilitate therapist-physician contact. Finally, as individuals and families move more quickly in and out of medical groups, networks, or HMOs, the communication difficulties become even more exacerbated unless the organization is prepared to facilitate the exchange.

Most therapists who work in private practice with people living with chronic illness can expect relatively little collaboration with physicians, although it is wise to make attempts to do so.

It is important to remember that physician-to-physician contact tends to be relatively rare except in group or hospital settings that favor face-to-face contact, by accident or design. Even in centralized HMOs (which are being replaced by off-site networks), the communication between professionals except through the reading of treatment notes is minimal. Just as working with a cotherapist is a luxury that few practitioners outside of some clinic settings enjoy, so is ongoing, or even incidental, contact with physicians around specific concerns of individuals and families.

People with chronic illness frequently bring therapists questions related to medical concerns but are reluctant to take the time for a medical appointment or to make an inquiry, which might get them an equivocal answer. Often people just want someone with whom to discuss their thoughts about a particular medication, treatment, care provider, or symptom. Therapists can assist individuals in clarifying their thoughts and feelings about the issue at hand. They can help people to formulate questions if in fact a call or visit to the physician seems appropriate. Transference issues, often based on the realities of the medical context, are frequently present. Some individuals do not want to bother the physician they so admire with their complaints or queries. Others are angry at their doctors and withhold information to demonstrate how little the physician is needed or to prove that they can arrive at medical conclusions or make decisions equally well. Many people simply do not know how to approach the physician and collaborate in their own care. They are shy in a physician's presence and allow the doctor to assume that their silence signifies their assent.

Phil, for example, had been bothered by chronic pain in his shoulder, upper back, and chest. The symptoms were due, he said, to damaged nerves in his upper abdominal area following an operation in that site for a cyst. He was referred to me by a chiropractor from whom his father had obtained relief from lower back pain some years before. Phil could barely raise his arms, turn his head, or twist his torso without suffering. At the time I saw him, he was being treated within his provider network by an anesthetist who apparently had an expertise in chronic pain and was giving Phil injections of what he thought might be steroids in the area of nerve damage. Phil had already been seen by gastroenterologists and physicians who ruled out other possible causes. He was unclear about the nature and possible side effects of the treatment he was receiving. The reasons for the injection, according to Phil, were that "it would stop the pain" and "it's what the doctor said to do."

Both Phil and his wife understood little of what the physician had told them but felt foolish and unable to acknowledge their confusion to him. I listened to the description of symptoms, the care that Phil's wife gave, and his own self-care, acknowledged the extent of their distress, demonstrated diaphragmatic breathing, and recommended that he play with the sensation of having his stomach gently expand when he breathed in and deflating when he exhaled. I also arranged to meet with other family members to discuss distributing more equitably the burden of care that was on Phil's wife.

By the time of our next visit, Phil had seen a neurologist who had told him to stop the injections and had prescribed amitryptiline, a drug he said was useful for pain. The neurologist had not identified it as an antidepressant but focused instead on its anodyne effects. Phil had also practiced the breathing and reported that it calmed him down and provided some relief. The eager expectancy with which he had greeted me at our first session was built upon with enthusiasm for the relief of pain he had experienced for the first time since the operation. Moreover, the opportunity for open discussion provided by the family meeting gave emotional comfort to Phil's wife.

It seemed to me that Phil was greatly influenced by transference to medical authorities. I thought that the good it may have done him, however, was threatened by the uncritical judgment he brought to his medical affairs. I could have proceeded to continue to work with him and decrease his painful symptoms by utilizing suggestion, relaxation, and helping the family to reorganize the assignment of roles and tasks. But to do that alone would have been a disservice that risked leaving Phil and his wife at the mercy of unexamined medical transference again. I made a brief phone call to his neurologist and related my concerns. He agreed that they were valid. He candidly indicated that he was unsure as well of the source of Phil's pain, although he thought it was possible that the distress was a consequence of the operation.

The third time I met with Phil and his wife (who agreed that he was improving), I told them I thought it was important that they be full collaborators in the healing process. If I ever said or suggested anything whose purpose or meaning they did not understand, they were to "pause" the session immediately. I also encouraged them to write down any questions, doubts, or thoughts about Phil's chronic condition or our work together and bring in the list to the next meeting. I told them I wanted to engage them in a continuing conversation about living with and lessening Phil's pain. My intent, I explained, was for us to model together the principles of patient participation in medical decision-making so they would be better prepared in any further health or illness encounters. I wanted to take account of three principles, or "tensions," as Katz (1984) calls them, of informed and humane patient care—*sharing authority, respecting autonomy,* and *acknowledging uncertainty.*

Within a couple of months, Phil's pain had significantly decreased, he no longer required any family care, and he was reporting the questions and answers he asked and received from the neurologist and primary care physician. We agreed that we did not know if improvement was due to amitryptiline (whose use as an antidepressant as well as for pain relief I had explained), relaxation breathing, our work together, the healing of Jesus (to whom Phil had always prayed), the ending of a cycle of pain and the guilt Phil felt about the weight his care put on his family, or something else entirely. We concurred that both Phil and his wife felt more empowered in medical situations. Both also agreed that they were better able and more likely to assert themselves in other contexts as well.

I encourage people to ask questions of health care providers, and I acknowledge that I occasionally feel a similar shyness or reluctance to admit my ignorance. Some physicians with whom I speak, whether for personal or professional reasons, assume that I am conversant in medical and technical terminology and jargon and do not explain phrases they would not use with non-professional patients. I appreciate the collegiality suggested by such discourse, but I try to avoid colluding in my own self-deception and instead choose to display my lack of knowledge and ask for clarification. In addition, some therapists need to be careful that their own feelings of inadequacy around health care professionals or with medical language and procedures do not lead them into joining their clients in disparaging physicians.

Individuals and families also frequently assume that my medical knowledge is as extensive as a physician's. I acknowledge that it is not. At the same time, I think it is useful to model how to think through and make informed medical choices in which individuals and family members have identified and articulated their own values and goals.

Many people, for example, want to discuss and talk through a decision to undergo particular medical treatments, ranging from operations to medications. Sometimes they have already made a preliminary judgment following conversation with their physician and family. We clarify together the purpose of our discussion: to air feelings, thoughts, fears, and hopes about taking a significant step; to reevaluate the consequences of consent or refusal; to assess risk or trace out consequences; and so on. We also discuss how the client wants me to respond. Does he or she want me to be a reflective listener, expressing no opinions and asking no questions? Am I expected to challenge my client's thinking, to poke holes in the logic of his or her emotions, to point out what might be overlooked in choosing one course of action rather than another?

REVEALING MYSELF

Often I am asked my opinion, what I would do if I were in the same position or facing an identical choice. Deciding how to respond to such a request isn't easy. My concern for my client's well-being comes first, and I consider the question within the overall context of our ongoing therapeutic relationship. I am not averse to sharing my own reflections. But the ability to make significant medical and moral decisions is an important strength and skill. We discuss how I can help a person or family learn to do so by weighing alternatives, looking at resources, assessing priorities, clarifying values, and so on. In some respects, I act as a moral counselor, encouraging individuals and families to sort out ethical claims and a variety of consequences from the choices they face, make, or avoid.

Jack is diagnosed with multiple sclerosis. He is about my age and identifies with me quite strongly because of the illness we share. Some of the difficulties, beliefs, and experiences Jack describes are similar to my own. On the other hand, many others are not. He often prefaces a comment about his life with illness with the comment, "As guys like us know. . . ." What, I ask myself, is an appropriate response to Jack's assumption? If I remain silent, Jack may take that as assent, and I will have allowed him to misrepresent me to himself at the same time that we both seek authenticity in the therapeutic relationship. If I tell Jack when I do not agree with his remark, I may deny him the identification that is helpful to him as he suffers and mourns the losses that have accompanied the diagnosis and progression of his illness.

Jack asks me intimate questions related to managing our shared illness, ones concerning bladder function, for example. His inquiries are neither intrusive nor prurient, but straightforward. On what grounds can I justify withholding the knowledge and tips I've accumulated over the years to aid me in my own coping? My purpose is to assist Jack in making sense of his illness experience. Should I tell him to ask such questions of his physicians, whose answers, I know, may not be as helpful as my own, based as mine are upon the trial and error of personal experience? I see the benefit of a continuing and intermittent relationship between Jack and me over the years of his illness. What purpose is served by suggesting he find another person to answer his questions? Would it be more helpful to Jack to encourage him to take his concerns to a health professional or agency worker, even though such a person is more likely than I am to move on to a new residence or other employment?

These issues are perhaps no different from those raised when I am questioned by couples with whom I work about my marriage and the ways my wife and I deal with this or that. Most therapists would agree that responding regularly to such questions is inappropriate. It is more useful to help the couple assume responsibility for working on the specific and personal ways in which they can create the kind of relationship they find satisfying, as well as examine the issues of boundaries, propriety, and roles that may be problematic in their own lives.

The psychoanalytic ideal of the nondisclosing therapist is typically justified by the need for the analyst to provide patients with a "blank screen" on which to project their fantasies, as well as to avoid influencing the patient with his or her own reactions, beliefs, or values. Putting aside the questions of whether the anonymous analyst is possible or desirable, this orientation is theoretically consistent with psychoanalytic practice. Even analysts, however, are increasingly likely to put much of their ongoing experience of the psychoanalytic encounter between themselves and analysands into play as a legitimate source of therapeutic inquiry.

Transference toward professionals associated with health care is, of course, not limited to physicians and therapists. Sid, diagnosed with multiple sclerosis, often spoke with a glowing admiration for his chiropractor, who "really knows this stuff"—that is, the care and treatment of his MS symptoms. Sid did not disparage his primary care provider or his neurologist but did express upset with the medical system for its failure to develop effective remedies for MS when "they know so much about how it works." Sid believed that there was a correlation between the spinal cord lesions that resulted from his disease and the efficacy of certain treatments his chiropractor offered. These involved the application of a handheld, battery-operated "stimulator" to his skull or back, a treatment that Sid believed stimulated the spinal cord and lower brain stem. The chiropractor never proposed that his work with Sid was a cure for MS. He only suggested that some symptomatic relief was possible. He also sold Sid some vitamin supplements that he said research showed were helpful to people with MS. Sid discontinued taking them after several weeks because he saw little benefit. He still uses the stimulator, however, because it relieves headaches and decreases fatigue.

Sid's chiropractor actively responded to Sid's need to do something for his illness, a response that is characteristic of many nonmedical practitioners. Although cures for chronic illnesses rarely, if ever, result from nonmedical treatments, these procedures usually avoid the adverse side effects that may accompany equally unsuccessful medical procedures or medications. The time and attention that many "alternative" practitioners give to patients such as Sid helps nurture a positive transference and feelings of hope. When patients eventually leave their care, they typically do not carry the same kind of animus toward the practitioner that they more commonly direct toward physicians. The explanations they give to individuals with illness are typically based upon a model of disease and dysfunction that satisfies the patient's need to know in a way that the more complex biomedical model does not.

WHEN THE THERAPIST LIVES WITH ILLNESS

Freud suggested that the countertransference was the effect of the patient upon the analyst's unconscious feelings. Concerned with the impact of the therapist's subsequent anxiety upon the patient's unconscious, Freud suggested ongoing self-analysis to help the analyst free himself or herself from these undesirable influences. The ideal analytic practice was marked by a bearing of benign unperturbability. The analytic attitude was similar to a deep pond that barely ripples when a tossed pebble breaks its surface.

Gradually analysts recognized that no matter how much they tried, it was impossible to separate out their own experience from what took place in the analytic field. They were inescapably in and of it. Since the analyst could not avoid countertransference, he or she might as well make it, as well as the transference, grist for the analytic endeavor. It became acceptable for a therapist to bring up his or her own emotional responses during the session and allow them to become part of the therapeutic process.

The ideal of personal anonymity places pressure upon therapists when they are confronted by certain conditions and circumstances. This is the case when a therapist is living with a chronic illness, particularly one whose symptoms or effects are visible and likely to elicit curiosity or empathy in relationships as intimate as the therapeutic one. Detachment or distance can be maintained only with great effort. It is no wonder that there has been little research on the impact on therapy of the therapist's illness given the potential anxiety that the confluence between the two can generate.

Initially, many people with chronic illness respond quite positively to a therapist whom they know to have a diagnosed illness or disability. The client may assume that the therapist is knowledgeable about his or her illness. Even if the therapist's illness is different, the client may imagine that he or she shares with the therapist similar experiences of illness, as well as attitudes and feelings toward physicians and medical care. Each and all of these assumptions may well be false.

Clark, for example, thought that he and I, both diagnosed with multiple sclerosis, would have the same orientation toward the search for a cure for MS. He was eager and willing to find and pursue any possibility for treatment he heard about, including megavitamins, bee stings, chiropractors, and Betaseron. I listened each time Clark told me about a new discovery and acknowledged the enthusiasm and hope with which he approached each potential treatment. Clark often gave me information about his latest trial and reported his experiential findings as well. His arguments for each treatment option were usually based on hearsay or an uncritical reading of the literature on it. I accepted the material and promised to read it, as I did.

One session, as Clark was telling me about his experiences with acupuncture, he asked me a question about one of his earlier forays in which he obviously assumed that I would have my experience to compare with his. When I told him I had not tried the treatment, he asked if I had attempted any of the treatments he had brought to my attention. I responded that, although I truly appreciated his concern, had read the literature he offered, and respected his determination, I had never followed through on any of his recommendations. He was surprised and disappointed.

In the conversations that followed his question and my disclosure, Clark discovered that even though we each were diagnosed with MS, there were significant differences in how we approached the illness experience and the search for cure. He was direct in his questions, and I thought it both appropriate and important to respond to him in a respectful and disclosing manner. Clark spoke a great deal about his struggles with his diagnosis and the impact the illness had upon his marriage, his work, his sense of competency and self. At first, he admitted, he was quite confident about his ability to "defeat this thing." As time went on, however, and he had tried one possible cure after another, his condition did not improve. He did not know what he was supposed to do or how he would feel if he stopped "trying to get better."

I shared with Clark my own coming to terms with my diagnosis over the past fifteen years. I told him of my preference for husbanding my energy and using it in activities I enjoyed, rather than expending it by trying out new treatments. I told Clark that my physician, family, and friends encouraged me to try Betaseron when it was approved for distribution. The drug was not a cure for MS, but a small number of trials indicated that it might decrease the frequency, duration, and severity of exacerbations for people with a certain type of MS. This was a category into which my illness seemed to fall, although as I pointed out to those advising me to try Betaseron, I had had no exacerbations for many years and would have no way of knowing whether the drug worked, only if it failed.

My concerns about its short- and long-term side effects were alleviated, and I agreed, although not wholeheartedly, to start the every-other-day mixing and injecting of the drug. Twice I halted the treatment, once after using the drug for one month, the second time for good. As I put it to Clark, "As foolish as it might sound to you, my reason for stopping was that I can't control the illness and what it does to my body, but at least I can control what I choose to do about my illness."

Clark was using Betaseron at the time of our conversation, and even though he had noticed no improvement, he had experienced no uncomfortable side effects either. He assured me that he was going to continue with his medication but appreciated my letting him know the route I had chosen to take. The next session, Clark said he felt relieved of a burden he had carried— the obligation to do "absolutely anything I can to beat this thing." Clark sees me as a companion along the road of illness in desperate quest for a cure. Now, however, he anticipates a future in which his having MS is not as crucial as the meaning and satisfaction he can draw from the life he was given to tend. He continues his Betaseron treatment.

Some therapists with a history of difficult medical experiences in their own lives may identify with the client's powerlessness, assume the role of rescuer, or share the client's intense emotions of anger, grief, and guilt. It could have been easy to fall into such a trap several years ago when I began work with Carter, a very bright engineer. Carter was very apprehensive about an initial appointment with a physician. He had recently moved to town from out of state, where he had lived for several years with a diagnosis of CFIDS. Carter's exhaustion contributed to his difficulty concentrating at work and irritability toward those at home. He readily acknowledged that he felt mildly depressed, but he also stated that he knew he was not more seriously emotionally distressed, because "I've been there, and I know what that black hole is like." Carter was concerned that his illness would not be taken seriously. He said that it was likely that "I'll have to prove myself to be ill."

Carter came to his next appointment angry that his new physician had made presumptions about his fatigue in exactly the reverse order of causality that Carter recognized. That is, the doctor "pushed his belief that I was tired because I was depressed, and not that I was depressed due to my fatigue. He pretty much ignored my diagnosis of chronic fatigue syndrome and focused instead on the depression, which he said he could treat."

I acknowledged Carter's anger and agreed that it was possible that the physician was insensitive to Carter's distress and overcommitted to his own beliefs and agenda. It would have been easy to join with Carter in a *choler à deux* at the doctor. But the reality of Carter's diagnosis was that he would often be met with suspicion and doubt. I thought it important that he develop adequate defenses to cope with the stigma attached to his illness. If he chose, he could also use his anger and disappointment to fuel political activity on behalf of people with his diagnosis, a cause in which he indicated he wanted to take part. We engaged in conversations about the difficulties of making diagnosis, somatization disorders, and the physical states of anxiety and depression.

The results were threefold. First, the process of intellectual inquiry allowed Carter to see the broader social contexts in which the experiences of disease and illness take place, and he did in fact get involved in CFIDS awareness action through the Internet. Second, the discussions gave him some defense against the fear and rage that had surged in him since his diagnosis. Third, Carter recognized that some of the symptoms he experienced were probably exacerbated by, if not the result of, anxiety and depression. At this point, he chose to make these his therapeutic focus.

A friend of mine, a psychotherapist, remarked to me that he has not yet recovered from the emotional wound opened up by the serious and life-threatening operation he underwent a year ago. "I always looked forward to a long, healthy, and happy retirement. That confidence has been shaken now. Although I know it can take a long time to recover from a major operation, I never thought it would drag on like this for me. And I never anticipated the kind of doubts and fears it brought up in me once the repair was made and the cut sutured. And none of *my* physicians wanted to talk about it, either before or after surgery. I left them openings to talk about my feelings once I was aware of what was going on, but you know how physicians are—they never said a thing. Once I returned to work in my group practice and my colleagues were assured that I was physically well, they no longer asked about how I was doing. The only people that seem to be still concerned and inquire about my health and recovery are some of my patients, especially those who also have suffered serious medical problems."

A short time ago, I was preparing to present a workshop for therapists with chronic illness, a topic that participants had never before seen offered. I came across a recent book, Schwartz and Silver's *Illness in the Analyst* (1990). The volume opens with a comment by one of its editors: "We are intrigued that it has taken the profession a century to acknowledge directly the specific effects of the morbidity and mortality of its practitioners" (p. 3). Reviewers on the book jacket confirmed that observation. "The first book to discuss at length the important and often vexing technical problems posed by an analyst's illness," wrote one. Another added, "Until now virtually ignored in the literature, the universality of the resistance [to discussion of analysts' illness] is at once evident in *Illness in the Analyst*."

Many therapists are themselves touched by chronic illness, whether their own or that of a significant family member. Rarely, however, are the personal and professional effects on patients, self, and colleagues of a therapist's life with illness examined. Freud, for example, suffered great pain owing to the cancer and more than thirty operations that ravaged his jaw for sixteen years before his death in 1939. Yet he never wrote of how his illness and disability affected his patients and his therapeutic work, although he believed for many years in his need for sound physical health to go on with his analytic work and discoveries (Schwartz, 1990). Few psychotherapists have written about their illnesses.

I am reminded of what Irvin Yalom (1980) wrote more than twenty years ago: "Denial plays a central role in a therapist's selective inattention to death in therapy. Denial is a powerful and ubiquitous defense ... [that] does not spare the therapist and in the treatment process the denial of the therapist and the denial of the patient enter into collusion" (p. 58).

Why does there appear to be so little literature on the impact of the illnesses of therapists and family members on their professional work? How are they and their families personally affected? Do therapists reveal the intimate details of chronic illness—illustrated throughout this book—when they work with individuals who are diagnosed with chronic illness? How do therapists' abilities to meet the challenges or fears associated with their own diagnoses interfere with or enhance their clinical attitudes and practice?

I live and work in a small town. Encounters between myself, my wife, my children, and individuals and families with whom I work are impossible to avoid, even if I were to wish to do so. When my children were younger, they were frequently asked by classmates whether I was their dad. When given an affirmative response, these youngsters often told mine that I saw them in therapy—reports that I neither confirmed nor denied to my children. Just as physicians, pharmacists, lawyers, and accountants—

people who share confidences with clients—go about town, meeting and greeting people at restaurants, the movies, town events, and festivals, so do I, often with cane in hand or, on occasion, seated in a wheelchair.

Just as physicians distance themselves from the sufferings they see or inflict, therapists too may be uncomfortable with the reality of illness before them. The characteristic therapeutic role of the participant-observer is ideally suited to defending against experiences of anxiety and distress when hearing of, seeing, or imagining the difficulties of a person with illness. If the therapist lives with illness, working with individuals and families similarly afflicted can result in a range of defensive behaviors. Some therapists with chronic illness, for example, want their clients to know as little as possible about their own illness, to protect clients from anxiety about their own or the therapist's health.

I have to be careful not to shrug off clients' expressions of sympathy or concern as if it were nothing to be ill. Potential consequences of such a dismissal might be clients believing they ought to be able to handle their much "smaller" problems without complaining or feeling guilty for burdening me with their legitimate concern. When people ask me why I tend to stand or walk stiffly, or tell me they have heard or read I have MS, I acknowledge my illness. I do so in what I hope is a receptive manner that signals my openness to further questions but also indicates that my health is not the focus of our time together. If people do seem apprehensive, I might also share my illness status to alleviate concerns they may have about my ability to work with them over the long run.

I am also frank if I must excuse myself briefly from the session to go to the bathroom. I explain that this is an unavoidable symptom of my MS. I apologize before and after my absence. Without exception, every individual and family has been gracious and patient, and we have always picked up where we left off. If necessary, I make some extra time available at the end of a session if I think someone has been cut short by my difficulty.

Some therapists compensate for their illness by demanding that the patient be "tough" or, conversely, encouraging the patient's expressions of helplessness to satisfy their own dependency needs. Therapists who feel anger and resentment over the necessity to work following a loss may envy their patients for "being taken care of." They may join with family members and prematurely push a person with illness to get over mourning his or her losses and move on. Caregivers, like mothers, aren't supposed to get sick. A therapist may attempt to prematurely lift a patient's burden or assign inappropriate blame to the patient's family owing to his or her own threatened ability to exercise control or influence events. Many therapists acknowledge that while going through their own loss experiences, they use attitudes of objectivity and detachment in the service of defenses such as denial, intellectualization, and rationalization. Doing so, however, leads to a lack of attention toward the painful particulars of a patient's loss.

A few therapists use the fact of their illness and their apparently successful coping to push their own philosophies of life or attitudes toward illness and healing on clients who are also ill. The magic healer role has powerful appeal, for it reflects fantasies of invulnerability that may serve to ward off fears of progression, recurrence, or exacerbation. Magic healers may also resent or belittle individuals with illness who do not respond as the therapists desire. Therapists with or without illness may think of individuals as unmotivated, uptight, self-defeating, or resistant if they do not follow through or agree with the therapists' health and illness beliefs or treatment strategies. The exciting but modest and ambiguous results to date of psychoneuroimmunological research invite some therapists and physicians to make grossly unwarranted claims about the effects of personality styles and the efficacy of attitudinal change on illness and disease.

Some clients withdraw from what they experience as the therapist's overprotective behavior, based on either the therapist's overestimation of the severity of illness or poor judgment of the individual's ability to handle suffering. Just as I, from the viewpoint of many of those close to me, tend to minimize the effects of my illness, I know that many others do so as well. A good therapist does not rush to attack and unmask an individual's defenses, but it is also wise to be careful of too much caring. Some therapists, for example, find it difficult to tolerate the self-sufficient character. They intrusively interpret such a client's behavior and reactions as denial, owing to their own need for expressions of vulnerability, warmth, or relatedness from those with whom they work. A therapist can forget that pride and silence are virtues as well as faults.

CHAPTER 10

Healing I. Spaces: Art, Imagination, and Computers

Art—and here it manifests its structural kinship to life—is capable of transforming noise into information.
Jurij Lotman, quoted in William Paulson,
"Literature, Complexity, Interdisciplinarity" (1991)

P AIN AND AFFLICTION call men and women to encounter the moral core of life. The great work of culture and art is to transform the helplessness of despair into the redemptive possibilities of suffering and healing. Homer sang of the destruction of the characters and lives of noble warriors under the awful lashings of war. The Greek tragedians wrote of men, women, and cities entangled in the inescapable nets of fate. The passions of the martyrs and the torments that awaited sinners were painted by the masters. Artists turn to classical myths to portray the ill fortune of mortals who remain the unhappy objects of the angers and lusts of the gods.

Shakespeare's dramas illuminate the inability of even the most powerful to undo deeds done in the heat of passion and pride. The paintings of Goya and Picasso express the cruelties visited upon the innocent by war. Novelists, poets, and play-

163

wrights—George Eliot, John Keats, Emily Dickinson, Eugene O'Neill—who among them has not looked clear-eyed at grief, aging, illness, and loss? The great modern mythmakers—Friedrich Nietzsche, Sigmund Freud, Carl Jung—tell of the human spirit at war with itself in a world without the consolations of religion.

Few works assert themselves with the stark immediacy of *The Scream* by Edvard Munch. Appearing on everything from ties to T-shirts, satirized and referenced by artists of all sorts, the print of an anguished woman grips the imagination and speaks to something unshakably real about the human condition. Most people appreciate the work as a wrenching depiction of existential, or "neurotic," anguish. What few may know is that tuberculosis was fatal to Munch's mother during the Christmas season of 1868, when the boy was only five years old. Munch's beloved sister died of the same disease a year after young Munch, at age thirteen, contracted and nearly succumbed to it. It is likely that the horror of *The Scream* is grounded in the facts of illness, loss, and grief.

Art, of course, can offer to neither the creator nor the viewer a guarantee of escape from suffering. At times, sorrow can only be endured. Much art, great as well as ordinary, exists as a memorial to those whose voices were strangled or stilled. Nevertheless, art can bring the possibility of healing to those living with illness. One purpose of art is to give form to that which is unspeakable, to render coherent the shattered and broken. Just as illness can be a vitiation of experience, art can give it both spirit and flesh. Art is a medicine for the suffering we call illness, just as it may function for those afflictions known as meaninglessness, despair, poverty, abuse, exile, and war. In the catalog for a recent exhibit, "Body and Soul: Contemporary Art and Healing," Mike Samuels (1994) reflects: "Into the heart of the artist yearning for meaning comes healing. Into the heart of the healer looking for meaning, emotion, and a language, comes art. And art becomes the doorway into the realm of the heart" (p. 67).

In the winter of 1995, the dance critic of *The New Yorker*, Arlene Croce, ignited a controversy when she refused to review the new production of the choreographer Bill T. Jones, *Still/Here*

(Oates, 1995). The piece used material, including video and audiotapes, that Jones, himself HIV-positive, developed during a process he called "Survival Workshops: Talking and Moving about Life and Death," which he conducted with people living with life-threatening illnesses. "We realized," the performance brochure notes, "that the participants living on the front lines of the struggle to understand our mortality are in possession of information—is their knowledge a gift or is it a burden?"

Croce labeled the work, which she had not seen, as an example of "victim art," "undiscussable," a "messianic traveling medicine show." She characterized such work as highly manipulative and argued that its focus on the suffering of real people made an objective review impossible. To dislike the performance was to risk being seen as unsympathetic to people with illness. The article seemed to many people a remarkable demonstration of ignorance of the nature of suffering and of the history and purposes of art. "The fact is," the essayist Nancy Mairs (1993), herself ill with multiple sclerosis, had written a year earlier,

> that the true victim—the person set apart from ordinary human intercourse by temporary or permanent misfortune—has little enough time and even less energy for sniveling. Illness and death, whether one's own or a beloved's, take *work*. . . . There are hands to be held and basins to be emptied and upper lips to be kept stiff. (p. 25)

There may be goods that illness delivers to us as well as the more obvious harms. Making contact with the capacity of imagination to generate new ways and possibilities of being is an event of significant therapeutic importance. As a person with illness draws symptoms and meanings into a new relationship, the illness itself becomes a source of its own healing. Prickly sensations and peculiar signs that once brought fear are now also objects of curiosity and sources of quickening symbols and forms. The painter Robert Farber (1994) expresses himself directly in an interview about his paintings, which evoke both the Black Death and the contemporary plague of AIDS:

I think part of my motivation is this virus that continues to eat away at my immune system. . . . The virus is on this inexorable path. And I think part of my motivation is that no one is in control of this virus. . . . Well, I'm going to take this virus and I'm going to make some art out of it. Then I'll be able to at least control this thing. It's not going to run over my life. I'm an artist, and I'm not going to stop just because I'm going to die. But last month, when my T-cell count went down to eight, during the rest of that day the last thing I wanted to do was make art. . . . Who cares about a painting in that moment? When I'm feeling okay, I do feel like I want to draw people into this and try and communicate my experience and hope that in doing that they'll recognize something in themselves in it.

The imagination is a bridge between the world of too much suffering and one of denial and no suffering at all. Imagination serves as a middle ground, an empty space, a terra incognita that, paradoxically, is filled with undiscovered continents and terrain. From this place that is not a place, one can draw images, metaphors, and sensations that give meaning, manageability, and shape to other voices and worlds within.

The surge of the body into consciousness and the strong emotions evoked by loss, uncertainty, and change awaken associations and fantasies linked to primal fears of the vulnerabilities of the flesh and to yearnings for security and coherence. In self-defense, symbol- and meaning-making capacities are animated. The organism attempts to reorganize and find new pathways for identity and behavior. When enlivening metaphors or opportunities for creative action are not available, however, the energy of adaptation and change is dampened. Loss without mourning cuts short the human potential for healing and transformation.

When one is sick, the body pushes its way into the mind, insisting on its own agenda. Doing art, the mind enters into the body, searching for the elusive sensation that will yield the next word, stroke, or note. Creative activity provides the opportunity and means to remake the interaction of body and mind once again.

The idea that art itself can be a healing experience is something the ancients knew, but it has only recently returned to professional favor. Occupational, art, or musical therapy was often treated as a kind of busy work for patients that permitted them to express their pathology in a socially acceptable way. It is only now being acknowledged that art can directly affect disease. Art enables individuals to knit together new kinetic melodies and patterns of meaning in the face of the unraveling of movement and order that chronic conditions incur.

We sing with our whole body. We use posture, breathing, the diaphragm, the sonic structure of the "mask" that gives our tones resonance, the feelings and thoughts we express to make our song. The self-as-voice reveals itself through sound. The same is true of painting. It is the hand that grips the brush, but the artist who places pigment on canvas. The firmness of the stroke, the response to light and color, the leaning toward and back from the work, the turning of the head to catch an angle, these are acts of the whole person, not of the arm alone. Writing is also an organic process. The writer searches for a word "on the tip of his tongue," tenses a fist, or wiggles a hip to capture just the right phrase, and he tunes into his gut to judge how well he has conveyed his meaning. The singer, painter, or sculptor no less than the author senses in his or her body for the proper note, tint, or plane. Throat, eye, and hand are not passive tools of the mind to be used for a purpose that is not their own. They are mind itself.

IMAGINING ILLNESS

Imagine that illness is a legitimate way of being, a local world like deafness or blindness. Think of the stiff gait of a person with Parkinson's, the labored breathing of one with emphysema, the explosive bursts of speech and twitches from those with Tourette's, as dance, song, poetry. Illness moves to a different tempo than we hear in the world of health.

Multiple sclerosis is my muse, a visitation from the gods to be shaped and reformed by my own genius. I imagine myself being kneaded in a slab of dough. The fingers of the baker touch me, inflicting a wound on my legs. My soul is being readied for the baking. Who is the baker? What is the bread? Or I picture my struggle with disease as if I were a farmer, constantly in close touch with local conditions, the terrain, my body on this particular day. The farmer cannot be sure when a hailstorm will pour down upon his crops or a drought might thankfully end. He knows that an infestation can plunder his fields and set upon him the even greater labor of saving what he gathers up. Likewise, I do not know when an exacerbation, temporary or more lasting, could force me to change plans, abandon goals, or even let go of my dreams. The farmer, like one who is handicapped, works at a different pace from other men. He moves more slowly, and with greater vigilance. He notices a little more. Perhaps he is simply grateful for small successes or minor defeats. I imagine myself that man.

Or imagine that illness is loaded with information. We construe as symptoms the unwanted noise that impedes our aims. The marks and signs of illness are a sort of static that interferes with the organism's prior acts and intentions. To perceive symptoms as signals and illness as information gives people a chance to break out of the narrow dichotomy of health and disease.

Complex systems are composed of unpredictable and chaotic processes that hide deeper structures of order. What appears to be either predictable or random has been shown to be neither. Instead, there is an order to disorder. Form and structure appear, only to disappear until reorganized into novel patterns once again. Psychologists recognize this process as one of insight and change. It is humbling to remind ourselves that we can predict neither.

One of the pleasures denied to many by illness is the feeling of flow, of "being in the groove," that emerges out of full involvement in a physical effort. A chef moves with confident ease in his busy kitchen, his senses alive with the odors, tastes, colors, and textures of his cooking. A runner hits her stride, arms, legs, breathing, working in ensemble as a dynamic whole, each step planted and raised with rugged grace. Tennis opponents raise their abilities a notch as each reaches shots and delivers serves that neither is in the habit of making. A spring day draws someone out to the backyard to rake, smell the freshening breeze, survey the landscape, clean chairs and tools, and finally to collapse, filled with exhilaration at jobs completed and

next chores planned. The organism thrives on ordinary pleasures. The hope for such simple achievements, however, is easily consumed by the conditions and demands of illness. If not
replaced, the loss of these achievements can undermine some of
the reasons we want to live.

Maslow (1962) describes a psychology of values that acknowledges what philosophers, poets, and artists have long known.
To flourish as an individual, it is necessary to have certain goods
in our lives. Just as we need B vitamins to be physically healthy,
there are values we must have to live well. Experiences of truth,
beauty, justice, order, richness, playfulness, and meaningfulness
are all food for the soul. Without them, we are vulnerable to the
sicknesses of cynicism, bleakness, mistrust, depression, grim-
ness, and despair.

Suffering increases when people living with chronic illness
are deprived of important nonmaterial values. Lives are more
constricted and sickness worsens when there are fewer opportunities to participate in and enjoy the making of beauty or the
study of truth. Music, gardening, reading, viewing nature, are
all therapeutic. No one lives by bread, work, or medication
alone.

Art is not the only process that can contribute to remaking a
broken world. Nor need conscious meanings be gathered from
this work. Many patients in psychiatric hospitals and other
institutions of the nineteenth century cared for herds of cattle
and sheep whose milk and wool they used and sold. With such
labor came feelings of productivity and pride. Unfortunately,
when medications, chemical restraints, and surgical interventions were introduced, the virtues of "moral therapy" were
forgotten.

Activities such as gardening have always had profound and
lasting effects on body, mind, and soul. The healers of many cultures often prescribe walks in nature. Monasteries had well-
tended gardens of flowers and herbs, and their inhabitants
devoted a great deal of time to the cultivation of plants for the
good of the soul and the body.

Today, once again, increasing numbers of hospital and reha-
bilitation centers encourage their patients to tend gardens and
plants. People with physically disabling illnesses enjoy the slow

pace and familiar touch of working the soil. Oliver Sacks notes that patients with severe cognitive difficulties who cannot tell the difference between forks and knives never place a plant upside down in the dirt. The use of hands, eye, and mind for purposes of order and pleasure is a deeply human satisfaction available to all.

Sarah, ill with Parkinson's, moved at the urging of her friends from a two-story home on the ocean to a one-floor condominium nearer the center of her seacoast town. She acknowledged that the change made sense, but she was not at peace about giving up the beauty of her site for a more mundane setting. Time showed her concern to be justified. She did not feel at ease with the intermittent sounds of traffic and the limited vista her new neighborhood offered. At my urging, Sarah searched the area, despite the physical strain entailed, for a small cottage that sat at the ocean's edge. She found one. Her friends warned her about its lack of conveniences and its distance from downtown, but the thoughtful owners of the cottage allowed Sarah to rent the cottage for one month before deciding whether to purchase it.

She has not slept a night anywhere else for nearly three years. The certain sight of rolling breakers and luminous sunsets and the reassuring crash and drag of surf over stones provides her with a welcome respite from the palsy of her illness. For Sarah, the ocean is a healing presence as necessary to the quality of her life as any medical treatment or logistical utility might be. However her disease might progress, she is sure her illness is getting better.

HEALING WITH THE SYMPTOM

Imagine illness as a text, a medium, a way. It is material with which one can work rather than simply an unwanted force to which one is subject. Everything about the illness—medicines, pains, postures, medical encounters—can be used. Leave out nothing. Who can count the wealth of themes, metaphors, possibilities, and forms that the detritus of illness offers? Like the grit in the oyster, the matter of illness becomes the substance of art.

Nancy is ill with lupus. As an adolescent and young adult, she studied to be an artist. But under the demands of parenthood and the need to work for a supplementary income, she had quit being an artist many years before. Art remained for her a vague longing and a persistent regret.

She entered psychotherapy seeking help for her mild depression and difficulties adjusting to an exacerbation. She said she remained in an unsatisfying marriage. Although she once had fantasies of escape after her children were grown, she had not left her husband. "I hated myself for being so dependent. I wish I could follow my heart and get out, but I'm afraid to do it now that my lupus is getting worse, and I also feel I would be abandoning Ted." Nancy's husband was aware of her wish to leave the marriage, but he was happy to have her companionship and content to live with the status quo for his own sake. Nancy thought of her illness as a punishing figure that condemned her to stay in a marriage precisely because she wanted out. She firmly stated that leaving the relationship was not an option she was willing to consider; she wanted help in feeling more autonomous despite the illness.

Nancy was able to begin a new world for herself despite its limitations by connecting with her youthful desires and abilities as an artist. She began to sketch the autumn leaves and winter branches in her yard. Previously, her attention had been compromised and her mood dragged down by the insistent nagging of her symptoms. Now a focus on uncomfortable sensations yielded colors and shadings that captured the changing scene outside her door. The melancholia and irritability that accompanied her illness and once threatened to overwhelm her served as a palette of tones she had rarely explored before.

The imagination is rooted in the body, and each possibility has its own feel. In the creative process, for example, one continually dips into the personal reservoirs of images and associations embedded in deeds, words, and memories. Different metaphors evoke distinct complexes of thought, emotion, and attitude. Poets especially are conscious of the physicality of language, including the literal force of punctuation. Poems spoken aloud, to oneself or another, are not the same works when scanned quietly. Reading is also an activity of the "live creature"

(Dewey, 1934). The eye lingers over the shapes of letters and words, the body senses the effects of dialogue, plot, and style.

Art is alchemy. Through art the distress of illness can be changed into something more valuable. The Nobel laureate and blind storyteller Jorge Luis Borges (1980/1994) wrote:

> A writer, or any man must believe that whatever happens to him is an instrument; everything has been given for an end. This is even stronger in the case of the artist. Everything that happens, including humiliations, embarrassments, misfortunes; all has been given like clay, like material for one's art. One must accept it. . . . Those things are given to us to transform, so that we may make from the miserable circumstances of our lives things that are eternal, or aspire to be. If a blind man feels this way, he is saved. Blindness is a gift. (p. 385)

"Wounded healer" is a phrase that has been used to characterize the shaman of traditional cultures who undergoes a time and trial of suffering as an initiation into his calling as a healer. The archetypal wounded healer of classical culture is wise Chiron the Centaur. He was the teacher of Aesculapius, among others, to whom he imparted knowledge of both music and medicine. Accidentally wounded by Hercules, Chiron could not heal himself. The immortal Chiron would have suffered unendingly had he not offered to die for Prometheus, himself condemned by the gods for his theft of fire. In honor of Chiron's nobility, Zeus granted the centaur the release of death. The mythic resonance between Chiron, Aesculapius, music, medicine, empathy, suffering, and the creative heat of Prometheus suggests that the suffering body and mind are also sources of their own transformations. Art and suffering are mated. "I create," wrote the artist Paul Klee, ill with sclerodoma at age forty, "not to cry."

Imagination is a middle way between realities too harsh or wearing to bear, yet too insistent to be shut out. The image offers a place at the table to the chronic illness, an uninvited but nonetheless unavoidable guest. Both therapist and patient search for symbols evocative enough to permit us to conceive of new possibilities, just as a rock cleared from a cave mouth allows a thirst-quenching stream to flow. What if we approach the illness experience as a work of art, a dramatic epic, for example, with moments of farce, terror, catharsis, and pity? Therapist, patient, and family could collaborate in creating and making sense of the illness experience. Such an attitude on the part of patient and therapist can restore the experience of illness and affliction to a place of honor at our human core.

THE PLEASURES OF COMPUTING

The interactive technology accessible through computers provides many benefits to people with illness. I want to focus on the changes in the experience of self and others that computer use may facilitate for those who feel limited by physical distress. Adaptive computer technology, information retrieval, and mediated communication, for example, offer individuals with illness and disabilities increased opportunities to:

initiate and maintain multiple social interactions with a wide range of people across a variety of different groupings, including but not limited to those arising from specific and general illnesses and disabilities;

retrieve and generate queries and information about specific illness and disabilities and their diagnosis and treatment, based on professional data and personal experience and anecdote;

work at home or in settings that offer greater flexibility and choice about mobility, time use, physical appearance, fatigue, and the need to exercise physical strength, dexterity, or sensory acuity;

engage in personal and political health advocacy by linking with individuals who share common concerns across lay, professional, geographic, diagnostic, and other boundaries;

participate in interpersonal and organizational encounters and contexts in which gender, physical health, age, status, and other traditional social cues are minimized;

use and interact with technology that is highly responsive and adaptable to specific and changing physical needs and displays extraordinary "patience," both in its use and in many of the purposes for which it is employed;

experiment with and develop new means of self-expression that have no physical or sensory limitations and, increasingly, require less specialized knowledge;

enjoy new forms of recreation and play that are rarely affected by illness and disability, ranging from fantasy games to visual and audio entertainment to "web surfing" to adult learning;

perceive fewer distinctions between those with and without illness and minimize the stigmas often associated with these differences; and

acquire membership in computer-related groups and subcultures that minimize barriers of time, space, and social anxiety and are distinguished by interests and competence.

Many individuals living with illness are making use of these resources now. Other advantages to computer technology that may not be as apparent are nevertheless among the most important; as with artistic activity, their use can lead to a reconfiguration of the relationships forged between body, consciousness, self, and world as a result of chronic illness. Through interactive technology, individuals

receive the satisfaction of quick and significant responsiveness to small actions within a context of ongoing, noncritical, skill-building learning;

enter the simultaneous vastness and interior of cyberspace, in contrast to the cognitive constriction and intrusion that often follow trauma; and

experience a new, rapidly evolving world with many unanticipated dimensions and possibilities, in contrast to the world of narrowing pathways and alternatives often characteristic of chronic illness.

Computer-mediated communication (CMC) can be a very satisfying way of sharing interests with other people in a non-coercive, relatively low-risk manner and with none of the constraints set by time, geography, and obstacles such as chronic illness and disability, racial or ethnic identity, physical appearance, and social anxiety. CMC is unique for the sheer number of potential communicants it allows, as well as the choices of what and how much to reveal it makes possible. Impression management, a frequent concern of individuals living with chronic illness, is under one's own control. When mutual interest builds, initial contact within anonymous group settings can move toward more reciprocal, long-term, disclosing conversation within the context of a community or in paired relationships.

FREEDOM IN CYBERSPACE

The absence of the facial and other gestural cues that characterize face-to-face interactions does not mean that computer-assisted engagements between people are emotionally impoverished. Humans have always relied on the mind's eye to create the image of another, more distant soul. Storytellers, troubadours, and poets sang and praised the deeds of heroes and strangers. Their lyrics and tales enraptured their listeners, who felt as if nothing could be more real than the world of words they had entered. Letters between strangers have crossed continents and oceans, bringing proposals of marriage and news about family members never seen. Pen pals who have never met exchange correspondence, each partner able to conjure up pictures out of phrases and never doubting that what they feel is real. Telephone conversations take place in cyberspace, and imagination fills in where sight and memory are lacking. Radio listeners and book readers empathize no less with characters because they are not visible on a television or movie screen. In fact, many people feel that the converse is true. The texture of CMC has a depth and feel to it that generate a uniquely expressive, emotional, and relational content. "What is essential," as Saint-Exupéry (1943) wrote in *The Little Prince*, "is invisible to the eye."

Cyberspace as a place is "the compelling focus of a field; it is a small world, the node at which activities converge" (Yi-fu Tuan, quoted in Gesler, 1991, p. 164). People with illness engage in resource-hunting and personal interactions through online services, message boards, and chat forums. Many smaller user networks, or "infonets," such as the WELL in the California Bay Area or specific illness forums on America Online, acquire a sense of community, spirit of participation, and personality of their own. Users develop a relationship with both the individuals and the electronic web of which they are a part, just as people identify with the city or town where they live. The web sites also provide opportunities for employment and leisure, appeals for help and expressions of concern, socializing, gossip, and even debates about the nature and quality of the interactive experience itself. In the long run, the accessibility of the "information highway" and the vehicles that cruise it will be as crucial, if not more so, to individuals living with illness as curb cuts.

Gesler (1991) distinguishes between space and place. The former is abstract and universal, whereas place suggests the concrete and particular. Space is measured. Meaning fills place. One of the challenges faced by users as well as developers of the World Wide Web and other computer-mediated networks is to transform the space of digital bits into places that matter. Just as in family, therapy, or medical settings, people online purposefully engage in patterns of interaction and create social structures that evoke affection and connection.

Virtual communities are not intended to replace encounters in the "real world" with either persons or nature. But there are many people for whom the real world is not navigable, friendly, or attractive. Online sites are examples of intermediate social spheres that share many of the same properties as clubs, fraternal organizations, pubs, and other informal associations. They serve important functions, providing sociality without the role and performance demands of work or home and drawing individuals out of the private interior of the self. The disappearance of such intermediate places from the lives of those living with illness and disability can be partially remedied by participation in CMC, just as many older people have enriched their lives through involvement with SeniorNet.

The way in which people communicate with each other and access information on the World Wide Web is through the non-sequential, densely connected multimedia interface known as hypertext. The use of hypertext may have cognitive and emotional effects of significant therapeutic value. Quite interestingly, the hypertext process appears to parallel the ways in which humans explore, encounter, make sense of, and organize cognitive experience and knowledge. Whether beginning with the clearest or vaguest of intentions, sooner or later we jump from one concept, idea, or site to another, making patterns out of fortuitous chance.

Unfamiliar concepts and unexpected coherence can occur. But such rapid, nonlinear activity easily generates a lot of excitement, even in the absence of any productive result. "A waste of time," some say.

"Isn't this play?" I say.

The fact that the simple tap of a finger can move a user back and forth from a chronic illness organization in Boston to a disabled artist in Tokyo and link them both to an art gallery in Caracas and bibliographical references to art and illness in New Zealand is a powerful stimulant. Cyberspace is vast and filled with people. For those whose mobility is impaired, the experience is dramatic and liberating.

Therapists may fail to recognize the powerful antidepressant effect of life in cyberspace. The success of antidepressant medication is often due to the initial "tidal lift" it gives people so they can initiate acts and contacts that, in turn, reinforce and support similar behaviors. Computer assisted technology, computerized information retrieval, and CMC have, I am convinced, stimulant effects as well. Some of the very characteristics of technology and the Internet that those without illness may fear—its anonymity, redundancy, commercialism, apparent isolation, and lack of reality—are for people with physical difficulties or limits a great boon.

The fantasy future of disembodied souls sailing through silicon space on digital wings is frightening or disheartening to many people. But for me, travel on spastic legs is not easy. Time is weighted with immediate worries such as urgent bladder and more distant concerns of possible progression and exacerbation to come. Cyberspace is as enticing to me as uneven and charming cobblestone lanes and long, ambitious hikes used to be. For others who share similar afflictions or fates, tomorrow offers gifts of greater freedom.

A major theme of this book is the impact that chronic illness has on an individual's sense of body, time, and space, relations with other people, assumptions about the meaning and values of life, and experience of consciousness and self. Computer-assisted technology, information retrieval, and communication, used within the intuitive frameworks of hypertext and other interactive processes, can fundamentally change the meaning and experience of illness. Therapists, physicians, and the individuals and families with whom they work can acquire from each other the confidence, knowledge, skills, and equipment to employ these new technologies and communication processes.

When the ability of people to function is dramatically enhanced and the possibility of new, continuing, and significant relationships with other people is realized; when the medium of expression, communication, shopping, and interaction is never in a rush, and useful connections are made and explored between individuals continents apart; when the constraints of weather upon activity are unimportant—for someone with illness these are extraordinary events. It is difficult to say that I am ill in the same way I was before, although my diagnosis may remain the same.

CHAPTER 11

Healing II. Gladness, Sadness, Values, God

In many ways disease and episodes of sickness remind people that meaning is an achievement.
Lawrence Sullivan, "Images of Wholeness" (1993)

THE LOT OF THOSE living with illness is not solely one of suffering and loss. Illness also provokes a counterresponse to keep and restore as much of one's world as one is able and to transform that which cannot be saved. From nothing, creation occurs.

"MS sucks!" Laughter and nodding heads greet my opening statement. I am facilitating a workshop for individuals and families living with multiple sclerosis. Participants are pleased that a professional who shares their diagnosis has a similar perspective on their situations. Group discussion is lively, but then a fellow about forty years old says something that gives me pause.

"Not that I'm glad that I have it [MS]," he remarks, "but I've become a better person since I was diagnosed ten years ago." His comment sounds familiar: I realize that several other participants have pronounced much the same thing. Each has described a change of personality since the onset of illness that

179

would be considered a worthwhile outcome of any psychotherapy process. One woman says she has become stronger, more self-reliant. Another claims she is less negative than before her diagnosis. A man states that he is more intimate and emotionally expressive in his personal encounters. Others in the group nod their heads in agreement.

Irvin Yalom (1980) reports similar findings in his work with terminally ill cancer patients. Many people describe "startling shifts" that "can be characterized in no other way than 'personal growth.'" Among the changes people identify are "a rearrangement of life's priorities," "vivid appreciation of the elemental facts of life," "fewer interpersonal fears," and "enhanced sense of living in the immediate present" (p. 35).

Yet, despite these warrants of significant and positive change, every single person in my workshop makes sure of adding, "Not that I'm glad that I have it." Why are people so reluctant to say they are glad to have experienced something from which good has been made? Of course, for some with illness, the losses are too recent or too great. They may fear worse days to come or feel unable to wrench any meaning from their fate. Yet it is possible for people to find or even imagine value where there appears to be none. One purpose of this book is to help individuals, families, and professionals to do just that.

THE FLIGHT FROM SORROW

"The idea that positive change is possible in the context of loss is poorly developed in the literature," suggests Viederman (1989, p. 188). Yet loss is all around us—losses in love and in life, of home and of health, of work and from war, of family and of friends, of esteem and of face, of senses and of faith. How often do we as therapists acknowledge the sheer abundance of loss to ourselves and to our patients? When do we allow ourselves to feel the sorrow of the world? Perhaps the most important work of therapy is to provide a place for helping another accomplish the task of mourning. Hopelessness and despair can be turned toward faith and renewal.

Would it make a difference if we were to converse with our

patients about their suffering rather than about their depression? If we talked about sadness instead of guilt? Sam is a young man who describes the guilt he feels about his inability to relieve his partner's suffering from AIDS. He works at a job he loves that requires frequent evening and occasional weekend commitments. He knows that his partner wants him to be providing care at home rather than working away from home. Sam knows there is little more he can do than to speak with his partner several times a week on the telephone. He knows that he ought not to feel guilty. There is, however, nothing he can do about it. He is aware of the irrationality of his guilt but feels unable to get away from the grip it has on his thoughts and from the ache in his chest. When I ask Sam why he labeled what he feels as guilt, he answers, "What else could it be?"

"Sadness," I reply, "for your partner's suffering." Sam bursts into tears and talks and talks about how sad and helpless he feels. I tell him that he has a right to feel sad. Sadness makes sense to him in a way that guilt does not. It is not irrational to be sad.

Why did the word *sadness* release such a flood of emotion and, paradoxically, leave Sam with more energy and, indeed, more hope? How many others interpret their experience of grief as one of guilt? It is not unusual for people to construe sadness and grief as anxiety, depression, or guilt. Yes, it could be that the young man was feeling "survivor's guilt." He possessed good health and a promising future, and his partner's life was on a fatal course. It is often easier to announce guilt or depression than sadness. The former are more easily used as weapons against others or oneself. Sadness can be too much feeling to bear. Maybe Sam's guilt masked a terror of his own vulnerability. To acknowledge his sadness might arouse the first stirrings of a richer understanding of life's transience.

Therapists who focus on guilt and avoid sadness attempt to keep their own sorrow at bay. Illness is often a threat to therapists' sense of identity and self. It forces upon their awareness knowledge of their own physical vulnerability and that of those they love. It causes them to question their own ability to endure suffering and to understand, manage, and find meaning in the larger world beyond the room, the clinic, the institution, the community in which they work.

We flee from sadness. "In twentieth century America," D. M. Dooling (1986) writes, "'sadness' is not at all commendable. One has only to be in a reflective mood, or in some way occupied with serious thought, to elicit from a friend or stranger this protest, 'Why are you so sad?'—as if one were committing some kind of social sin" (p. 3). Attempts to discuss sadness are often deflected by people unable, apparently, to tolerate their own fears of loss and distress.

In families with illness, children and intimates are often shielded from the sadness that is a common partner of loss. Some do not wish to express sadness around children, fearing that their trust and faith in a safe or good world will be harmed. Many parents believe that children who know of grief or danger will suffer unnecessarily. Sadness, from such a point of view, is a trauma to be avoided. How often is a child who expresses sadness met with the simple, quiet acceptance of a parental hug? More often we point out why a child need not feel so sad, or we propose a plan of action so that sadness won't happen again. It can be easier to devise strategies to cope with guilt than it is simply to sit still with sadness. Arthur Frank (1991) may be quite right when he says: "Most people's problems with mourning are not caused by compounded losses; their problems are caused by other people's desires to get mourning over with" (p. 40).

In our culture, the work of mourning is attempted through a vocabulary of affects—anxiety, depression, angst, stress, and the like—that locates the source of anguish in the individual's body or mind rather than in the community, environment, or transcendent order in which individuals also live. "All of us who concern ourselves with the human psyche know," Mitscherlich-Nielsen (1989) reminds us, that "without mourning there can be no development in the inner life of the individual" (p. 414). What is there about the mourning process that seems so essential? How can it be used to facilitate the healing of individuals and families afflicted with illness?

"The successful completion of the mourning process results in creative outcome," suggests George Pollack (1989, p. 28), in a discussion of painters, musicians, writers, and other artists whose work flourished in spite of, and possibly owing to, their physical afflictions and other experiences of loss and grieving.

Why would this not also be true of the less artistically gifted? Are not richer relationships, accomplishments in the face of great odds, experiences of joy and humor, battles for social justice, taking a stand for one's own dignity, and the simple satisfaction of making it through the day also creative possibilities that people living with illness may realize through their grief?

Lifton (1979) describes the "inability to mourn" as "part of a breakdown in the symbolizing process. . . . The image . . . is integral to human life. Its absence . . . threatens human life. Indeed human life itself can be understood as a quest for vitalizing images and image-constellations" (p. 295).

Many people diagnosed with chronic illness carry an ongoing sense that an old world is falling apart and another needs to be claimed. For others, the realization of what has been lost and what may be required to go on arrives with sudden force. The blows of fate delivered by blindness, double vision, terrifying paralysis, persistent fever or cough, or bloody stools easily overwhelm individuals and their families. The beliefs by which they have previously organized and built their lives no longer hold. Self and others, time and space, body and soul, are in upheaval. The threat and reality of progression, exacerbation, and accumulating losses continue.

LIMINAL TIME

It is little wonder that those with illness and their families often enter a sort of "in-between" time to come to grips with shock, grief, and mourning. The struggles of adolescence around issues of competency, autonomy, and values rise up with great force. Similarly, one's identity is threatened by illnesses that lack clear physical, social, or psychological definition. How helpful it would be if those with illness could participate in some sort of socially sanctioned moratorium to rest, recover, reorganize, and go through such a profound psychosocial transition. Such an opportunity too rarely exists. Instead, many with illness enter a sort of exile, not necessarily from the affections and cares of family, friends, physicians, and others, but from the world of the self that existed before.

In our culture, the need for a respite and retreat from the world and self that existed before is recognized for a short time after childbirth, during the honeymoon after marriage, and for the ever briefer period of mourning following death. Most people understand that people may not be themselves, in mood or actions, at these times. Each such event involves the addition or loss of a significant person or identity in one's life, in the membership of the family, and, traditionally, within the community.

The acts that deepen, halt, or relieve suffering do not take place in a moment. It is important for therapists to show respect for the invalid, the victim, the exile, and other archetypal ways of being that emerge with illness. One is wise not to attempt a premature solution to these problems. We try to help individuals or families adapt to loss by cheering or hurrying them up because we cannot abide their pain. We don't tolerate victims very well, and we have subtle and more openly stated expectations that suffering will be used as an opportunity for growth. Individuals need to wrestle with their own answer to the question, "Why me?"

Rites of initiation in traditional cultures often include the intentional infliction of disenchantment on the newly initiated. They discover that the masked figures they have assumed since childhood to be gods are people like themselves. The neophyte learns that the responsibility of adulthood is to introduce the young into the tradition and to uphold its ways for the invisible gods. For a time the novice remains between two worlds as his or her state of consciousness and behavior oscillate back and forth between those appropriate to the former status and those of the newly emergent one. Both the passages themselves and the selves traveling through them are liminal.

"Liminality," rooted in the Latin for *threshold* and *doorway*, is a concept that some anthropologists and psychotherapists in recent years have applied to rites of initiation, physical disability, midlife, and other phenomena. It offers a fruitful approach to examining chronic illness for several reasons. First, chronic illness commonly brings with it, as a result of medication, fatigue, fear, anxiety, parathesis, and many of the phenomena described above, a liminal consciousness that differs from the wide-awake consciousness of our daily lives. Second, as a result of the potential disability and ambiguity associated with the sick role, chronic illness places many patients in a liminal location vis-à-vis many social norms and expectations. Third, chronic illness moves a person into a liminal space in relation to spouse and family, especially around issues of autonomy, reciprocity, moral judgments, and mutual responsibilities and obligations. Fourth, for many individuals the experience of chronic illness is a transitional process between differing and changing dimensions of body, time, and self.

Liminality represents both structure and process, just as a door is both wood and way. The liminal zone is for some a temporary place of abode, housing them as the camp shelters the refugee. For others it is a more permanent place of being, whether as exile, invalid, wise man, or fool. For many therapists who work with individuals and families living with chronic illness, the ability to understand liminality and work with it constructively is of great importance.

William Gesler (1991) uses the felicitous term "fields of care" to refer to places that leave those who enter with a deep reservoir of memories of affection, familiarity, and concern. The therapist's office has the potential to provide refuge during a client's explorations of the geography of illness. Within its safe harbor, individuals and families can venture out to map the terrain of the land they have entered, using the leisure that trust brings to describe what has been left behind. One goal of psychotherapy with individuals and families with chronic illness is to help them construct a home, and to build a place to dwell in a new world, especially one that holds up to predictable dangers as well as unexpected threats.

COHERENCE AND MEANING

What makes a difference in how people respond to illness? Antonovsky (1990) developed the concept of a "sense of coherence" with which to investigate the human capacity to endure suffering and maintain a sense of personal integration and hope. The three core characteristics of a sense of coherence are:

1. Comprehensibility: the ability to structure the painful events (e.g., illness) into some graspable pattern
2. Manageability: the availability and use of resources to cope with affliction
3. Meaningfulness: the sense that there is something to be gained from living through difficulties

Meaningfulness, he found, was the most important of these characteristics.

Antonovsky's work is consistent with one of the earliest and simplest models for looking at how families cope with crisis and catastrophe—the ABCX model developed by Reuben Hill (Figley & McCubbin, 1983). In the 1930s, 1940s, and 1950s, family researchers looked at the responses of families to financial difficulties, death, wartime separation, alcoholism, and other stressful and catastrophic circumstances. They reported that the severity of crisis a family experienced (X) was a result of interactions between the stressor event (A), the resources available to a family to respond to the stressor (B), and the definition or meaning the family made of the stressor (C). The central role that issues of meaning play in the making and remaking of illness experiences by both individuals and families is highlighted by Antonovsky and the ABCX models.

People with illness confront a fate in which achievement is measured by small increments of increased mobility or a lessening of pain. They are forced to question their commitment to the unexamined myths of progress, purpose, and problem-solving. Unable to go further, faster, higher, people with illness do have the capacity—although they didn't choose it—to reflect upon the virtues, values, and goods that make their lives worthwhile.

Illness is not only a process of disease and disruption. It is also the caring involvement of family, friends, physicians, therapists, and other people of significance. The presence of a resilient network of social support is crucial for healing. People need to know that they are valued despite the burdens their care imposes and their lessened capacities to fulfill former roles. Relationships offer substantial portions of the meaning people need to hold each other up.

When a family member receives a diagnosis of chronic illness, not only the individual but the family needs to cope successfully with its uncertain, depleting, and accumulating demands. As financial resources and those of time, energy, and labor, among others, are drawn down, their lack becomes itself a source of distress and potential illness. Some families, like some individuals, seem better able to avert the full disaster that chronic illness and other changes and losses might become. There are even those families, or individuals within the family, who seem the better for what has happened to them.

Therapists can be most useful to their clients by helping them to approach questions of meaning. They can do little to directly change or alter disease processes, and their ability to call up new resources is limited. By focusing on the disease process rather than on the specific meanings that illness has for the person before us, we use medical terminology as one of "the structures . . . to exorcise the fear that we may lose control—indeed, that we are really not in control at all" (Gilman, 1988, p. 2). By applying a diagnostic term, be it chronic illness, multiple sclerosis, cancer, or lupus, clinicians can lose sight of the accumulating personal losses or unexpected strengths that are hidden by that term.

A physician's diagnosis can lead one to ask, "How do I connect the fact that I am ill with how I choose to live my life?" In the second edition of *Motivation and Personality* (1970), Abraham Maslow addresses the collegiate readers of his text who questioned whether they were "self-actualized." (Maslow had borrowed the term "self-actualization" from the pioneering neurologist Kurt Goldstein, who studied the capacity and drive of brain-injured people to function as well as they could.) Maslow responds by listing his criteria for self-actualization, the first two of which are the achievement of identity and autonomy. It is interesting to see how many of the remaining conditions for self-actualization are consistent with a recognition of limits, imperfection, and humility and have little to do with progress, individuality, or health. Young people, he writes, have not

> had time enough to experience an enduring, loyal post-romantic love relationship, nor have they generally found their calling, the altar upon which to offer themselves. Nor have they worked out

their own system of values; nor have they had experience enough (responsibility for others, tragedy, failure, achievement, success) to shed perfectionistic illusions and become realistic; nor have they generally made their peace with death; nor have they learned how to be patient; nor have they learned enough about evil in themselves and others to be compassionate; nor have they had time to become post-ambivalent about parents and elders, power and authority; nor have they generally become knowledgeable and educated enough to open the possibility of becoming wise; nor have they generally acquired enough courage to be unpopular, to be unashamed about being openly virtuous.

Illness does not stand in the way of any who aim for such ends.

HEALING

The experience of chronic illness is one of a major disruption in the taken-for-granted world of ordinary life. The ability to be the author of one's life is seriously harmed. Those who live with chronic illness acquire an amphibious nature—they live in two worlds, one of illness, the other of the not-yet-ill. As Jerome Frank (1974) long ago pointed out, the experience of feeling demoralized is the common characteristic of people seeking the help of psychotherapists. The healing activities of most cultures are oriented toward restoring an individual's morale to better meet the demands or losses that have come his or her way. It is unfortunate that the idea of healing has become synonymous with the concept of cure at the same time that chronic illness and other medical misfortunes most susceptible to healing effects are increasing in number. Although cures for chronic illnesses are unlikely, therapists can fill a healing role by offering empathic attention to the story of change and disruption and helping those with illness to make some sense of their circumstances and fate.

Individuals and families cast a wide net in their search for relief of their suffering. They have a broad view of what constitutes illness and possible sources of treatment and healing. They make use of biomedical physicians, nurses, psychotherapists, other licensed and unlicensed practitioners of the healing arts, the advice and instruction of friends and books, and the testimonials of strangers and advertising. Physicians and psychotherapists are only two among the many possible sources of help and information for people in need or distress.

I received my original diagnosis of multiple sclerosis from a neurologist. Although I was raised in a physician's family with a healthy dose of skepticism for the claims of nonmedical practitioners, I consulted a naturopath when I learned there was no medical treatment for the illness. In the years since, I have also had brief and helpful sessions with chiropractors and acupuncturists, and a longer relationship with my psychotherapist. Currently I use medications to decrease spasticity at night and to combat fatigue. I also briefly tried Betaseron as a possible way to prevent future exacerbations. The number of physicians, "alternative" healers, somatic treatments, diets, vitamins, drugs, and other methods and regimens I have encountered is on the small side compared to the efforts of many others similarly diagnosed. I also am aware that despite my good relationships with and respect for my current neurologist and my primary care physician, I have spoken very little of my use of nonmedical approaches with them. In this, I am, of course, not unique. The people I work with in therapy tell me more of their involvement with both biomedical and alternative approaches than they tell their physicians.

In most cultures, healing activities take place over a relatively short period of time, often in public, with family members present; they emphasize social roles and obligations, make use of religious and communal symbols, and often involve direct bodily contact and manipulation. Many psychotherapists, on the other hand, sit in offices with a single individual over a number of months or years, have little knowledge of or contact with the community in which they practice, emphasize individual autonomy and development, are primarily secular in orientation, and provide little somatic intervention beside the recommendation of medications.

Most therapists also practice very differently from most biomedical professionals. They engage in a form of symbolic healing that places great emphasis on the use of rhetoric, trust, empathy, and skilled listening. Therapists acknowledge that bodily symptoms may have multiple meanings that express emotional and social distress. In contrast, medical education tends to underemphasize the importance of the subjective elements in patient recovery and compliance, as well as overvalue the effectiveness of medical and technological interventions. The placebo effect, for so long seen as no more than a nuisance in clinical trials or a sign of a patient's gullibility or unrealistic expectations, is given too little credit.

The writer and counselor Kat Duff (1993), ill with chronic fatigue and immune dysfunction syndrome, draws on the powerful imagery of alchemy, introduced into modern Western psychology by Jung, to illuminate her own experience with illness. To imagine that one's personal suffering is part of a larger process of transformation gives some consolation and hope. The painful process of physical breakdown and emotional scorching can yield a small pearl of wisdom, which in turn can give hope and healing to others.

In the Western culture of psychotherapy, the imaginations of Freud and Jung continue to exercise tremendous influence on our fantasies of human behavior and development. Despite the claims and findings of biopsychiatry, sociobiology, evolutionary psychology, and cybernetics, no one else in the human sciences has yet matched the breadth of knowledge, humanism, audacious reach, and sense of the tragic that mythmaking requires and our need for meaning thirsts for.

Jung suggested that symptoms, whether of physical or psychological distress, were the calls of the suffering soul. What most people view as pathological are the cries of the psyche as it struggles with the conflicting and complex demands within its own nature and in its relation to culture and society.

Hillman (1989) and Berry (1982) emphasize the role of image as the guide of the soul. One approaches a dream or a symptom as a creation of psyche in her own right. The particular images, colors, and shadings of a dream are appreciated not just for what they appear to mean, but because in giving them close attention, *one quickens the life of the soul*. Respect for the image and the symptom offers individuals a way to work with the marks and signs of suffering and loss. Every apparent harm as well as success is potential food for the soul. We lick our wounds to heal them and are nourished and transmuted as well by what they leave on our tongue.

Mogenson (1989) approaches the Bible as a psychological document. He uses its language and symbols, including the core metaphor of God, the *imago dei*, to give trauma and other secularized descriptions of suffering the dignity usually reserved for the struggles and heroism of Moses, Jesus, or Job. From Mogenson's point of view, the problem of unending trauma comes not from the event itself but from the pinioning of the particulars and individuality of an individual's injury within the hardened casement of diagnostic categories—whether post-traumatic syndrome or multiple sclerosis.

Ziegler (1983) calls his psychotherapeutic work "archetypal medicine." He attends to symptoms as conduits for the amplification of images and associations relevant to an individual's subjective experience. Ironic, provocative, hermetic, Ziegler acknowledges that his therapy for organic diseases and disturbance is "verbal and extremely impractical" (p. 38). Archetypal medicine does not seek to avoid or eliminate biomedicine or disease but to use illness in the service of healing. The exchange of words is a kind of hydrotherapy, facilitating the flow of meaning through the dry desert of disease.

Sardello (1992) connects disease with the condition of what he calls the soul of the world, the ancient *anima mundi*. If we view disease and its treatment as discrete phenomena of the body, invading virus or bacteria, and medicine, we miss the larger web of meanings and terrain in which we live. In response to antibiotics or antiviral agents, for example, microscopic life forms change. Our bodies, formerly protected, are now vulnerable. A continuous process of mutation between two beings, one small, the other larger, takes place within the body and the environment. How is it possible to separate such interrelated parts? How can the complexity of these processes of life be teased into separate strands? If the individual is ill, the larger world she inhabits is ill. If we approach medical treatment as if it were only our body that is in need, we miss a sense of participation in a greater whole. To care for the world because it is ill is a way of taking care of oneself.

THE WORSHIP OF HEALTH AND THE CALL OF ILLNESS

There are dangers implicit in our concept and worship of health. Dare I suggest that illness is not only inevitable but necessary in our culture? Yes, the messiness and pain of illness erupt into the sunlit clarity of the taken-for-grantedness of daily life like a ragged man at a politician's ball. But illness is one of the few remaining humble and personal forces to oppose the powerful social ideals of health, adaptation, and productivity. Without illness as a grave reminder, our personal and social fantasies of mastery and wealth might recognize no limit.

Psychological thought has been patronizing, neglectful, or disrespectful of religion. The investigation of religious experience, one of the most significant dimensions of many people's lives, has rarely been taken seriously. Most modern psychologies focus on the crucial influence of family and parents upon personality. Therapists routinely show much less interest in their clients' religious or spiritual histories. It is possible, however, that an individual's sense of the sacred and of fundamental good has a more significant impact on his or her life than parents and family.

Modernization and its accompanying attitudes have undercut the plausibility of religious belief for many. But it has not removed, as Peter Berger (1974) reminds us,

> the experiences that call for them. Human beings continue to be stricken by sickness and death; they continue to experience social injustices and deprivation.... What [modernity] has accomplished is to seriously weaken those definitions of reality that previously made our human condition easier to bear. This has produced an anguish all its own. (p. 185)

Both therapist and patient are in need of opportunities and images to adequately symbolize and make meaning out of loss experiences. Religion and myth are abundantly provisioned storehouses of such images and meanings.

From a traditional religious perspective, illness and symptoms reflect humanity's fallen state of being. The presence of physical suffering is an outward display and reminder of the distress and distance from perfection and wholeness all humans share. People with cancer, multiple sclerosis, Parkinson's, or any other diagnosis bear witness, not to their own shortcomings, but to the community's unwillingness to care; all too often, people with illness reflect the community's failures of mercy. Morally, the sight of a physically ill person ought to evoke the wish to harbor, comfort, and heal. Our communal failure to do so demonstrates, from a spiritual orientation, that we are *all* ill. The religious attitude is important, because it calls us to witness and care for the suffering other as we wish to be healed ourselves.

Religious, spiritual, and archetypal meanings are among the few frameworks that can bear the weight of loss, uncertainty, and change with dignity and love. The victim has a place of honor here. Particular images and experiences of God's benevolence—the bosom of Abraham, God's will, the hand of God, the intelligent universe—can offer tremendous support to people in need, as well as to those who attempt to help them.

It makes little sense to rule out or ignore religious meanings as part of the process and content of therapy. In my experience, many individuals and families are eager to discuss the application to their lives and illness of their religious and spiritual beliefs. People often find and make use of spiritual resources at the same time they are visiting a therapist or physician because serious illness has entered their lives. Most are also willing and able to look at not only the confirmations of their professed beliefs in their actual behavior but the contradictions as well. Religious and spiritual concerns inform people in matters ranging from the meaning and cause of illness, suffering, and death to specific religious practices. In many cultures, the experience and healing of chronic illness take place within a less secular context than in our own. Biomedicine, science, and the psychological perspective find their place among, not replacing, other values.

There are, of course, profound differences between psychotherapy and religion. The emphasis in psychotherapy is on helping individuals make and act on choices consistent with the values to which they are committed following examination and reflection on the story of their own lives. Within a religious framework, a person's behavior is guided by the moral teachings and mystery that come from a divinely inspired source of authority and meaning. In psychotherapy, individuals are often asked to search within, to listen for the voice of the real or true self. In religious traditions and pastoral settings, one prays to hear the call of the absolute Other. The doctrine, authority, and fellowship of the sacred texts, minister, and congregation serve as a check that prevents the word of the Lord from being confused with the appetites of the self.

Yet it is the individual person who seeks the Other. Therapists can help people to identify the personal factors that may (or may not) account for their ability to live up to religious commitments and ethics. Individuals and families living with illness can benefit from therapists who acknowledge the help that may come from religious traditions and spiritual paths, both conventional and more idiosyncratic.

Fortunately, therapists can draw from both medicine and other traditions. The vocabulary of medicine, pain, disease, cure, and suffering constitutes one of the few remaining languages in our culture through which people can struggle with the facts and place of affliction, healing, and meaning in the order and disorder of self and life. Psychotherapists must help to tease open the constructs of illness.

Let us bring illness out from its isolation within the medical setting, where it has been subordinated to our cultural ideals of wellness and health. When chronic illness is approached as a form of suffering, a therapeutics of the psyche as well as of the body is indicated. In such a context, clinicians can orient their practice toward care as well as cure, acceptance as well as treatment. They are able to acknowledge and embrace weakness, limits, unknowing, and loss.

People commonly grapple with important questions about life's design and significance under the hard hand of illness. The presence of disease pushes therapists and clients to work on identity, autonomy, and values. What is happening to me? Why am I suffering? How can I be healed? These are questions with which the ill and their families are seized. Who am I? What is my life worth? Is my life a "good" life? What do people in families and communities owe to themselves and each other? How much suffering is too much suffering? Is there any goodness or meaning to be found amid pain and loss? Individuals in distress benefit from a relationship with a person who cares, is committed to giving help, and joins them in finding answers to such fundamental questions.

In the central narratives of many religious traditions, it is often that which is most neglected or despised that is the source of new spirit and hope. For many suffering individuals, neither priest nor rabbi, philosopher nor physician, provides what they wish for or need. The therapist is often the one who listens to their story, sees their losses, and has compassion for their pain. A sensitive clinician helps individuals and their families hold onto or recover hope, meaning, and morale during the continuing and unwelcome presence of illness and disability. Perhaps illness *is* a visit from the gods, who leave a mystery behind of value unknown—danger? a gift? a new capacity for love? death? a summons to listen for meaning? Sometimes, Rabbi Adin Steinsaltz (1994) reminds us, "the call comes not through any kind of a voice; sometimes the call comes because you are put into a position in which a choice is made for you which you never imagined. It may begin from anything—from an accident to a disaster" (p. 29).

The archetype of the healer need no longer be embodied in another. The healer is within. That healer is not, however, the positive-thinking, cancer-slaying hero who still lives in the dualistic paradigm of illness and health. The healer is one well suited to this age, opposed to its dominant ideologies, fragmented, uncertain, and suffering. The healer is the illness experience itself. Through art and craft, the paths of service and reflection, the vocations of work and relationship, people with chronic illness find and prepare the ground for another way of being in the world.

SOURCES

Abt, T. (1989). *Progress without loss of soul*. Wilmette, IL: Chiron Publications.

Agich, G. (1990). Reassessing autonomy in long-term care. *Hastings Center Report, 20*(6), 12–17.

Allert, G., Sponholz, G., & Baitsch, H. (1994). Chronic disease and the meaning of old age. *Hastings Center Report, 24*(5), 11–13.

Antonovsky, A. (1990). Pathways leading to successful coping and health. In M. Rosenbaum (Ed.), *Learned resourcefulness* (pp. 31–63). New York: Springer.

Arno, P., Bonuck, K., & Padgug, R. (1994). The economic impact of high technology homecare. *Hastings Center Report, 24*(5), S15–S19.

Bair, B., & Cayleff, S. (eds.). (1993). *Wings of gauze: Women of color and the experience of health and illness*. Detroit: Wayne State University Press.

Bakan, D. (1971). *Disease, pain, and sacrifice*. Boston: Beacon Press.

Baumeister, R. (1991). *Meanings of life*. New York: Guilford Press.

Becker, E. (1973). *Denial of death*. New York: Free Press.

Beresford, E. (1991). Uncertainty and the shaping of medical decisions. *Hastings Center Report, 21*(8), 6–11.

Berger, P. (1967). *The Sacred canopy*. New York: Anchor Books.

Berger, P., Berger, B., & Kellner, H. (1974). *The Homeless mind*. New York: Vintage.

Berger, P., & Luckman, T. (1966). *The Social construction of reality*. Garden City, NY: Doubleday.

Berry, P. (1982). *Echo's subtle body*. Dallas, TX: Spring Publications.

Bilu, Y., & Witztum, E. (1993). Working with Jewish ultra-orthodox patients: Guidelines for a culturally sensitive therapy. *Culture, Medicine, and Psychiatry, 17*(2), 197–233.

Bloom, H. (1994). *The western canon*. New York: Harcourt Brace & Company.

Borges, J. L. (1994). Blindness (Trans. Eliot Weinberger). In P. Lopate (Ed.), *The Art of the personal essay* (pp. 377–386). New York: Anchor Books. (Originally published 1980)

Bowlby, J. (1980). *Loss*. New York: Basic Books.

Brody, H. (1987). *Stories of sickness*. New Haven: Yale University Press.

Brody, H. (1992). *The Healer's power*. New Haven: Yale University Press.

Broyard, A. (1992). *Intoxicated by my illness and other writings of life and death*. New York: Fawcett Columbine.

Campion, E. (1993). Why unconventional medicine? *New England Journal of Medicine, 328*(4), 282–283.

Carlsen, M. B. (1995). Meaning-making and creative aging. In R. Neimeyer & M. Mahoney (Eds.), *Constructivism in psychotherapy* (pp. 127–153). Washington, DC: American Psychological Association.

Carotenuto, A. (1992). *The Difficult art*. Wilmette, IL: Chiron Publications.

Cassell, E. (1976). *The Healer's art*. Philadelphia: Lippincott.

Cassell, E. (1990). *The Nature of suffering*. New York: Oxford University Press.

Charmaz, K. (1991). *Good days, bad days: The self in chronic illness and time*. New Brunswick, NJ: Rutgers University Press.

Cohn, K., & Rapgay, L. (1994). A Meeting of traditional Tibetan and Western medicine. In L. Sullivan (Ed.), *The Parabola book of healing* (pp. 137–157). New York: Continuum Press.

Connell, C., Davis, W., Gallant, M., & Sharpe, P. (1994). Impact of social support, social cognitive variables, and perceived threat of depression among adults with diabetes. *Health Psychology, 13*(3), 263–273.

Danieli, Y. (1989). Mourning in survivors and children of survivors of the Nazi Holocaust: The role of group and community modalities. In D. Dietrich & P. Shabad (Eds.), *The Problem of loss and mourning* (pp. 427–460). Madison, CT: International Universities Press.

Danis, M., & Churchill, L. (1991). Autonomy and the commonweal. *Hastings Center Report, 21*(1), 25–31.

DesPres, T. (1976). *The Survivor*. New York: Oxford University Press.

Dewey, J. (1934). *Art as experience*. New York: Capricorn Books.

Di Matteo, M., et al. (1993). Physicians' characteristics influence patients' adherence to medical treatment: Results from the Medical Outcomes Study. *Health Psychology, 12*(2), 93–102.

Doherty, W., & Baird, M. (1983). *Family therapy medicine*. New York: Guilford Press.

Dooling, D. M. (1986). Focus. *Parabola, 11*(3), 3–4.

Duff, K. (1993). *The Alchemy of illness*. New York: Bell Tower.

Eisenberg, D., Kessler, R., Foster, C., Norlock, F., Calkins, D., & Delbanco, T. (1993). Unconventional medicine in the United States. *New England Journal of Medicine, 328*(4), 246–252.

Eisenberg, L. (1992). Treating anxiety and depression in primary care. *New England Journal of Medicine, 326*(16), 1080–1084.

Epstein, S. (1993). Bereavement from the perspective of cognitive-experiential self-theory. In M. Stroebe, W. Stroebe, & R. Hansson (Eds.), *Handbook of bereavement* (pp. 112–125). Cambridge: Cambridge University Press.

Erikson, E. (1959). Identity and the life cycle. *Psychological Issues*, monograph. I, 1. New York: International Universities Press.

Erikson, E. (1978). Reflections on Dr. Borg's life cycle. In E. Erikson (Ed.), *Adulthood* (p. 25). New York: Norton.

Family Psychologist. (1994). [special issue on disabilities], *10*(4).

Farber, R. (1994). [interview]. In H. Goldfarb, *Art's lament* (exhibition catalog). Boston: Isabella Stewart Gardner Museum.

Farmer, P., Lindenbaum, S., & Good, M. (1993). Women, poverty and AIDS. *Culture, Medicine, and Psychiatry, 17*(4), 387–397.

Feinberg, J. (1989). Autonomy. In J. Christman (Ed.), *The Inner citadel* (pp. 27–53). New York: Oxford University Press.

Feyerabend, P. (1978). *Against method*. London: Verso.

Figley, C., & McCubbin, H. (eds.). (1983). *Stress and the family: Vol. 2, Coping with catastrophe*. New York: Brunner/Mazel.

Fingarette, H. (1963). *The Self in transformation*. New York: Harper & Row.

Fins, J., & Callahan, D. (1992). Commentaries on palliation in the age of chronic disease. *Hastings Center Report, 22*(1), 41–42.

Flanagan, O. (1991). *The Varieties of moral personality*. Cambridge, MA: Harvard University Press.

Fleishman, J., & Fogel, B. (1994). Coping and depressive symptoms among people with AIDS. *Health Psychology, 13*(2), 156–169.

Fox, R. See Zaner.

Frank, A. (1991). *At the will of the body*. Boston: Houghton Mifflin.

Frank, J. (1974). *Persuasion and healing* (rev. ed.). New York: Schocken Books.

Freidson, E. (1988). *Profession of medicine* (rev. ed.). Chicago: University of Chicago Press.

Geertz, C. (1983). *Local knowledge*. New York: Basic Books.

Gergen, K. (1991). *The Saturated self*. New York: Basic Books.

Gesler, W. (1991). *The Cultural geography of health care*. Pittsburgh: University of Pittsburgh Press.

Gilman, S. (1988). *Disease and representation*. Ithaca, NY: Cornell University Press.

Goffman, E. (1963). *Stigma*. New York: Simon & Schuster.

Good, B. (1992/3). Culture, diagnosis and comorbidity. *Culture, Medicine, and Psychiatry, 16*(4), 427–446.

Good, B. (1994). *Medicine, rationality and experience*. Cambridge: Cambridge University Press.

Good, B., Brodwin, P., Good, M. J., & Kleinman, A. (eds.). (1992). *Pain as human experience*. Berkeley: University of California Press.

Gordon, G. (1966). *Role theory and illness*. New Haven: College and University Press.

Griffith, J., & Griffith, M. (1994). *The Body speaks*. New York: Basic Books.

Hall, J., Epstein, A., DeCiantis, M., & McNeil, B. (1993). Physicians' liking for their patients: More evidence for the role of affect in medical care. *Health Psychology, 12*(2), 140–146.

Hampshire, S. (1983). *Morality and conflict*. Cambridge, MA: Harvard University Press.

Hardwig, J. (1990). What about the family? *Hastings Center Report, 20*(2), 5–10.

Harris, M. (1991). *Sisters of the shadow*. Norman: University of Oklahoma Press.

Hawkins, A. (1993). *Reconstructing illness*. West Lafayette, IN: Purdue University Press.

Heath, D., & Rabinow, P. (eds.). (1993). Bio-politics: The anthropology of the new genetics and immunology. *Culture, Medicine, and Psychiatry, 17*(1), 1–97.

Heller, A. (1988). *General ethics*. Oxford: Basil Blackwell.

Herman, J. L. (1992). *Trauma and recovery*. New York: Basic Books.

Hillman, J. (1976). *Suicide and the soul*. Dallas, TX: Spring Publications.

Hillman, J. (1989). *A Blue fire*. New York: Harper & Row.

Horowitz, K., & Lanes, D. (1992). *Witness to illness*. Reading, MA: Addison-Wesley.

Hull, J. (1991). *Touching the rock*. New York: Pantheon Books.

Hunter, K. (1991). *Doctor's stories*. Princeton, NJ: Princeton University Press.

James, W. (1890). *The Principles of psychology*. 2 vols. New York: Henry Holt.

Jecker, N., Carrese, J., & Pearlman, R. (1995). Caring for patients in cross-cultural settings. *Hastings Center Report, 25*(1), 6–14.

Jennings, B., Callahan, D., & Caplan, A. (1988). Ethical challenges of chronic illness. *Hastings Center Report* (special supplement), *18*(2), 4.

Johnson, M. (1993). *Moral imagination*. Chicago: University of Chicago Press.

Jonas, H. (1992). The Burden and blessing of mortality. *Hastings Center Report, 22*(1), 34–40.

Jones, B. T., & Arnie Zane Dance Company. (1995). *Still/Here* (performance brochure).

Kafka, F. (1925, 1979). *The Metamorphosis*. In *The Basic Kafka*. New York: Pocket Books.

Katz, J. (1984). *The Silent world of doctor and patient*. New York: Free Press.

Katz, R. (1993). *The Straight path*. Reading, MA: Addison-Wesley.

Katz, R. (1994). The Kung approach to healing. In L. Sullivan (Ed.), *The Parabola book of healing* (pp. 164–174). New York: Continuum Press.

Kemeny, M., Weiner, H., Taylor, S., Schneider, S., Vischer, B., & Fahey, J. (1994). Repeated bereavement, depressed mood, and immune parameters in HIV seropositive and seronegative gay men. *Health Psychology, 13*(1), 14–24.

Kestenbaum, V. (ed.). (1982). *The Humanity of the ill.* Knoxville: University of Tennessee Press.

King, K., Reis, H., Porter, L., & Norsen, L. (1993). Social support and long-term recovery from coronary artery surgery: Effects on patients and spouses. *Health Psychology, 12*(1), 56–63.

Kirmayer, L. (1993). Healing and the invention of metaphor: The effectiveness of symbols revisited. *Culture, Medicine, and Psychiatry, 17*(2), 161–196.

Kirmayer, L. (1994). Improvisation and authority in illness meaning. *Culture, Medicine, and Psychiatry, 18*(2), 183–214.

Kleinman, A. (1980). *Patients and healers in the context of culture.* Berkeley: University of California Press.

Kleinman, A. (1988a). *The Illness narratives: Suffering, healing, and the human condition.* New York: Basic Books.

Kleinman, A. (1988b). *Rethinking psychiatry.* New York: Free Press.

Kleinman, A., & Kleinman, J. (1985). Somatization: The Interconnections in Chinese society among culture, depressive experiences, and the meanings of pain. In A. Kleinman & B. Good (Eds.), *Culture and depression* (pp. 429–490). Berkeley: University of California Press.

Leder, D. (1990). *The Absent body.* Chicago: University of Chicago Press.

Levin, D. (1985). *The Body's recollection of being.* London: Routledge and Kegan Paul.

Levin, D. (1989). *The Listening self.* London: Routledge.

Levin, D. (ed.). (1987). *Pathologies of the modern self.* New York: New York University Press.

Lewis, C. S. (1962). *The Problem of pain.* New York: Macmillan.

Lifton, R. J. (1979). *The Broken connection.* New York: Simon & Schuster.

Luepnitz, D. (1988). *The Family interpreted.* New York: Basic Books.

Lusseyran, J. (1985). Sense and presence. *Parabola, 10*(3), 59–65.

Lynn, J. (1993). Travels in the valley of the shadow. In H. Spiro, M. Curnen, E. Peschel, & D. St. James (Eds.), *Empathy and the practice of medicine* (pp. 40–53). New Haven: Yale University Press.

Lyons, J. (1994). The American medical doctor in the current milieu: A matter of trust. *Perspectives in Biology and Medicine, 37*(3), 442–458.

Mahoney, M. (1991). *Human change process.* New York: Basic Books.

Mairs, N. (1993, February 21). When bad things happen to good writers. *New York Times Book Review.*

Maslow, A. (1962). *Toward a psychology of being* (rev. ed.). Princeton, NJ: Van Nostrand.

Maslow, A. (1970). *Motivation and personality* (2nd ed.). New York: Harper & Row. (Originally published 1954)

McCubbin, H., & Patterson, J. (1983a). Chronic illness: Family stress and coping. In C. Figley & H. McCubbin (Eds.), *Stress and the family: Vol. 2, Coping with catastrophe* (pp. 21–36). New York: Brunner/Mazel.

McCubbin, H., & Patterson, J. (1983b). Family transitions: Adaptation to stress. In C. Figley & H. McCubbin (Eds.), *Stress and the family: Vol. 1, Coping with normative transitions* (pp. 5–25). New York: Brunner/Mazel.

McDaniel, S., Hepworth, J., & Doherty, W. (1992). *Medical family therapy.* New York: Basic Books.

McNiff, S. (1992). *Art as therapy.* Boston: Shambala Publications.

Mitscherlich-Nielsen, M. (1989). The Inability to mourn—Today. In D. Dietrich & P. Shabad (Eds.), *The Problem of loss and mourning* (pp. 405–426). Madison, CT: International Universities Press.

Miller, J. (1992). Energy deficits in chronically ill persons with arthritis: Fatigue. In J. Miller (Ed.), *Coping with chronic illness* (pp. 196–221). Philadelphia: E. F. Davis Co.

Miller, S. (1990). To see or not to see: Cognitive informational styles in the coping process. In M. Rosenbaum (Ed.), *Learned resourcefulness* (pp. 95–126). New York: Springer.

Moerman, D. (1991). Physiology and symbols: The anthropological implications of the placebo effect. In L. Romanucci-Ross, D. Moerman, & L. Tancredi (Eds.), *The Anthropology of medicine* (pp. 129–143). New York: Bergin and Garvey.

Mogenson, G. (1989). *God is a trauma.* Dallas, TX: Spring Publications.

Morrison, A. (1990). Doing psychotherapy while living with a life-threatening illness. In H. Schwartz & A. Silver (Eds.), *Illness in the analyst* (pp. 227–250). New York: International Universities Press.

Moss, D. (1978). Brain, body, and world: Perspectives on bodily image. In R. Valle & M. King (Eds.), *Existential-phenomenological alternatives to psychology* (pp. 73–93). New York: Oxford University Press.

Murphy, R. F. (1990). *The Body silent.* New York: Norton.

Niederland, W. (1989). Trauma, loss, restoration, and creativity. In D. Dietrich & P. Shabad (Eds.), *The Problem of loss and mourning* (pp. 61–82). Madison, CT: International Universities Press.

Nuland, S. (1994). *How we die.* New York: Knopf.

Nussbaum, M. (1986). *The Fragility of goodness.* Cambridge: Cambridge University Press.

Oates, J. (1995, February 19). Confronting head-on the face of the afflicted. *New York Times.*

O'Connor, F. (1979). *The Habit of being.* New York: Farrar, Straus & Giroux.

Oths, K. (1994). Communication in a chiropractic clinic: How a D.C. treats his patients. *Culture, Medicine, and Psychiatry, 18*(1), 83–113.

Ovid. *The Metamorphoses.* C. Boer (Trans.). (1989). Dallas: Spring Publications.

Parkes, C. (1993). Bereavement as a psychosocial transition: Processes of adaptation to change. In M. Stroebe, W. Stroebe, R. Hansson (Eds.), *Handbook of bereavement* (pp. 91–101). Cambridge: Cambridge University Press.

Parsons, C., & Wakeley, P. (1991). Idioms of distress. *Culture, Medicine, and Psychiatry, 15*(1), 111–132.

Paulson, W. (1991). Literature, complexity, interdisciplinarity. In N. K. Hayles (Ed.), *Chaos and order* (pp. 37–53). Chicago: University of Chicago Press.

Pollack, G. (1989). The Mourning process, the creative process, and the creation. In D. Dietrich & P. Shabad (Eds.), *The Problem of loss and mourning* (pp. 27–59). Madison, CT: International Universities Press.

Post, S. (1993). Psychiatry and ethics: The problematics of respect for religious meanings. *Culture, Medicine, and Psychiatry, 17*(3), 363–384.

Ramsey, C. N., Jr. (ed.). (1989). *Family systems in medicine.* New York: Guilford Press.

Reiss, D., & DeNour, A. (1989). The Family and medical team in chronic illness: A transactional and developmental perspective. In C. N. Ramsey, Jr. (Ed.), *Family systems in medicine* (pp. 435–444). New York: Guilford Press.

Remen, R. (1993). Wholeness [interview with Bill Moyers]. In B. Moyers, *Healing and the mind* (pp. 343–363). New York: Doubleday.

Richardson, H. (1989). Quoted in D. Ransom, Development of family therapy and family theory. In C. N. Ramsey, Jr. (Ed.), *Family systems in medicine* (p. 30). New York: Guilford Press.

Rolland, J. (1991). Helping families with anticipatory loss. In F. Walsh & M. McGoldrick (Eds.), *Living beyond loss* (pp. 144–162). New York: Norton.

Rolland, J. (1994). *Family, illness, and disability.* New York: Basic Books.

Romanucci-Ross, L., & Moerman, D. (1991). The Extraneous factor in Western medicine. In L. Romanucci-Ross, D. Moerman, & L. Tancredi (Eds.), *The Anthropology of medicine* (pp. 389–406). New York: Bergin and Garvey.

Rosenberg, C. (1992). *Explaining epidemics and other studies in the history of medicine.* Cambridge: Cambridge University Press.

Rosenblatt, P. (1994). *Metaphors of family systems theory.* New York: Guilford Press.

Ruddick, W. (1994). Transforming homes and hospitals. *Hastings Center Report, 24*(5), S11–S14.

Sacks, O. (1984). *A Leg to stand on* (rev. ed.). New York: HarperCollins.

Sacks. O. (1989). *Seeing voices.* Berkeley: University of California Press.

Saint-Exupéry, A. (1943/1968). *The Little prince.* New York: Harcourt Brace & Company.

Samuels, L. (1992). When the analyst cannot continue. *San Francisco Jung Institute Library Journal, 10*(4), 27–38.

Samuels, M. (1994). Art as a healing force. In *Body and soul: Contemporary art and healing* (exhibition catalog) (pp. 66–77). Lincoln, MA: DeCordova Museum and Sculpture Park.

Sandblom, P. (1995). *Creativity and disease* (rev. ed.). London: Marion Boyars Publishers.

Sardello, R. (1992). *Facing the world with soul.* Hudson, NY: Lindisfarne Press.

Savage, J. (1989). *Mourning unlived lives.* Wilmette, IL: Chiron Publications.

Schutz, A. See Wagner.

Schwartz, H. (1990). Illness in the doctor: Implications for the psychoanalytic process. In H. Schwartz & A. Silver (Eds.), *Illness in the analyst* (pp. 115–149). New York: International Universities Press.

Schwartz, H., & Silver, A. (eds.). (1990). *Illness in the analyst.* New York: International Universities Press.

Shay, J. (1994). *Achilles in Vietnam.* New York: Atheneum.

Shuman, R., & Schwartz, J. (1988). *Understanding multiple sclerosis.* New York: Scribner's.

Smith, T., Christensen, A. J., Peck, J. R., & Ward, J. R. (1994). Cognitive distortion, helplessness, and depressed mood in rheumatoid arthritis. *Health Psychology, 13*(3), 213–217.

Sontag, S. (1990). *Illness as metaphor and AIDS and its metaphors.* New York: Anchor.

Sourkes, B. (1982). *The Deepening shade.* Pittsburgh: University of Pittsburgh Press.

Stein, J., & Stein, M. (1987). Psychotherapy, initiation, and the midlife transition. In L. Mahdi & S. Foster (Eds.), *Betwixt and between* (pp. 287–303). LaSalle, IL: Open Court.

Stein, M. (1983). *In midlife.* Dallas, TX: Spring Publications.

Steinsaltz, A. (1994). The Command is to hear [interview with Jean Sulzberger]. *Parabola, 19*(1), 26–33.

Stout, J. (1988). *Ethics after Babel.* Boston: Beacon Press.

Sullivan, L. (ed.). (1989). *Healing and restoring.* New York: Macmillan.

Sullivan, L. (ed.). (1993). Images of wholeness [interview with Ellen Draper and Virginia Baron]. *Parabola, 18*(1), 4–13.

Sullivan, L. (ed.). (1994). *The Parabola book of healing.* New York: Continuum Press.

Trungpa, C. (1985). Acknowledging death as the common ground of healing. *Naropa Institute Journal of Psychotherapy, 3,* 3–10.

Turner, V. (1987). Betwixt and between: The liminal period in rites and passages. In L. Mahdi & S. Foster (Eds.), *Betwixt and between* (pp. 3–19). LaSalle, IL: Open Court.

Varela, F., Thompson, E., & Resch, E. (1991). *The Embodied mind.* Cambridge, MA: MIT Press.

Viederman, M. (1989). Personality change through life experience: 3. Two creative types of response to object loss. In D. Dietrich & P. Shabad (Eds.), *The Problem of loss and mourning* (pp. 187–212). Madison, CT: International Universities Press.

Wagner, H. (ed.). *Alfred Schutz on phenomenology and social relations.* Chicago: University of Chicago Press. (Originally published 1945)

Ward, J. (1994). Some thoughts on healing in Western medicine. In L. Sullivan (Ed.), *The Parabola book of healing* (pp. 111–117). New York: Continuum Press.

Whan, M. (1987). Chiron's wound: Some reflections on the wounded healer. In N. Schwartz-Salant & M. Stein (Eds.), *Archetypal processes in psychotherapy* (pp. 197–208). Wilmette, IL: Chiron Publications.

Whyte, S. (1995). Constructing epilepsy: Images and contexts in East Africa. In S. Whyte & B. Ingstad (Eds.), *Disability and culture* (pp. 226–245). Berkeley: University of California Press.

Whyte, S., & Ingstad, B. (eds.). (1995). *Disability and culture*. Berkeley: University of California Press.

Wilcox, V., Kasl, S., & Berkman, L. (1994). Social support and physical disability in older people after hospitalization: A prospective study. *Health Psychology*, *13*(2), 170–179.

Wilson, B., & Jung, C. (1994). Spiritus contra spiritum. In L. Sullivan (Ed.), *The Parabola book of healing* (pp. 128–133). New York: Continuum Press.

Wolstein, B. (ed.). (1988). *Essential papers on countertransference*. New York: New York University Press.

Wright, D. (1990). *Deafness: A personal account*. London: Faber and Faber.

Yalom, I. (1980). *Existential psychotherapy*. New York: Basic Books.

Zaner, R. (1982). Chance and morality: The dialysis phenomenon. In V. Kestenbaum (Ed.), *The Humanity of the ill* (pp. 39–68). Knoxville: University of Tennessee Press.

Ziegler, A. (1983). *Archetypal medicine*. Dallas, TX: Spring Publications.

Zola, I. (1991). Communication barriers between "the able-bodied" and "the handicapped". In R. Marinelli & A. Dell Orto (Eds.), *The Psychological and social impact of disability* (3rd ed., pp. 157–164). New York: Springer.

RESOURCES

T HE FOLLOWING LIST of organizations and services is designed to help people take advantage of computers, and especially the World Wide Web (WWW). When an organization is not online, I have added other online sites with related information. Addresses, whether regular mail, e-mail, Internet, or World Wide Web (URL), are up-to-date as of spring 1996. WWW addresses change more frequently than others, but forwarding addresses are often available online. I would appreciate hearing of any unlisted web sites that are useful resources (rshuman@www1.usa1.com/).

ASSOCIATIONS AND ONLINE INFORMATION SOURCES

Johns Hopkins Medical Institutions Information Network
E-mail: www@infonet.welch.jhu.edu
URL: http://infonet.welch.jhu.edu/advocacy.html

American Self-Help Clearinghouse
Puts callers in touch with any of several hundred self-help groups covering a wide range of illnesses and disabilities; national database of over 750 national and model groups.
Northwest Covenant Medical Center
25 Pocono Rd.
Denville, NJ 07834
(201) 625–7101
(TDD) (201) 625–9053

National Health Information Center (NHIC)
Database includes 1,100 organizations and government offices that provide health information upon request, including toll-free numbers.
URL: http://nhic-nt.health.org/

Chronic Illness Resources
URL: http://asa.ugl.lib.umich.edu/chdocs/support/chronic.html

The Complete Guide to Sites Related to Psychology
URL: http://pegasus.acs.ttu.edu/~civelek/newII/thanatos2.html

Disability Resources
URL: http://disability.com/cool.html

Disability Resources on the Web
URL: http://primes6.rehab.uiuc.edu/pursuit/dis-resources/inet-dis/inet-dis.html

RESOURCES BY DISEASE/DISABILITY

AIDS/HIV

Online information:
E-mail: QRDstaff@vector.casti.com
URL: http://vector.casti.com/QRD/www/AIDS.html

CDC National AIDS Clearinghouse (NAC)
PO Box 6003
Rockville, MD 20849–6003
(800) 458–5231
Fax: (301) 738–6616
HIV/AIDS Treatment Information Service: (800) HIV–0440 (448–0440)
TTY access: (800) 243–7012
Direct log-in: (800) 521–7245 (modem configuration: 8, N, 1, VT100)
E-mail: aidsinfo@cdcnac.aspensys.com
URL: http://cdcnac.aspensys.com:86

KAIROS Support for Caregivers Material
E-mail: bhunter@interramp.com (Brett N. Hunter)
URL: http://www.catalog.com/kairos/material.htm

ALZHEIMER'S DISEASE
URL: http://medhlp.netusa.net/general/ALZHEIM.TXT

Alzheimer's Association
919 N. Michigan Ave., Suite 1000
Chicago, IL 60611–1676
(312) 335–8700 (main reception)
(800) 272–3900 (24-hour information and chapter referral)

TDD: (312) 335–8882
URL: http://www.alz.org/

Benjamin B. Green-Field National Alzheimer's Library
(312) 335–9602
Fax: (312) 335–0214
E-mail: greenfld@alz.org

AMYOTROPHIC LATERAL SCLEROSIS
URL: http://www.caregiver.org/text/fs_als.html

Amyotrophic Lateral Sclerosis Association
21021 Ventura Blvd., Suite 321
Woodland Hills, CA 91364
(800) 782–4747

ARTHRITIS
URL: http://weber.u.washington.edu/~dboone/key/subjects/
arthritis/xzzzzzzz1_1.html

Arthritis Foundation
1314 Spring St., NW
Atlanta, GA 30309
(800) 283–7800
E-mail: help@arthritis.org.
URL: http://www.arthritis.org/

ASTHMA AND ALLERGY
URL: http://www.asthma.comm/what.html

Asthma and Allergy Foundation of America
Offers a newsletter and referrals to affiliated support groups and specialized medical services throughout the country.
1125 15th St. NW, Suite 502
Washington, DC 20005
(800) 624–0044 or (800) 7–ASTHMA (727–8462)

American Academy of Allergy Asthma and Immunology (AAAAI)
611 East Wells St.
Milwaukee, WI 53202
(414) 272–6071
(800) 822–ASMA (822–2762) (physicians' referral and information line)

Allergy and Asthma Network/Mothers of Asthmatics, Inc.
3554 Chain Bridge Rd., Suite 200
Fairfax, VA 22030
(703) 385–4403
(800) 878–4403

National Jewish Center for Immunology and Respiratory Medicine
The leading research and treatment center for asthma in the world.
1400 Jackson St.
Denver, CO 80206
(800) 222–LUNG (222–5864)

CANCER

URL: http://oncolink.upenn.edu

American Cancer Society
1599 Clifton Rd., NE
Atlanta, GA 30329
(800) ACS–2345
(800) CANCER (cancer information service)
E-mail: mneitzel@mindspring.com
URL: http://www.cancer.org

CEREBRAL PALSY

URL: http://asa.ugl.lib.mich.edu/ch.docs/support/chronic.html
/#palsy

United Cerebral Palsy Association, Inc.
1522 K St., NW, Suite 1112
Washington, DC 20005
(202) 842–1266
(800) USA–5–UCP
Fax: (202) 842–3519
America Online address: UCPA INC

CHRONIC FATIGUE SYNDROME

Online information:
E-mail: J.Hellwege@latrobe.edu.au (Jason Hellwege)
URL: http://www.dds.nl/~me-net/meweb/cdcfacts.txt
URL: http://www.ncf.carleton.ca/ip/social.services/cfseir
/cfseir.hp.html#3-Other-www
URL: http://metro.turnpike.net/C/cfs-news/faq.html
URL: http://www.latrobe.edu.au/Glenn/CFS.html

CROHN'S DISEASE AND COLITIS

Online information about Crohn's disease, ulcerative colitis, and irritable bowel syndrome:
E-mail: billr@bu.edu (Bill Robertson)
URL: http://128.197.93.205/cduchome.html

Crohn's and Colitis Foundation of America
386 Park Ave. South, Floor 17
New York, NY 10016–7374
(212) 685–3440
(800) 932–2423
Fax: (212) 779–4098
CCFA brochures (free of charge): (800) 343–3637
E-mail: MHDA37B@prodigy.com.

CYSTIC FIBROSIS
Online information:
E-mail: rcalhoun@mit.edu (Rob Calhoun), mernst@theory.lcs
.mit.edu (Mike Ernst)
URL: http://www.ai.mit.edu/people/mernst/cf/

Cystic Fibrosis Foundation
6931 Arlington Rd.
Bethesda, MD 20814
(800) 344–4823 (FIGHT–CF)

DIABETES
Online information:
E-mail: belve@delphi.com (Belver Ladson)
URL: http://www.biostat.wisc.edu/diaknow/dfan/dfanidx.htm

American Diabetes Association
1660 Duke St.
Alexandria, VA 22314
(800) DIABETES (342–2383) (state offices)
(800) 232–3472 (national office)
URL: http://www.diabetes.org

EPILEPSY
Online information:
URL: http://www.swcp.com/~djf/epilepsyindex.html

Epilepsy Foundation of America
4351 Garden City Dr.
Landover, MD 20785
(301) 459–3700 (voice)
(800) 332–1000 (information/referrals)
(800) 642–0500 (epilepsy information service)
E-mail: postmaster@efa.org

HEART DISEASE AND STROKE
    URL: http://www.stroke.org

American Heart Association
    7272 Greenville Ave.
    Dallas, TX 75231–4596
    (800) AHA–USA1 (553–6321)
    E-mail: chuck@amhrt.org
    URL: http://www.amhrt.org/

National Stroke Association
    8480 E. Orchard Rd., Suite 1000
    Englewood, CO 80111–5015
    (303) 762–9922 (voice)
    (800) STROKES (787–6537) (voice)

HEMOPHILIA
    Online information:
    E-mail: Davon@web—Depot.com
    URL: http://www.web-depot.com/hemophilia/organizations.html

National Hemophilia Foundation
    110 Greene St., Suite 303
    New York, NY 10012
    (212) 219–8180
    (800) 424–2634
    Fax: (212) 966–9247
    HANDI phone: (800) 42–HANDI
    HANDI fax: (212) 431–0906

Hemophilia Federation
    Advocacy for persons with clotting disorders, and for their families.
    906 D St., NE
    Washington, DC 20002
    (800) 230–9797

KIDNEY DISEASE
    URL: http://www.cc.utah.edu/~cla6202/KPR.htm

American Association of Kidney Patients
    100 S. Ashley Dr., Suite 280
    Tampa, FL 33260
    (800) 749–2257
    E-mail: aakpaz@enet.net

LIVER DISEASE
    URL: http://sadieo.ucsf.edu/alf/alffinal/homepagealf.html

American Liver Foundation (ALF)
1425 Pompton Ave.
Cedar Grove, NJ 07009
(201) 256–2550
(800) 223–0179

LUPUS

Lupus Foundation of America
4 Research Pl., Suite 180
Rockville, MD 20850–3226
(301) 670–9292
(800) 558–0121
E-mail: lupus@piper.hamline.edu
URL: http://www.hamline.edu/lupus/index.html

MULTIPLE SCLEROSIS
URL: http://www.ifmss.org.uk

National Multiple Sclerosis Foundation
733 Third Ave.
New York, NY 10017
(800) FIGHT–MS (344–4867)
E-mail: help@nmss.org
URL: http://www.nmss.org

MUSCULAR DYSTROPHY
Online information:
URL: http://www.softconn.co.za/~mpeters/mdas2.html#usa

Muscular Dystrophy Association
3300 E. Sunrise Dr.
Tucson, AZ 85718
(602) 529–2000
URL: http://www.compuserve.com/mda/about.html

MYASTHENIA GRAVIS
Online information:
URL: http://www.infohiway.com/way/mgacolorado/ (Myasthenia Gravis Association of Colorado)

Myasthenia Gravis Association
222S Riverside Plaza, No. 1450
Chicago, IL 60606
(800) 541–5454
Fax: (312) 258–0461

PARKINSON'S DISEASE

Online information:
URL: http://neuro-e-e.mgh.hjarvard.edu/parkinsonsweb/Main /Support/USA.html

National Parkinson Foundation
Miami, FLA
(800) 327–4545
Fax: (305) 243–4407
E-mail: mailbox@npf.medmiami.edu
URL: http://www.Parkinson.org

Parkinson's Action Network
Founded in 1991 to provide a unified, national voice for the Parkinson's community.
822 College Ave., Suite C
Santa Rosa, CA 95404
(707) 544–1994
(800) 820–4716
Fax: (707) 544–2363
E-mail: ParkActNet@AOL.com

POLIO AND POST-POLIO SYNDROME

Online information:
E-mail: dempt@eskimo.com (Tom Dempsey)
URL: http://www.eskimo.com/~dempt/polio.html

SCLERODERMA

URL: http://www.iacnet.com/health/11063052.html

United Scleroderma Foundation
21 Brennen St., Suite 21
PO Box 399
Watsonville, CA 95077
(408) 728–2202
(800) 722–4673
Fax: (408) 728–3328
URL: http://www.scleroderma.com

Scleroderma Research Foundation
Pueblo Medical Commons
2320 Bath St., Suite 307
Santa Barbara, CA 93105
(805) 563–9133
(800) 441–CURE

TOURETTE SYNDROME

Online information:
  URL: http://www.umich.edu/~infinit/tourette.html

Tourette Syndrome Association
  42–40 Bell Blvd.
  Bayside, NY 11361
  (718) 224–2999
  (800) 237–0717
  URL: http://vh.radiology.uiowa.edu/Patients/IowaHealthBook/
  Tourette/HomePage.html

CAREGIVER SUPPORT

The Caregiver's Handbook **(online)**
Assisting both the caregiver and the elderly care-receiver.
  URL: http://neuro-chief e.mgh.harvard.edu/parkinsonsweb
  /Main/Coping/caregiver.html

The Caregiver Education and Support Services
  Seniors Counseling and Training Case Management Services of San
  Diego County Mental Health Services
  Robert Torres-Stanovik, LCSW
  1250 Moreno Blvd.
  San Diego, CA 92110
  (619) 692–8702
  E-mail: johnc@idafw.net

The Well Spouse Foundation
Support and advocacy for spouses and children of the chronically ill.
  PO Box 801
  New York, NY 10023
  (212) 644–1241
  (800) 838–0879
  Fax: (212) 644–1338
  URL: http://nhic-nt.health.org/htmlgen/htmlgen.exe/
  Entry?HRCode='HR2456'

INTERNET AND OTHER RESOURCES FOR PHYSICAL LOSS, CHRONIC ILLNESS, AND BEREAVEMENT

Online information:
  URL: http://asa.ugl.lib.umich.edu/chdocs/support/emotion.html
  URL: http://asa.ugl.lib.umich.edu/chdocs/support/chronic.html
  URL: http://www.lib.umich.edu/chdocs/support/emotion.html

Academy of Dentistry for Persons with Disabilities
211 E. Chicago Ave., Suite 948
Chicago, IL 60611
(312) 440–2660

American Academy of Ophthalmology
(800) 628–6733

American Optometric Association
(800) 262–3947

American Paralysis Association
5000 Morris Ave.
Springfield, NJ 07081
(800) 225–0292
Fax: (201) 912–9433
URL: http://teri.bio.uci.edu/paralysis

Help for Incontinent People, Inc. (HIP)
PO Box 544
Union, SC 29379
(803) 579–7900
(800) BLADDER

National Center for Nutrition and Dietetics (NCND) of the American Dietetic Association
Provides consumers with direct and immediate access to reliable nutrition information.
216 W. Jackson Blvd.
Chicago, IL 60606–6995
(800) 366–1655 (consumer nutrition hot line)

The National Easter Seal Society
230 W. Monroe St., Suite 1800
Chicago, IL 60606
(312) 726–6200
(800) 221–6827
TDD: (312) 726–4258
URL: http://seals.com

National Organization for Rare Disorders
Acts as a clearinghouse for information about rare disorders and brings together families with similar disorders for mutual support.
PO Box 8923
New Fairfield, CT 06812–1783
(203) 746–6518
(800) 999–6673

The Simon Foundation for Continence
PO Box 835
Wilmette (Chicago), IL 60091
(708) 864–3913
(800) 23–SIMON

United Ostomy Association, Inc. (UOA)
36 Executive Park, Suite 120
Irvine, CA 92714–6744
(714) 660–8624
(800) 826–0826

INTERNET AND OTHER RESOURCES FOR CREATIVE ACTIVITIES AND THERAPIES

American Art Therapy Association, Inc.
1202 Allanson Rd.
Mundelein, IL 60060
(708) 949–6064
Fax: (708) 566–4580
URL: http://nhicnt.health.org/htmlgen/htmlgen.exe
/Entry?HRCode='HR2175'

American Dance Therapy Association
2000 Century Plaza, Suite 108
Columbia, MD 21044
(410) 997–4040
Fax: (410) 997–4048
URL: http://www.citi.net/ADTA/

American Horticultural Therapy Association
Works to promote and develop the practice of horticulture as a therapy to improve human well-being.
362A Christopher Ave.
Gaithersburg, MD 20879
(301) 948–3010
(800) 634–1603
Fax: (301) 869–2397
URL: http://http.tamu.edu:8000/~pnw3384/ahta.html
Internet: 75352.122@compuserve.com

Creative Arts Therapies Society (CATS)
E-mail: LEVYB or RDWing @Aol.Com
URL: http://www.users.interport.net/~levyb/cats.html

National Association of Drama Therapy
44 Taylor Pl.
Branford, CT 06405
(203) 481–1161
Fax: (203) 483–7373
URL: http://csep.sunyit.edu/~joel/nadt.html (unofficial)

National Association for Music Therapy
8455 Colesville Rd., Suite 930
Silver Spring, MD 20910
(301) 589–3300
Fax: (301) 589–5175
URL: http://nhic-nt.health.org/htmlgen/htmlgen.exe
/Entry?HRCode='HR0506'

Society for the Advancement of Travel for the Handicapped (SATH)
Dedicated to barrier-free access for travelers with disabilities and to the widest possible circulation of information concerning travel conditions for disabled travelers.
(770) 641–9900
(800) 969–6419
Fax: (770) 641–8061
URL: http://www.travelagency.com/page13.html

Wheelchair Sports, USA
3395 E. Fountain Blvd., Suite L–1
Colorado Springs, CO 80910
(719) 574–1150
Fax: (719) 574–9840
URL: http://nhic-nt.health.org/htmlgen/htmlgen.exe
/Entry?HRCode='HR1657'

ASSISTIVE TECHNOLOGY RESOURCES—OTHER ONLINE SERVICES

Online information:
America Online: See Clubs and Interests/Better Health
CompuServe: See Disabilities+ Forum
Prodigy: See Health Forum

Adaptive Computing Technology Center
Campus Computing
University of Missouri—Columbia
200 Heinkel Bldg.
Columbia, MO 65211
(314) 882–2000
Fax: (314) 884–5240

E-mail: cckevin@mizzou1.missouri.edu
URL: http://www.missouri.edu/~ccact

Alliance For Technology Access

Provides access to empowering technology for children and adults with disabilities. Publishes the book Computer Resources for People with Disabilities, *with a foreword by Stephen Hawking.*

2173 E. Francisco Blvd., Suite L
San Rafael, CA 94939
(415) 455–4575
E-mail: atafta@aol.com
URL: http://marin.org/ata/

American Speech-Language-Hearing Association (ASHA)

Professional association of speech-language pathologists and audiologists who develop computer technology to assist the disabled.

10801 Rockville Pike
Rockville, MD 20852
301–897–5700 (voice/TDD)
800–638–8255 (voice/TDD)

Apple Computer, Inc.

Created the industry's first disability solutions group.

1 Infinite Loop, M/S 38–DS
Cupertino, CA 95014
(800) 600–7808
TTY: (800) 755–0601
Fax: (800) 462–4396 (to receive free comprehensive database of access products called the Mac Access Passport (MAP), you must have a fax machine)
E-mail: webmaster@apple.com (Apple on the Internet)
URL: http://www.apple.com or http://www.info.apple.com.
URL: http://www.apple.com/disability/welcome.html. (Apple Computer's disability solutions home page)

Apple's Disability Resources Online

Four short videotapes are also available ($8/each) through Apple's Starting-Line; call (800) 825–2145 for a catalog.

1. *Access*—the lives of four people with disability are transformed by Apple technology. 10 min. Part #APL829.
2. *Chapter One*—shows ways that future technologies might enable people with disabilities. 10 min. Part #APL830.
3. *Curb Cuts*—shows what makes Macintosh the most accessible computer. 8 min. Part #APL831.
4. *Independence Day*—Macintosh helps individuals with disabilities improve quality of daily lives. 10 min. Part #APL832.

Berkeley Systems
Adaptive software for people with visual disabilities.
2095 Rose St.
Berkeley, CA 94709
(510) 883–6280
Fax: (510) 883–6270
TTY: (510) 540–0709
Peter Korn, Project Manager, Access: korn@berksys.com
Marc Sutton, Product Manager, Access: msutton@berksys.com
General Berkeley Access questions: access@berksys.com
outSPOKEN Mac tech support: osmac@berksys.com
outSPOKEN Windows tech support: osw@berksys.com
inLARGE Macintosh tech support: inlarge@berksys.com
GUI Access questions/support: guiaccess@berksys.com
Placing orders and customer service: cs@berksys.com
URL: http://access.berksys.com/

Equal Access to Software and Information (EASI)
An affiliate of the American Association for Higher Education.
(714) 830–0301 (Pacific time zone)
Fax: (714) 830–2159
E-mail: EASI@EDUCOM.EDU
URL: http://www.rit.edu:80/~easi/

Closing the Gap
A bimonthly newsletter about assistive technology for the disabled.
PO Box 68
Henderson, MN 56044
(612) 248–3294

Handicap News Archive
Comprehensive information for those with disabilities, including Americans with Disability Act and related legislation, listings of national and local support groups, newsletters, sources of state and federal assistance. Shareware for the disabled computer user can be downloaded. Anonymous ftp (file transfer protocol) site: log on as "Anonymous" to HANDICAP.SHEL.ISC-BR.COM
(203) 337–1518 (contact Bill McGarry)
E-mail: wtm@bunker (Bitnet) or wtm@Shelden.Shel.isc-br.com (Internet)

HEATH Resource Center
National clearinghouse for information about assistive technology.
1 Dupont Cir., NW, Suite 800
Washington, DC 20036
(202) 939–9320
(800) 544–3284
E-mail: heath@ace.nche.edu

IBM Special Needs Systems/Independence Series Information Center
> 1000 NW 51st St.
> Boca Raton, FL 33431
> (800) 426–4832
> TDD: (800) 426–4833

National Braille Press
Publishes Solutions: Access Technologies for People Who Are Blind, *updated guide for the blind and visually impaired in print, cassette, and computer disk versions.*
> 88 St. Stephen St.
> Boston, MA 02115
> (617) 266–6160

Trace Research and Development Center
Information on on adaptive hardware and software.
> (608) 262–6966
> TDD: (608) 263–5408

WebABLE!
Dedicated to promoting the interests of adaptive, assistive, and access technology researchers, users, and manufacturers.
> E-mail: mpaciello@www.webable.com
> URL: http://www.webable.com/

PUBLICATIONS

Barasch, Marc. (1994). *Healing Path: A Soul Approach to Illness* (Jeremy Tarcher).

Bayles, David, & Ted Orlando. (1993). *Art and Fear* (Capra Press).

Bosnak, Robert. (1988). *A Little Course in Dreams* (Shambhala).

Cameron, Julia. (1992). *The Artist's Way: A Spiritual Path to Higher Creativity* (G. P. Putnam's Sons).

Edwards, Betty. (1993). *Drawing on the Right Side of the Brain* (Harper-Collins).

Edwards, Paul. (1994). *Working from Home* (Jeremy Tarcher).

Enteen, Robert. (1992). *Health Insurance: How to Get It, Keep It, or Improve What You've Got* (Paragon House).

Franck, Frederick. (1973). *The Zen of Seeing* (Vintage).

Garfield, Patricia L. (1981). *Creative Dreaming* (Ballantine).

Goldberg, Natalie. (1986). *Writing down the Bones* (Shambhala).

Goldman, Charles D. (1987). *Disability Rights Guide: Practical Solutions to Problems Affecting People with Disabilities* (Media Publishing).

Hecker, Helen. (1985). *Travel for the Disabled: A Handbook of Travel Resources and 500 Worldwide Access Guides* (Twin Peaks Press).

Hecker, Helen. (1991). *Directory of Travel Agencies for the Disabled* (Twin Peaks Press).

Isaacs, Stephen, & Ava Swartz. (1992). *The Consumer's Legal Guide to Today's Health Care* (Houghton Mifflin).

Judy, Stephanie. (1990). *Making Music for the Fun of It* (Jeremy Tarcher).

Kane, Rosalie, & Robert Kane. (1987). *Long-Term Care: Principles, Programs, and Policies* (Springer).

Keyes, Margaret. (1983). *The Inward Journey: Art as Therapy* (Open Court).

Kroll, Ken, & Erica Levy Klein. (1995). *Enabling Romance: A Guide to Love, Sex, and Relationships for the Disabled* (Woodbine House).

Lasher, Margot. (1992). *Art and the Practice of Compassion* (Jeremy Tarcher).

Mathieu, W. A. (1991). *The Listening Book: Discovering Your Own Music* (Shambhala).

McNiff, Shaun. (1992). *Art as Medicine: Creating a Therapy of the Imagination* (Shambhala).

Messervy, Julie Moir (photographs by Sam Abell). (1995). *The Inward Garden: Creating a Place of Beauty and Meaning* (Little, Brown).

Milam, Lorenzo. (1993). *Crip Zen: A Manual for Survival* (Mho & Mho Works, San Diego)

Moyers, Bill. (1993). *Healing and the Mind* (Doubleday).

Nachmanovitch, Stephen. (1990). *Free Play: The Power of Improvisation in Life and the Arts* (Jeremy Tarcher).

Progoff, Ira. (1979). *At a Journal Workshop* (rev. ed.) (Jeremy Tarcher).

Rainer, Tristine. (1978). *The New Diary* (Jeremy Tarcher).

Richards, M. C. (1962). *Centering: Poetry, Pottery, and the Person* (Wesleyan University Press).

Rico, Gabriele. (1983). *Writing the Natural Way* (Jeremy Tarcher).

Rico, Gabriele. (1991). *Pain and Possibility: Writing Your Way Through Personal Crises* (Jeremy Tarcher).

Rogers, Judith, & Molleen Matsumura. (1992). *Mother to Be: A Guide to Pregnancy and Birth for Women with Disabilities* (Demos Publications).

Roth, Wendy, & Michael Tompane. (1992). *Easy Access to National Parks* (Sierra Club Books).

Sandblom, Philip. (1995), *Creativity and Disease* (Marion Boyars Publishers).

Strong, Maggie. (1988). *Mainstay: For the Well Spouse of the Chronically Ill* (Little, Brown).

Sullivan, Lawrence (ed.). (1994). *The Parabola Book of Healing* (Continuum).

Trieschman, Roberta. (1987). *Aging with a Disability* (Demos Publications).

MEMOIRS, NOVELS, STORIES OF ILLNESS AND DISABILITY

Brookes, Tim. (1994). *Catching My Breath: An Asthmatic Explores His Illness* (Times Books/Random House).

Broyard, Anatole. (1992). *Intoxicated by My Illness and Other Writings of Life and Death* (Clarkson Potter).

Duff, Kat. (1993). *Alchemy of Illness* (Pantheon).

Frank, Arthur. (1991). *At the Will of the Body* (Houghton Mifflin).

Grealy, Lucy. (1994). *Autobiography of a Face* (Houghton Mifflin).

Hockenberry, John. (1995). *Moving Violations* (Hyperion).

Kleinman, Arthur. (1988). *The Illness Narratives: Suffering, Healing, and the Human Condition* (Basic Books).

Mairs, Nancy. (1992). *Plaintext* (University of Arizona).

Mukand, Jon, (ed.). (1990). *Vital Lines: Contemporary Fiction About Medicine* (Ballantine Books).

Murphy, Robert. (1987). *The Body Silent* (Henry Holt and Co.).

Pensack, Robert Jon, & Dwight Arnan Williams. (1994). *Raising Lazarus* (G. P. Putnam's Sons).

Price, Reynolds. (1995). *A Whole New Life* (Plume/New American Library).

Sacks, Oliver. (1984). *A Leg to Stand On* (Summit Books).

Sarton, May. (1988). *After the Stroke: A Journal* (Norton).

Sheed, Wilfred. (1995). *In Love with Daylight* (Simon & Schuster).

Tourette, Paul. (1990). *Borrowed Time: An AIDS Memoir* (Avon).

INDEX